D0373428

Grammar
for
Journalists

E. L. CALLIHAN

Professor and Chairman, Emeritus
Division of Journalism
Communication Arts Division
Southern Methodist University

CHILTON BOOK COMPANY
Radnor, Pennsylvania

Grammar for Journalists

THIRD EDITION

Published in Radnor, Pennsylvania 19089, by Chilton Book Company
and simultaneously in Scarborough, Ontario, Canada,
by Nelson Canada Limited

Manufactured in the United States of America
Designed by Arlene Putterman

Library of Congress Cataloging in Publication Data
Callihan, E. L.
    Grammar for Journalists.

    Bibliography: p. 300
    1. English language—Grammar—1950-
1. Title.
PE1116.J6C3 1979   428.2'024'097   78-22114
ISBN 0-8019-6823-2

4 5 6 7 8 9 0   8 7 6 5 4 3 2

To my wife Lillian

Without her help
this edition could not have
been published

. . . .

Contents

Foreword

It is a good thing that Lee Callihan does in the pages of this book. Someone should worry about the writing behavior of both practicing and student journalists. He does it well.

My own distant background badly needs revisiting. And I suspect many of my colleagues will welcome this completely revised third edition of *Grammar for Journalists* as a reference book for the media as well as a textbook for students.

In these moments of constant news developments, it is imperative that newspaper and broadcasting practitioners write clearly, concisely, interestingly—and correctly. In the related areas of magazines, public relations and industrial journalism there is the same obligation.

We assume that the journalism graduate comes properly equipped when he enters the professional field. But the assumption is not always correct. We find ourselves conducting newsroom "classes" and refresher courses in elementary grammar. And we patiently wonder whatever happened to spelling books.

Professor Callihan advises that his meticulously programmed book "is intended only to help cure 'grammaritis,' which journalism employers rank as the No. 1 ill of journalism graduates and other beginners in journalism." Further, its flexibility makes it serviceable in the classroom and laboratory in any number of courses.

But most important for those of us already out in the field, the new edition of *Grammar for Journalists* is so devised that self-instruction is easy. The use of short quizzes at the beginning of most of the chapters is continued in this new edition. By taking these, the practicing journalist may be surprised to find how much he needs a thorough review, at least, of grammar.

The author has numerous exhibits of poor grammar, spelling, punctuation and sentence structure—all taken from newspapers, magazines and broadcasts. He graciously apologizes for his invasion into the professional field and then pricks our hides with the comment that the examples "indicate that even the professional journalist's knowledge of grammar leaves something to be desired."

Over the years it has been my privilege to work with many of Professor Callihan's products. Many have graduated to the staff of *The Dallas Times Herald*. I always found the same qualities in the Callihan product. They do know how to spell. They do know how to structure a sentence. They do know the basic rules of grammar.

The author does not waste words in presenting the elements of grammar. He starts with the journalist's chief tool, the sentence, and moves through the parts of speech, the framework of the sentence, the correct use of verbs, nouns, pronouns, verbals, adjectives and adverbs, prepositions and conjunctions, etc. Part 2 is devoted to unity, emphasis, clarity, and variety of expression in sentence construction, and Part 3 has important chapters on punctuation and spelling. A glossary of usage has been added. Mr. Callihan's approach is brisk, anything but boring.

One very valid point is made in the presentation. It is to be assumed that the aspiring journalist is attracted to writing and has a certain facility with words. The desire and the interest are there—but can he put them together?

Actually, writing flows at a swifter, smoother pace if the writer does not hesitate to ponder the rules of grammar. It gives the confidence that leads to real creativity in writing.

So, thank you again, Lee Callihan, for the contributions you have made in these three editions. The latest should be on the shelves of newspaper libraries. Or, better, on the desks of reporters.

FELIX R. MCKNIGHT
Vice Chairman and Editor, Ret.
The Dallas Times Herald
President (1961–62)
The American Society of Newspaper Editors

Introduction

No more timely book could appear at this stage in the development of journalism and mass communication education, and the industries and professions they serve, than this third edition of E. L. Callihan's time-honored and highly useful book, *Grammar for Journalists*.

For just when the new technology is placing greater demands than ever upon journalists to be proficient in grammar, punctuation and spelling, many young people seeking careers in news, advertising, public relations and other communication fields find themselves severely handicapped by today's educational system, which places its priorities elsewhere.

Scores of journalism schools now require that students pass grammar proficiency tests before they may gain admission. Within the schools, emphasis is increasing upon the development of writing and editing skills. Many news, advertising and public relations employers test job applicants in these areas before hiring them. In fact, there are few fields of mass communication employment in which a command of the English language is not essential.

Most newspaper offices, for example, now are equipped with video display terminals. In these offices reporters and editors find that they also must be compositors, for the modern newsroom encompasses some of the functions, often including proofreading as well, that formerly were performed in the composing room. Because fewer eyes than previously scan copy before publication, the journalist's spelling and sentence structure must be impeccable and the style clear and interesting.

That's why *Grammar for Journalists* is essential. Students knocking at the doors of journalism schools use the book as a self-study guide; instructors throughout the country require its study in beginning mass communication courses of all kinds; and news, advertising and public relations men and women already on the job keep well-thumbed copies at ready reference.

Published first in 1957 and completely revised in 1969, this pioneering book has long been the No. 1 text-reference in its field. The new edition—with extensive revision and updating of the rules of grammar and of the examples that are largely taken from the media—should be an invaluable aid for the countless writing and editing courses being added to curricula through-out the country. A recent nationwide study revealed that approximately one-fourth of all the courses added during a three-year period involved news writing and reporting. Another similar study disclosed that more copywriting courses were being added to advertising curricula than any others. Still a third such study revealed that courses in news writing had been added as requirements for public relations majors at twice the rate of any other courses. New internship courses—all requiring proficiency in grammar—were at or near the top of the list of courses added in all three areas of study: news-editorial, advertising, and public relations.[1]

Grammar for Journalists thus has assumed an importance, on a broad school-wide scale, as never before. It is fully equal to the task.

Users of this book will be pleased to learn that a new edition of an accompanying workbook entitled *Exercises and Tests for Journalists,* pub-lished in 1970, will be issued shortly. Based on *Grammar for Journalists,* the book contains drill exercises written by Callihan, and grammar, punctuation and spelling tests developed and tested by Dean Wayne A. Danielson of the School of Communication, University of Texas at Austin, and Dr. Harold L. Nelson, professor and former director of the School of Journalism and Mass Communication, University of Wisconsin at Madison. The tests originally were tried out in 20 universities and in 1977 were re-standardized nationally through the participation of 38 schools in 25 states.

Together, *Grammar for Journalists* and *Exercises and Tests for Journalists* will help thousands of students to attain the finely honed proficiency in grammar, punctuation and spelling that is essential in almost all fields of mass communication.

WARREN K. AGEE, Ph.D.
Professor and Former Dean
Henry W. Grady School of
Journalism and Mass Communication
University of Georgia

[1]The news-editorial study, entitled "Coping With the Seventies: Recent and Projected Changes in News-Editorial Curricula in Schools of Journalism," by Warren K. Agee, was published almost in its entirety in *Journalism Educator* 32:3 (October 1977). Publication of the other two studies was pending at the time of publication of this book.

PART 1

Elements of Grammar

1

Advice for Journalists

Either you are preparing yourself for a career in journalism, or you already are working on a newspaper or a magazine, in public relations, advertising or in radio or television broadcasting, or perhaps free-lancing.

No matter what area of mass communications you plan to enter or in which you now are working, you certainly must have a certain facility with words and you like to write. But also—quite probably—you make your share of mistakes in grammar and spelling.

"What are the greatest weaknesses of men and women who are entering the broad field of journalism today?" This question put to the editors of 100 newspapers throughout the United States brought the reply: grammar, spelling, punctuation.

The journalist who aspires to reach the top in his profession cannot afford to ignore the warning and the advice offered by these editors, who are representative of thousands of editors who hire—and sometimes fire—young men and women entering journalism.

Advice from these editors boils down to this: Get a good foundation in grammar and spelling if you want to go far in journalism. Get it, preferably, while you are still in school. Don't wait to acquire it the hard way—after you go out on your first job.

Grammar for Journalists is not a panacea for all the ills from which journalism students and practicing journalists suffer. It is intended only to help cure "grammaritis," which employers, as well as journalism school directors, rank as the No. 1 ill of journalism graduates and other beginners in journalism.

This book deals with the fundamentals of American grammar. It does not go in for subtleties but aims at being plain, explicit and useful. The standard of correctness in the book is not academic but journalistic; in other words, it is the standard of most good editors.

As the author pointed out in the second edition, there is no quarrel with ending a sentence with a preposition or with splitting an infinitive or a verb phrase. It is now considered proper to end a sentence with a preposition or to split an infinitive phrase when such a construction makes the sentence clearer or more emphatic or more natural.

In the first revision of *Grammar for Journalists*, the author was more permissive than he was in the first edition. Now, in this third edition we have gone much further in recognizing usage changes. Although language usage in most newsrooms and magazine offices remains fairly conservative, we must accept certain changes in use, although we don't have to go all the way in using *Webster's Third International Dictionary* as our Bible!

We must be more permissive, for example, in accepting the use of *will* for *shall*. We must recognize that *further* is rapidly displacing *farther*, but we also must realize that many editors—and the press associations—still insist on the use of *farther* in referring to distance or space. Certainly we must yield ground on the use of *like* as a conjunction in the place of *as*, particularly in the area of advertising. Imagine what would have happened to Winston sales if the copywriter had used *as* instead of *like* in the "Winston tastes good *like* a cigarette (cigaret) should" slogan.

The rules may be different for radio and television news writing. We have recognized in *Grammar for Journalists* that there is a distinction between spoken language and written language. The electronic journalist, therefore, must be granted more freedom than newspaper reporters in the use of colloquialisms. For example, the weather forecaster on television should be permitted to say that "the temperature tomorrow will be *around* 80 degrees," and the newscaster to quote the newly elected mayor as saying that he "would *try and* live up to the great responsibilities of the office." Whereas, the newspaper reporter probably will be required by the editor to make it "*about* 80 degrees" and "*try to* live up to."

In other words, the newspaper editor must insist that staff members cannot write it "just the way they talk" because they are working for a printed medium, rather than for a speech medium, and the *written* word is much more permanent than the *spoken* word. Therefore newspaper editors, and most magazine editors, must insist on good *written* English usage, which must be more precise, formal and literary than the colloquial language of the electronic journalist.

Whatever medium you work for, you should always strive to use "good

English,'' which is not necessarily "correct English,'' as advocated by strict grammarians. Let your chief objective be to write carefully, precisely, logically, directly and clearly—and you will find you are writing *correctly!*

This book, the first edition of which was published in 1957, was the first grammar written specifically for journalism students and practicing journalists. Most of the examples used in the book to illustrate common errors in grammar, spelling, punctuation and sentence structure were taken from the columns of various newspapers and magazines and from radio or television newscasts. Some changes were necessary to conceal names of individuals and of publications.

As Dr. Agee pointed out in the Introduction, this book was planned for use almost anywhere in a mass communications program. It can be used in any course in news writing, reporting, feature writing and editing, and also in advertising and public relations. It is used as a textbook, especially in courses in journalistic writing, in reporting and in editing. It is used in many schools as an auxiliary text or as a self-study text-reference. With more than half of the accredited schools in journalism now requiring students to pass tests in grammar, spelling and punctuation, *Grammar for Journalists* is the book used in most of the schools as a self-study text-reference in preparing students for testing.

Students in many schools that use *Exercises and Tests for Journalists,* a workbook based on *Grammar for Journalists* and keyed to the textbook, will welcome a second completely revised edition of the workbook. It can be used, together with the textbook, in class or in the lab or in self-study.

Practicing journalists should find this third edition of *Grammar for Journalists* suitable to refresh their knowledge of grammar, spelling, word usage and sentence structure. Journalists should think of themselves as "continuing students" of our language. Any time that they spend on this book will pay for itself handsomely. Working journalists might note that the second edition of *Grammar for Journalists,* published by Chilton in 1969, was listed in *Editor & Publisher* Bookshelf's "Ten Best Sellers" list for 1978.

When students or practicing journalists find themselves getting beyond the "depth" of this book, they should refer to modern guides to English usage and style. By far the most valuable reference—along with *Webster's New Collegiate Dictionary* (1977)—used by the author in revising *Grammar for Journalists* this time was the 1977 *Associated Press Stylebook and Libel Manual.* (United Press International published a similar stylebook at the same time.) In writing a new glossary on usage and style for this edition, we made maximum use of the *Associated Press Stylebook.* Practicing journalists, of course, are using the AP or the UPI book, or both, often in addition to their publication's own stylebook. Use of a stylebook for references on usage as well as style is essential also for students preparing to enter any area of mass communications.

Two guides that have been quoted often in this edition are: Theodore M. Bernstein, *The Careful Writer: A Modern Guide to English Usage* (New York, Atheneum, 1965) and Roy H. Copperud, *A Dictionary of Usage and Style* (New York and London, Hawthorne Books, Inc., 1964). Rudolf Flesch's *Look It Up: A Deskbook of American Spelling and Style* (New York, Harper & Row, 1977) also was very useful. Incidentally, pay no attention to the publication dates of the Copperud and Bernstein books, which are just as up-to-date on grammatical usage as they need to be and which are still the most highly regarded, authoritative references for journalists.[1]

Henry Ward Beecher, an outstanding pulpit orator of the last century, used to boast: "When the English language gets in my way, it doesn't stand a chance." Mr. Beecher could afford to speak as he pleased, as long as he was interesting to his audience, but a reporter cannot adopt the same attitude. The reporter is working with raw material—the news—which must be made not only interesting but accurate. To make the news accurate, the reporter must use sound grammar, unless he is quoting certain persons whose slips in grammar are characteristic of those individuals. And certainly there is little excuse for the writer to use incorrect spelling and punctuation.

Imagine what confusion would result if a reporter made a grammatical blunder like this one:

> "When six years old, my Grandma died,"
> A freshman wrote today.
> Do you suppose Grandma's playmates cried
> When Grandma passed away?[2]

A newspaper editor would see no humor in it. Nor would he like the remark of the journalism teacher who said that "some students believe that learning spelling and grammar is pointless since newspapers have their own rules."

It is true that newspapers have their own rules, but these rules deal largely with what is called *newspaper style* and are concerned primarily with such mechanics of writing as capitalization, abbreviations, use of figures and use of titles. This book, then, is not overly concerned with so-called newspaper style. Instead, it treats the fundamentals of expression which cannot be

---

[1] Bernstein has a new book on the market: *Dos, Don'ts and Maybes of English Usage* (New York: Times Books, 1977). Material was drawn almost entirely from his thrice-weekly, nationally syndicated column "Bernstein on Words." The book has an alphabetical format.

[2] From *Word Study*—Used by permission of G. & C. Merriam Company.

handled in the ordinary newspaper stylebook—fundamentals which an editor will expect you to know before you join his staff.

And if you are tempted to cut corners in studying this book, or if you begin to think the subject is of minor importance, simply recall the words of one distinguished editor: "Journalism graduates are more concerned with news gathering than anything else. This is necessary, but if they do not know grammar and spelling, all is lost. *There is no other foundation upon which they can build.*"

2
The Sentence:
The Journalist's Chief Tool

Journalists do not manufacture facts, but they do manufacture sentences which go into building news stories, feature stories, feature articles, editorials and advertisements. Almost anyone can make sentences, but journalists are expected to be experts in such work. Putting words together to make good sentences—sentences that can be read with maximum profit and pleasure—is the basic job of the journalist, and *grammar is simply the correct use of words in sentences.*

Our logical starting point, then, is a brief overview of what the sentence is and what it is not. Can you tell the difference between a whole sentence and a fragment of a sentence? Can you tell the difference between one sentence and two sentences run together? Fundamental knowledge for the journalist is to know unerringly whether a group of words is a complete sentence; to know the various forms of the sentence; and to know how to avoid errors in sentences and how to keep sentences varied in form and pleasing to the eye.

To test yourself on these important questions, why not take the short quiz that follows? You may take the quiz either by rewriting the sentences, making all necessary corrections, or by using copy-editing marks. Don't forget to look for errors in punctuation.

QUIZ

1. "Orange Juice" Simpson hesitated for a split second; then he reversed his field and went 68 yards for a touchdown.
2. The team of 24 Americans, 16 Canadians and 12 Australians were soon developed into a highly effective unit.
3. Herbert Asbell of Brooklyn, as well as two unidentified South Vietnamese, were killed in the skirmish.
4. "Umbarger now has lost five and won only two, therefore I have to take him out of the starting rotation," Hunter said.
5. Both owners finally relented and sent their animals to the country. But still no ordinance against livestock, so Mrs. Bilbeck brought in the eleven pigs.
6. It is not my problem, it's yours.
7. The sister as well as the two brothers have been charged with the murder; however the police are still seeking a man who boarded with the Smiths until a month ago.
8. The NFC has now won two big ones lately, so there must be some balance. Although it would not be surprising if the AFC makes a comeback.
9. Rain, hail and wind, along with the recent tornado, has caused an estimated $22-million damage to crops and livestock.
10. When two of the jurors became violently ill, the jury of eight men and four women were discharged.

Turn to the quiz answers at the end of the chapter to see how many errors you missed.

WHAT A SENTENCE IS

A sentence is a group of words that expresses a complete thought.

A sentence is made up of words, and words are classified as *parts of speech*. There are eight parts of speech: *nouns, pronouns, adjectives, verbs, adverbs, prepositions, conjunctions* and *interjections*.

Let us, then, review what a sentence is and what it is not. We begin with a study of what it takes to make a sentence.

SUBJECTS AND PREDICATES

A group of words that expresses a complete thought has two essential parts: a subject and a predicate.

The subject of a sentence names a person, thing or idea, and the predicate tells something about the subject. In other words, the subject of a sentence is what is spoken about, and the predicate is what is said about the subject.

You know, of course, that the essential part of the predicate must be a verb or a verb phrase that usually expresses action or being.

The subject usually is a noun or a personal pronoun. Certain other constructions may be used as subjects and these will be discussed later.

To test whether a group of words is a sentence or not, find the predicate first. Then ask a question by putting *who* or *what* before the predicate.

The deputy shot the fleeing robber.

Shot is the predicate. Who shot? The *deputy* shot. Then (the) *deputy* is the subject.

You might note here that many verbs which express action require an object to complete the meaning of the sentence. Here the direct object is *robber;* it is acted upon by the subject. In this sentence, *shot* is a transitive verb. Transitive verbs are action words or phrases that take an object. However, an action verb is not always transitive, as in this sentence: He *shot* into the air. Here *shot* is intransitive because it takes no object.

Study three more examples:

He *whirled* around and left hurriedly. (*Whirled* is an intransitive verb; it expresses action but takes no object. (*Whirled* can be used as a transitive verb also: Will Rogers *whirled* a rope expertly.)

Ms. Jory Graham *is* a popular columnist. (*Is* expresses being.)

Is is used in this sentence as a linking verb. Linking verbs do not indicate action, but simply couple subjects to nouns, pronouns or adjectives that are called complements because they either complete or describe the subject. In the foregoing example, *columnist* is a predicate noun that refers back to the subject. If the sentence is changed to read "Ms. Jory Graham is *popular,*" *popular* is a predicate adjective that describes the subject.

Forms of the verb *be*, such as *is, are, was* and *were,* may be used as linking verbs. The other class of linking verbs includes such verbs as *smell, seem, feel, look* and *appear.* These verbs link the subject to a predicate adjective, as in these examples: The garbage smells *bad* (not *badly*). The doctor's patient feels *bad* (not *badly*) today.

(Linking verbs, along with transitive and intransitive verbs, are treated extensively in Chapter 4.)

A sentence may consist of only a subject and a predicate without any modifiers: James Earl Ray has been recaptured. (Note here that the subject, James Earl Ray, has been acted upon instead of performing the action. It is, therefore, in the passive voice, compared with such a verb as *shot,* which is in the active voice because it has a direct object. This is known as the passive sentence pattern, in which the object in an active sentence becomes the subject in a passive sentence. For example, "They have recaptured James Earl Ray" becomes "James Earl Ray has been recaptured." Journalists prefer the active voice to the passive, but they must know to use the passive voice when the person or thing acted upon is more important than the actor. Certainly the well-known name *James Earl Ray* should replace the vague pronoun *They* here. Journalists should recognize this as a fourth sentence pattern, to be added to the other three: a subject and a verb; a subject, an active verb and one or more objects; and a subject, a linking verb and a predicate noun, pronoun or adjective. You will have a detailed study of verbs, voice, tense and the correct usage of these later.

Here's an excellent example of the subject-predicate sentence with no modifiers. It is the opening sentence in the lead of an article by William N. Knoedelseder Jr. of *The New York Times.*

> Cheryl Tiegs has graduated. With 14 years of modeling and about 100 fashion magazine covers behind her, Tiegs has moved into the mainstream as a *Time* magazine cover subject. The household face is becoming a household name.

However, you certainly know that most sentences a reporter writes will contain modifiers—words that are used to describe the subject or the verb or to complete the verb.

Let us recall, then, the difference between the complete subject and the simple (or essential) subject, and the difference between the complete predicate and the simple (or essential) predicate. You need to be able to identify them unerringly if you are to avoid making errors in grammar.

Always remember that the *simple subject* is the essential noun or pronoun, or its equivalent, that tells what or who is spoken about in the sentence, and that the simple predicate is the essential verb or verb phrase which says something about the subject.

A reporter has no difficulty in writing a simple sentence like this: Gerald Smathers is dying. This sentence consists of only the simple subject *Gerald Smathers* and the simple predicate *is dying.* But more words usually are added to both subject and predicate.

> The frail, 70-year-old Gerald Smathers, together with his two younger brothers, is dying of malaria in the tropics.

When a writer adds words like this to the simple subject and simple predicate, he may run into grammatical trouble unless he keeps in mind the simple subject and makes the verb agree with it in number. In the sentence above, the simple subject, stripped of all its modifiers (the article *The* and the adjectives *frail, 70-year-old*), is *Gerald Smathers.* The phrase *together with his two younger brothers* is parenthetical; it is not essential in making the construction a complete sentence. Therefore the verb phrase *is dying* (not *are dying*) is the correct simple predicate since it must agree in number with the singular subject *Gerald Smathers.* (Agreement of subject and predicate is treated fully in Chapter 8.) In the sentence, note that the phrases *of malaria* and *in the tropics* are prepositional phrases used adverbially to modify the predicate *is dying*.

The *complete subject,* then, is the simple subject together with all the words grouped about it that modify it. The *complete predicate* is the simple predicate and its modifiers. Until you can distinguish unerringly between the complete subject and the simple subject, and between the simple predicate and the complete predicate, you will have difficulty constructing sentences that are grammatically correct.

In addition to the noun and the personal pronoun, other constructions that may be used as subjects include these substantives: the gerund or gerund phrase, the infinitive phrase and the noun clause. Also, demonstrative and interrogative pronouns may be used as subjects.

You may find the following tips helpful in determining the simple subject when it is something other than a noun or a pronoun, thus enabling you to avoid errors in agreement of the subject with the predicate in number and also in the use of the wrong case.

A gerund is a verbal, always ending in *ing*, that is used as a noun. Study some examples.

> *Jogging,* as well as hiking, has become a popular exercise. But many men and
> women prefer swimming.
> *Uncovering corporate fraud* is his primary duty.

In the first sentence, *jogging* is the simple subject. Since *as well as hiking* is a parenthetical phrase, the predicate *has become* (not *have become*) is correct. *Hiking,* of course, is also a gerund. In the second sentence the gerund *swimming* is the object of the predicate *prefer*. Test it: Men and women prefer *what*? *Swimming* is the answer.

In the second sentence the complete subject of the predicate *is* is the phrase *Uncovering corporate fraud*. The simple subject is the gerund *Uncovering,* but of course it takes the whole gerund phrase to make sense.

An infinitive is a verbal in which the verb form is usually preceded by *to*. The infinitive may be used as a noun, an adjective or an adverb. Note how the infinitive is used as a noun in this sentence: *To get parents to help their children with homework* is the superintendent's objective. The infinitive phrase is the subject of the predicate *is*. Incidentally, *is* is used as a linking verb here; it links the subject to *objective,* a predicate noun that refers back to the subject and means the same thing as the subject.

Now take a look at an inverted sentence, in which the predicate comes ahead of the subject: Hiding behind the shed were a frightened woman and two men.

You find that the predicate is the verb phrase *were hiding*. *Who* were hiding? A frightened *woman* and two *men,* a plural subject that takes the plural verb *were hiding*.

Try analyzing this sentence: Whom has the committee on rezoning chosen for its new chairman?

The predicate is the verb phrase *has chosen*. Test it: *Who* has chosen? *Committee* is the simple subject. Because the subject is a collective noun, acting as a unit instead of individually, it requires the singular verb *has chosen* and the singular pronoun *its*. Be especially careful to have correct agreement in this kind of interrogative sentence. (Collective nouns are treated on pages 29–30, 105–06.) You might note, too, that *Whom* instead of *Who* is correct because it is the object of the predicate.

Here's one final example: *Who* (not *Whom*) will be named chairman concerns the group very much.

The predicate of the sentence is *concerns*. Who or what concerns? *Who will be chairman*—a noun clause—is the answer. In the noun clause itself the predicate is *will be named*, and *Who* is the subject. Although the subject is acted upon here rather than doing the acting, the pronoun *Who*, not *Whom*, is correctly used because the subject must always be in the nominative case.

(In following chapters, full treatment is given to the usage of the gerund; the infinitive; the collective noun; and the interrogative pronouns, especially *Who* and *Whom*. A full chapter is devoted to use of the verbals—gerunds, infinitives and participles.)

Now that we have had a review of what a sentence is and what is needed to make a sentence—a subject and a predicate—let us proceed to classes of sentences. After that we will have an overview of the two common kinds of sentence errors that the journalist must avoid making. These are the fragmentary sentence and the run-on or comma-fault type of sentence.

CLASSES OF SENTENCES

In reviewing the sentence briefly, you should recall that sentences are classified in two ways: (1) as to use or meaning, and (2) as to form or structure.

Classification as to Use

The journalist need not be too concerned about classifying sentences as to *use*. The main thing here is to learn how to punctuate correctly—whether to use the period, the comma, the exclamation mark (point) or the question mark.

1. A *declarative sentence* tells something; it states a fact or a possibility.

The jet fighter pilot died in the crash. (Fact)
The jet fighter pilot may die. (Possibility)

The declarative sentence ends with a period.

2. The *interrogative sentence* asks whether something is a fact or not a fact.

> Is the pilot a Jordanian? Is he lying about the crash?
> "Who wouldn't like to get a doctorate by correspondence?" Mrs. Foster said.

The interrogative sentence usually ends with a question mark.

3. The *imperative sentence* makes a request or gives a command or an order.

> Please help me with this problem.
> Don't enter that room.

The imperative sentence usually ends with a period.

4. The *exclamatory sentence* expresses strong or sudden feeling or emotion. It may be written with or without an interjection.

> Oh, I can't move my leg!
> My God! The plane is falling!
> Ouch! That hurts!
> I won't do it! (Note that there is no interjection in this one.)

The exclamatory sentence ends with an exclamation mark (point). However, don't use the mark in sentences which are not really exclamatory. If an interjection is used in the sentence, it may be followed either by a comma (as *Oh*, above) or by an exclamation mark (as *Ouch*!). Note that the use of an exclamation mark after the interjection makes it necessary to capitalize the next word. Remember that every sentence begins with a capital letter.

Some interrogative sentences and some imperative sentences may be considered exclamatory, in which case it is correct to end them with exclamation marks.

> Is your mother injured!
> Sock it to him!

Classification as to Form

Sentences are classified into four groups according to their form or grammatical structure—the simple, the compound, the complex or the compound-complex sentence.

It is most important that you study the classification of sentences as to grammatical structure. Unless you can readily recognize the difference between a compound sentence and a complex sentence, for example, you cannot possibly write sentences that are grammatically correct, that are punctuated correctly and that are effective.

No matter what the length of a sentence is or how many independent clauses, subordinate clauses and phrases it may contain, the sentence must have unity—oneness of thought. It must be one complete unit of thought. If the sentence contains two or more clauses or parts, the writer must make sure that these are closely related and that the parts are fitted together to make up one unified larger thought or idea.

You must, then, become thoroughly familiar with sentences classified as to form or grammatical structure. Otherwise, you likely will violate sentence unity by writing fragmentary or incomplete sentences; by running two sentences together as if they were one—the run-on sentence; by cramming too many minor details into one sentence; or by joining two or more unrelated ideas—usually two independent clauses—in a sentence. (The two main violations of sentence unity—the fragmentary sentence and the run-on sentence—are treated in the last part of this chapter and in Chapter 13.)

To write effective sentences that satisfy your readers, you must recognize the importance not only of unity but also of coherence (clarity) and emphasis. You need to make the single thought that you are expressing in a sentence perfectly *clear* to readers. And you must learn how to use *emphasis*—how to stress the important idea of the sentence and how to subordinate the lesser words, phrases and clauses. (Sentence coherence and emphasis, along with sentence unity and variety of expression, are covered in separate chapters in Part II, Sentence Construction.)

Let's take a close look, then, at the four kinds of sentences according to grammatical structure.

Simple Sentences

A *simple sentence* consists of one independent (main or principal) clause which contains one subject and one predicate and which expresses one complete idea, thought or meaning.

> Red Brigades terrorists assassinated ex-Premier Aldo Moro yesterday.
> The body of kidnapped ex-premier Aldo Moro was found in a car outside Communist headquarters in Rome today.
> The body of Moro, kidnapped 55 days ago by Red Brigades terrorists, was found in a red Renault R4 just off the Street of the Dark Shops, site of Communist headquarters.

You probably had no difficulty identifying the first two examples as simple sentences since each is clearly composed of only one independent clause and no dependent clause. Possibly you hesitated over the third example if you at first thought *kidnapped* was a verb, but then you probably recognized *kidnapped* as a participle in the past participle phrase that is used adjectivally to modify Moro. In the independent clause, the predicate is *was found* and the simple subject is *body*.

Although the simple sentence has only one subject and one predicate, either the subject or the predicate or both may be compound. Two or more nouns or pronouns tied together form a *compound* (double) *subject*, and two or more verbs joined together form a *compound predicate.*

> *The pilot and the co-pilot* died in the crash. (Compound subject)
> The private *stopped and saluted* the general. (Compound predicate)
> *The pilot and the co-pilot* both *lived and died* together. (Compound subject and compound predicate)

Each of these three sentences is a simple sentence.

Not all simple sentences are short sentences. Both the subject and the predicate may have many modifying words and phrases, and these words and phrases may also have modifiers. For example:

> MOSCOW—Pyotr Grigorenko, the 70-year-old Red Army general turned dissident, has been stripped of his Soviet citizenship and barred from returning to his homeland for conduct allegedly damaging to the prestige of the Soviet Union, according to a government decree disclosed here Friday.

The sentence contains only one subject, *Pyotr Grigorenko*, and one predicate—a compound predicate—*has been stripped* and *barred*. The subject is modified by the appositive, *the 70-year-old former Red Army general turned dissident*. *Turned dissident* is a participial phrase used adjectivally to modify *general*. The prepositional phrase *from returning* is an adverbial modifier of *barred*; *to his homeland* is another prepositional phrase modifying *returning* and answering *where*; *for conduct* is another prepositional phrase modified adjectivally by the participial phrase *allegedly damaging*, with the whole phrase used adverbially to answer the question *why*; and finally comes the reporter's commonly used phrase of attribution introduced by the preposition *according to*.

Most good journalists use simple sentences often and to good effect in their writing. You are urged to do likewise. Use but don't abuse the simple sentence. Don't use it exclusively. Other kinds of sentences serve definite purposes and give variety to one's writing.

Compound Sentences

The *compound sentence* consists of two or more connected simple sentences. Each simple sentence that forms part of a compound sentence is an independent (principal or main) clause.

> Serious shortages exist in many drought-stricken areas, and the only permanent solution is the construction of more dams.

The coordinating conjunction *and* connects the two independent clauses, each of which could stand alone as a simple sentence.

> This mark would be far short of the 51-foot crest of the mammoth July overflow, but businessmen in the three threatened industrial districts were taking no chances.

The coordinating conjunction *but* connects two independent clauses.

> "I accept the appointment; I must finish the job my father began."

Here two related independent clauses form a compound sentence. A semicolon is used between the two parts of a compound sentence when they are not connected by a conjunction. Each clause could stand alone as a simple sentence.

> The cold weather was subsiding; so the people began to come out from behind doors and walk along Bourbon Street again.

A semicolon is necessary in this sentence because *so* is considered to be a conjunctive adverb that introduces a second independent clause. This is a compound sentence not joined by a coordinating conjunction; therefore a comma would not be sufficient punctuation. (This type of sentence error will be discussed next in this chapter.)

Remember that all the clauses in a compound sentence must be equal in rank. They must all be independent (principal) clauses. Such clauses may be called *coordinate*, because no one clause is subordinate to the other.

Journalists usually find less use for the compound sentence than for simple and complex sentences. However, the compound sentence does serve a specific purpose, and it can be used to lend variety to journalistic writing.

Complex Sentences

The *complex sentence* consists of two or more clauses which are not coordinate (of equal rank).

You have seen that the simple sentence is made up of one independent clause, and that the compound sentence is composed of two or more independent (principal or main) clauses which are said to be coordinate (equal in rank).

The complex sentence comprises two or more clauses that are not of equal rank or of equal importance. One of the clauses—and not more than one—is independent. At least one of the clauses in a complex sentence will be dependent upon the independent or principal clause. Such a clause is called a *subordinate* (dependent) *clause*.

Remember that the complex sentence may contain only one independent clause, but it may contain any number of dependent clauses.

As a journalist, you should soon discover that the complex sentence ranks next in importance to the simple sentence. Some journalists employ it more often than the simple sentence. Turn to the front page of any newspaper and check a few of the stories. You may find that more complex sentences have been used than any other kind. In writing for newspapers or magazines you often will wish to express at least two ideas in the same sentence, and you will realize that one of the two ideas is more important than the other. The best way to put the two ideas into the same sentence is to make one of them subordinate to the other in a complex sentence.

Study carefully the following example of a complex sentence:

> President Anwar Sadat was the first to step from the plane and walk down the steps when the Egyptian white Boeing 707, its red trim glistening under kleig lights, rolled to a stop at Tel Aviv's Ben Gurion Airport.

Note here that the main idea is expressed in the independent clause *President Anwar Sadat was the first to step from the plane and walk down the steps*. The second idea, *when the Egyptian white Boeing 707 . . . rolled to a stop at Tel Aviv's Ben Gurion Airport*, is subordinate to the independent clause and depends upon the independent clause to give it meaning. Even if you reverse the order of the two clauses, you still have a complex sentence with the same idea subordinated to the main idea. You would have what is called a periodic sentence in which the main idea is withheld until the end, making the sentence more dramatic. Note that in either construction the subordinating conjunction *when* joins the dependent clause to the independent clause.

> The conference will get under way Tuesday, although Soviet Foreign Minister Andrei Gromyko may not arrive before Wednesday morning.
> Or: Although Soviet Foreign Minister Andrei Gromyko may not arrive before Wednesday morning, the conference will get under way Tuesday.

The subordinating conjunction *although*, which introduces the dependent adverbial clause, joins the dependent to the independent clause.

Subordinating conjunctions used most frequently to introduce a dependent clause that is used adverbially are *when, although, where, because, so that*, etc. (Subordinating conjunctions and their use in the complex sentence are treated on pages 43–46.)

If the subordinate clause is used adjectivally instead of adverbially, the subordinating conjunction must be a relative pronoun such as *who, that* or *which*, as in this example: The president is the only man who can give the order. The dependent clause *who can give the order* is used adjectivally to modify the noun *man* in the main clause. The relative pronoun *who* joins the clauses. (Relative pronouns and their use, particularly the correct use of *who* and *whom*, are treated in Chapters 7 and 9.)

Here are examples of complex sentences in which the dependent clauses, introduced by the relative pronoun *that*, are used as nouns:

> That the Kissinger-Nixon tandem "could well have ordered a nuclear war between Russia and China" was charged in Haldeman's book.
> General LeMay told Keene that he and Broker had discussed the role of the Air Force until midnight.

In the first sentence, the noun clause *That the Kissinger-Nixon tandem "could well have ordered a nuclear war between Russia and China"* is used as the subject of the main predicate *was charged*. This subordinate clause is the only subject that *was charged* could have. It answers the question *"What was charged?"*

In the second sentence, the dependent (subordinate) clause *that he and Broker had discussed the role of the Air Force until midnight* is used as the direct object of the verb *told* in the independent (principal) clause, *LeMay told Keene*. It answers the question: LeMay told Keene *what*? Noun clauses are discussed later.

As suggested earlier, look at several stories in a newspaper and note how often the complex sentence is used by reporters.

Compound-Complex Sentences

The *compound-complex sentence* is made up of a compound sentence (composed of at least two independent clauses) and one or more dependent (subordinate) clauses.

> Curlee figured the values of several pieces of property which lie within the city limits, and he then wrote each property owner that the average cost of curbing would be about $180.

The sentence above contains two independent clauses joined by the coordinating conjunction *and*. The sentence has two dependent (subordinate) clauses. The relative clause *which lie within the city limits* is used adjectivally to modify the noun *property*. The noun clause *that the average cost of curbing would be about $180* is used as the direct object of the verb *wrote*. It answers the question "What did he write?"

You may be able to deal with the Chinese, who have produced 900 million people partly because they stayed home and didn't play golf, and you may be able to handle the Japanese, who are nutty about golf, but you can't conquer the world and conquer golf at the same time.

This compound-complex sentence includes three independent clauses, one more than the required number to make it a compound sentence. They are: *You may be able to deal with the Chinese*; *you may be able to handle the Japanese*; *but you can't conquer the world and conquer golf at the same time*. The dependent clauses are *who have produced . . .*; *because they stayed home and . . .*; *who are nutty about golf*.

Journalists, particularly newspaper reporters, have little use for the compound-complex sentence because it is likely to run too long and to become too involved for the average reader. Editorial writers and columnists are the most likely users of this type of sentence. For example, the last sentence analyzed was taken from a James Reston column.

KINDS OF SENTENCE ERRORS

There are two common sentence errors that the journalist must avoid making: fragmentary sentences and run-on sentences. The ability to recognize complete sentences is the first step in writing correctly.

Fragmentary Sentences

Fragmentary sentences are either *phrases* or *dependent clauses* which should not stand alone as complete sentences.

A phrase is a group of two or more associated words not containing a subject and a predicate. A phrase does not make a complete statement; it is only a part of a clause or a sentence. A phrase is never a clause, and certainly it is not a sentence.

The following example from a newspaper shows how a reporter made the error of writing a phrase as if it were a sentence:

One body was recovered last night. That of T/Sgt. William G. Seymour.

The first construction is a sentence. It passes the first sentence test. The verb, or predicate, is *was recovered*. What was recovered? *One body* was recovered. *One body* is the complete subject; *body* is the simple subject. The second test proves that the construction is a complete sentence, since the words make sense standing alone. But what about the second group of words, *That of T/Sgt. William G. Seymour?* It contains no verb. As there is no verb, there can be no subject. The construction is only a phrase—a fragmentary sentence. Both the reporter and the copyreader must share the blame for this error's getting into print, but the reporter will be held chiefly responsible for punctuating a phrase as a complete sentence.

Many grammarians call this the period fault, occasioned by placing a period at the end of a sentence fragment.

A clause is a group of related words that form part of a sentence. A clause must have a subject and a predicate. There are two types of clauses: *independent* (principal or main) *clauses* and *dependent* (or subordinate) *clauses.*

Study this sentence from a metropolitan newspaper:

> The challenger never won a round on the United Press International score sheet. Although he fought on even terms in the first session.

In the first construction, you see that *(never) won* is the verb—the predicate. *Who* won? *(The) challenger (never) won.* Is it a complete sentence? Yes, for it makes sense standing alone. Incidentally, *never* is an adverb. This first construction would be considered an independent clause, of course, if placed in a longer sentence with one or more other clauses.

Now test the second part of the construction. The verb is *fought.* Who fought? *He* fought. The pronoun *He* is the subject. Is it a complete sentence? No, for it does not make complete sense standing alone. It seems to be suspended in air. Apparently it depends on something that has gone before to make complete sense. This group of words is a dependent or subordinate clause punctuated as if it were a complete sentence—another form of fragmentary sentence. This is an error which the journalist must recognize and avoid.

An *independent clause* is one which can stand alone. It makes a complete statement or asks a question or gives a command or makes an exclamation. An independent clause, therefore, can stand as a complete sentence, but it may be combined with one or more dependent clauses or with one or more independent clauses.

A *dependent* or *subordinate clause* does not make complete sense. It cannot stand alone as a sentence. It depends on an independent clause which precedes or follows it for its meaning; it is subordinate to the independent or main clause.

In the foregoing example, the sports writer should have recognized the subordinate clause for what it is, a dependent clause that should be joined to the preceding independent clause to make a complex sentence. This could be done by eliminating the first period and by putting *Although* in lower case. Thus the sentence fragment is easily converted into a subordinate clause used adverbially to modify the predicate *won* in the independent clause.

Let's take a look at another type of fragmentary sentence:

> Muhammad Ali had one great remaining ambition. To win the heavyweight crown three times.

Here the fragment is a phrase instead of a dependent clause. *To win the heavyweight crown three times* is an infinitive phrase used as an appositive that designates what Ali's ambition is. The phrase should be combined with the independent clause. Because it is in apposition with *ambition,* the phrase should be set off by a comma, or possibly by a dash.

Most editors frown on both forms of the fragmentary sentence and consider it a serious error for a journalist to punctuate either phrases or dependent clauses as if they were complete sentences. An ace reporter or columnist may occasionally be allowed to use a fragmentary sentence for stylistic or rhetorical effect, but until you reach top rank on a newspaper staff you should refrain from turning in copy with phrases and clauses used as sentences. Most editors will assume you made the error through ignorance.

Bob Considine, who was an outstanding reporter and columnist, wrote the following:

> Queen Mary stays active and alert in her eighties. Likes a sherry or so before dinner and a cigaret after.

You recognize the second construction as a fragmentary sentence because it has no subject. The only grammatically correct sentences in which there is no subject are imperative sentences in which the subject—usually *you*—is understood: Shut the door. Halt!

Established columnists and journalists, such as Jim Murray of *The Los Angeles Times,* Mary McGrory of *Washington Star* Syndicate and top press association writers, can use fragmentary sentences effectively, for stylistic effect. Note these examples—with fragments italicized—from Murray, McGrory and a UPI writer:

> Joe Louis stands for something in this country. Joe stands for a lot in this country. *In the world.* Joe came along at a time when a black man couldn't play baseball in this country, or football, or basketball. *With white people, that is.*
>
> (Senator) Jennings Randolph wasn't particularly proud of what he had done. *Or happy, either.* It was simply a matter of survival, and he made no bones about it. (He was representing his West Virginia constituency, he said, in voting against the Panama Canal treaties.)
>
> That's Dixy. *Blunt. Independent. And still a maverick, popular or not.* (The subject was Gov. Dixy Lee Ray of Washington.)

But beginning journalists, remember, will do well to use a subject in every sentence they write and to avoid all kinds of sentence fragments—until they attain established bylines.

Run-on Sentences

The second type of sentence error is two sentences written as one sentence with only a comma to separate them or with no mark of punctuation between them. Study the sentences that follow.

> The Fountain of Youth is not in Florida, it's in Russia.
> Polls are showing that Democrats prefer Ted Kennedy for the party's nomination for president, however, the Massachusetts senator shows no inclination to enter the race in 1980.
> As our estimated landing time approached, we began wondering what was going on so I went forward to the crew's quarters.

The type of error committed in the first two sentences is what English teachers call the comma blunder or the comma fault. In these two sentences some mark of punctuation other than the comma was needed between the two complete statements.

In the third example not even a comma appears, although a comma before *so* would not make the construction correct in the eyes of most editors.

The comma blunder occurs when a writer runs together two independent clauses or sentences with only a comma between them or without any punctuation mark at all. The comma is not sufficient unless a coordinate conjunction is used to join the two complete statements, thus:

> The Fountain of Youth is not in Florida, but it's in Russia.

A better form, however, would be to shorten the sentence by reducing the second clause to a phrase, thus:

> The Fountain of Youth is not in Florida but in Russia.

Another correct form would be to use a semicolon between the two statements, thus:

> The Fountain of Youth is not in Florida; it's in Russia.

But remember that unless the clauses are rather closely related, it is always correct to make two separate sentences of two complete statements, like this:

> The Fountain of Youth is not in Florida. It's in Russia.

To avoid the comma blunder, remember that a comma placed between two independent clauses is not sufficient unless a coordinating conjunction also is used to join the clauses. You are likely, then, to commit this error as long as you fail to recognize the coordinating conjunctions. There are six simple *coordinating conjunctions* commonly used to join two independent clauses. They are easily remembered in the following rhyming form:

> and, or, nor,
> but, yet, for

Note the correct use of a comma before the coordinating conjunction in each of the following sentences:

> The tabulations will be made available to any groups wishing to use them, and the council itself will provide the speakers.
> In the past we have considered the diversified farm as necessary, but we must look at this idea now in the light of today's conditions.
> Commissioner Dirksen abstained from voting on the question, for he had not had time to read the petitions thoroughly.

Most editors recognize one exception to the rule of using a comma before a simple coordinating conjunction that joins two independent clauses: If the clauses make a *short* compound sentence, no comma is needed.

> Steve Cauthen showed up at Churchill Downs Friday and everybody forgot about the horses.

It is always safe to use the comma, however, even with short clauses. If there is any possibility that readers may misunderstand the meaning of the sentence, use the comma before the conjunction.

When the conjunction is omitted, it is always safe to use a semicolon between the two independent clauses. If the two clauses will make more sense if they are completely separated, punctuate them as two complete sentences.

Writers often make the comma blunder when they use conjunctive adverbs (*however*, *therefore*, etc.) as transition words between two main clauses. Used this way, conjunctive adverbs become connectives, and the writer must be careful to punctuate the two independent clauses correctly. A semicolon must be used between main clauses joined with a conjunctive adverb.

Take a second look at the second example of a run-on sentence on page 23. Here *however* is a conjunctive adverb that connects the two independent clauses. A semicolon must precede the conjunctive adverb. The alternative would be to convert the run-on sentence into two complete sentences. Ex.: Polls are showing that Democrats prefer Ted Kennedy for the party's nomination for president. However, the Massachusetts senator shows no inclination to enter the race in 1980.

The comma after *however* (*However*) is correct. Since conjunctive adverbs are transition words as well as connectives, they may be set off by the comma, but such punctuation is not necessary in most cases. But *however* is almost always set off. (Conjunctive adverbs are listed and discussed in detail on pages 37-43.)

Also, let's review the third example: As our estimated landing time approached, we began wondering what was going on so I went forward to the crew's quarters.

If the reporter had placed a comma before *so*, some editors would accept the sentence as correct because they consider *so* a true conjunction that may be used to link two main clauses. But most editors—and the press associations—regard *so* as a conjunctive adverb used as a connective to introduce the second clause and relate it to the first clause. Since a conjunctive is not a pure coordinating conjunction like *and* or *for*, a semicolon is required before it. Most editors, however, condemn the use of *so* as a connective and recommend elimination of its use from journalistic writing.

Some editors might go even further and recommend the elimination of such connecting adverbs as *accordingly*, *also*, *consequently*, *hence*, *indeed*, *nevertheless*, *thus*, *in fact* and *of course*. They are used too often by many writers.

Study the following run-on sentence and note the five ways given below to correct the error.

> Dry climates are good for persons with tuberculosis, doctors often advise tuberculars to go to New Mexico.

This sentence error can be corrected in any one of three ways: (1) by using a semicolon in place of the comma; (2) by using a coordinating conjunction like *and* following the comma; (3) by using a period after *tuberculosis* to make two sentences.

However, there are two other ways to avoid this sentence error and to achieve stronger sentence construction; (4) using a phrase in place of the initial independent clause; (5) using a subordinate clause in place of the first independent clause.

> Dry climates being good for tuberculars, doctors often advise patients to go to New Mexico. (Phrase)
> Because dry climates are good for tuberculars, doctors often advise patients to go to New Mexico. (Subordinate clause)

In studying and working with the remainder of the material in this book, which deals largely with correct usage of the parts of speech and with spelling and punctuation, never lose sight of your main objective. You are reviewing grammar to make sure that, as a journalist, you will be able to write sentences which give your readers a maximum amount of information, which are easy to read and which are pleasing to the eye in their variety.

QUIZ ANSWERS

1. Substitute semicolon for comma, or make it two sentences.   2. *was* for *were*.   3. *was* for *were*.   4. Substitute semicolon for comma. A comma may be used after *therefore* but is not necessary.   5. Both owners finally relented . . . to the country, but since there was still no ordinance against livestock, Mrs. B. brought in the eleven pigs. Or, may start separate sentence with *But since* . . . .   6. Semicolon for comma, or use two sentences.   7. *has* for *have*; replace comma with semicolon; use comma after *however*. Or, start new sentence with: However, the police . . . . Commas may be used to set off *as well as the two brothers* but are not necessary.   8. Must use semicolon before *so*. Convert fragmentary sentence into a dependent concessional clause.   9. *have* for *has*.   10. *was* for *were*.

3

Know the Parts of Speech

Until he becomes adept in recognizing the parts of speech unerringly, the journalist cannot hope to write correct English consistently.

Test your ability to avoid making errors that result from failure to recognize the eight parts of speech and their correct usage in the sentence. See how well you can do with the quiz that follows.

QUIZ

In the first five sentences you are to choose the correct word or phrase.

1. (*Who*, *Whom*) did the police come for?
2. The jury (*has*, *have*) finally reached a verdict.
3. The monument inscription will read: "To (*he*, *him*) who gave his life—the soldier. To (*she*, *her*) who bore life and gave a son—the mother.
4. Either of the answers you have given (*are*, *is*) incorrect.
5. The woman (*who*, *whom*) police believed took the jewels was cleared.

Correct whatever errors you find in the following ten sentences.

6. There's four major bowl games on New Year's Day.
7. Neither the sheriff or his deputies was able to catch the robber.
8. You can see, moreover, why we must try to pass this bill.
9. That book is not yours, its her's.
10. Eisenhower, himself, did the job.
11. Those three men are the ones which must be given most serious consideration.
12. She is the woman who's purse was snatched.

27

13. Clark's knee has failed to heal completely, therefore he may see little action against Ouachita Baptist Saturday.
14. "If you are thinking of switching to teaching its best to have at least five years newspaper experience," he advised the city editor.
15. Oh, how my head hurts!

To see how you scored on the quiz, turn to the end of the chapter. If you missed parts of the quiz, you need at least an overview of the *parts of speech* that are used in the construction of sentences. If you made a perfect score on the quiz, then you may wish to skip this chapter. Only a brief review of the eight parts of speech is presented here. Later chapters have more detailed discussion of the correct use of each part of speech.

All the words which make up the English language are classified into eight groups called *the parts of speech*. These eight parts of speech are: *verbs, nouns, pronouns, adjectives* (including *articles*), *adverbs, prepositions, conjunctions* and *interjections*.

VERBS

The verb is the most important word in the sentence. The word *verb* is derived from the Latin word *verbum* which means "word". The verb is the word which gives life and purpose to the sentence, and without a verb the group of words cannot be a complete sentence. Even a single word can be a sentence if it is a verb with an understood subject, as in the command: Halt! The subject *You* is understood: You halt!

In the preceding chapter you observed how a knowledge of verbs helps you to develop sentence sense. You found that unless you can recognize verbs, it will be difficult to determine whether certain groups of words are sentences or not, and you may continue to make sentence errors.

A verb is a word that denotes action, being or a state of being.

Most verbs are action verbs, but many verbs merely assert being or a state of being. Note the three types of verbs in the following sentences:

The heavyweight champion *rushed* from his corner. (Action)
The handlers *were* in the champion's corner. (Being)
The champion's wife *is* beautiful. (State of being)

Verbs are treated in detail in Chapters 5 and 6.

NOUNS

Nouns rank next in importance to verbs in building sentences. A sentence must have not only a predicate but also a subject. The subject is a noun or a pronoun or any word or group of words used as an equivalent to a noun. Noun equivalents include pronouns, gerunds, infinitives, noun phrases and noun clauses. In journalistic writing most subjects are nouns. Of course you know that nouns are not limited to use as sentence subjects. They also are used as objects of verbs and prepositions, as indirect objects, as predicate nouns, and in other ways.

Nouns are names of persons, animals, things, places, ideas, actions, qualities and the like. Any word used as a name is a noun. There are four kinds of nouns: common nouns, proper nouns, abstract nouns and collective nouns.

Common nouns are the ordinary names of common objects, human beings, animals, places, etc.

> bed   man   cat   town   battle
> black (as in: And black is beautiful.)

Proper nouns are the names of particular persons, places and things, and they are always capitalized. Also, you should follow press association style by capitalizing common nouns such as *party, river* and *street* when they are an integral part of the full name.

> Robert   Mr. Dawson   Delaware   Bible   Wednesday
> Lake Erie   Democratic Party   Colorado River   Wall Street
> White Rock Lake

Journalists should note that press association style now calls for capitalizing regions. Lowercase nouns like *north, south, northeast* and an adjective like *northern* when they indicate compass direction, but capitalize these words when they designate regions: The cold front that developed in the *Northeast* is moving *south* (or *southward*). Others include: the *South*, the *West Coast*, the *Midwest*, the *South Pacific*, the *Orient*, the *Middle East*, *Western Europe*, *Southeast Asia*, the *Western* states, a *Southern* accent, a *Northern* liberal and so on. But the preferred form for a section of a state or city is lowercase: western Wyoming, southern Atlanta.

Abstract nouns are the names of conditions and qualities.

> sadness   beauty   hope   speed   bravery   redness   kindness

Collective nouns are the names of collections or groups of persons, animals or things.

> team   jury   covey   fleet   army   group   crowd   family
> mob   crew   committee   class   gang   herd   breed   brand
> flock   number   remainder

Journalists must be able to recognize collective nouns if they are to avoid making errors in agreement. For example, note how the collective noun *committee*, which denotes a unit, takes the singular verb *is* and the singular pronoun *its* in this sentence: The committee *is* meeting to set *its* agenda.

The ability to recognize common nouns, proper nouns, abstract nouns and especially collective nouns will enable you to avoid many common errors in capitalization, in agreement of subject and predicate in number, and in agreement of pronouns with antecedents. (Agreement of subjects and predicates is treated thoroughly in Chapter 8. Correct use of collective nouns is discussed on pages 29–30, 105–06. Agreement of the pronoun with its antecedent in number, person and gender is covered on pages 119–22.)

PRONOUNS

Pronouns are words that are used in place of nouns.

A pronoun designates a person, a place or a thing without naming it. The prefix *pro* means "for"; so *pronoun* means "for a noun."

There are six classes of pronouns: personal pronouns, demonstrative pronouns, indefinite pronouns, distributive pronouns, interrogative pronouns and relative pronouns.

Personal Pronouns

A *personal pronoun* is one that shows by its form whether it denotes the speaker (first person), the person or thing spoken to (second person), or the person or thing spoken of (third person). The reporter soon learns to use the third person in news stories. First and second person, of course, may be used in direct quotes.

You must be able to recognize the personal pronouns and know when to use the nominative case (*I, he*) instead of objective (*me, him*) if you are to be a good writer. You must also know that the pronoun *you* always takes a plural verb (*you are, you were*) and that the pronouns *he* or *she* must not be used with *don't*, the contraction of *do not*.

(See pages 105–06, 112–13 for more on usage of personal pronouns.)

Review the following declensions of personal pronouns:

	SINGULAR FIRST PERSON	PLURAL
Nominative	I	we
Possessive	my,mine	our,ours
Objective	me	us

SECOND PERSON

Nominative	you	you
Possessive	your, yours	your,yours
Objective	you	you

THIRD PERSON

	Masc.	*Fem.*	*Neuter*	
Nominative	he	she	it	they
Possessive	his	her,hers	its	their,theirs
Objective	him	her	it	them

The personal pronouns, unlike nouns, do not use the possessive sign—the apostrophe—to indicate possession.

The gun is *yours.* (not your's)
That book is *hers.* (not her's)
The dog scratched *its* back. (*It's* is a contraction of *it is*.)

Compound personal pronouns are formed by adding *self* and *selves* to some of the personal pronouns. There are no possessive compound personal pronouns.

myself	ourselves
yourself	yourselves
herself,himself,itself	themselves

Compound personal pronouns are used in two ways: (1) for emphasis; (2) as reflexives.

Eisenhower *himself* (or *He himself*) is given credit for the victory.

The compound personal pronoun in this sentence is in apposition with the noun (pronoun) to which it refers: *Eisenhower (He).* Such pronouns are sometimes called *intensive pronouns* because they add emphasis or force to the noun or pronoun. The intensive pronoun is usually placed next to the word to which it refers, but it may come elsewhere: *Eisenhower* did the job *himself.* Note that intensive pronouns are not set off by commas. Incorrect: Eisenhower, himself, did the job.

When a compound personal pronoun is used as a reflexive, the subject is indicated to be acting upon itself.

The *general* blamed *himself* for the defeat. (Reflexive pronoun)

(For correct usage of reflexive and intensive pronouns, see pages 112–13.)

Demonstrative Pronouns

The *demonstrative pronouns* point out: *this* and *that* (singular); *these* and *those* (plural).

This is mine; *that* is yours; but *those* over there belong to Tom.

Indefinite Pronouns

The *indefinite pronouns* point out vaguely and indefinitely, and they often cause trouble in agreement of the subject with the predicate in number. (See pages 114–15.) The most common indefinite pronouns are:

SINGULAR		PLURAL		SINGULAR OR PLURAL
one	someone	both	many	all
anyone	everybody	few	several	none
everyone	another			some

Distributive Pronouns

The *distributive pronouns* separate groups into individuals. There are only three distributive pronouns: *each, either, neither.* Don't confuse the distributive pronouns *either* and *neither* with the *correlative conjunctions either/or* and *neither/nor* that are discussed on pages 42, 153–54 and 185.

Relative Pronouns

A *relative pronoun* connects (relates) a dependent clause to an antecedent (noun) in another clause.

Kennedy is the man *who* must run for president in 1980. many party members believe.

Kennedy is the man *whom* liberal Democrats believe they must nominate. the poll shows.

Who and *whom* both introduce a dependent clause and refer to the antecedent *man* in the independent clause. In the first sentence *who* is the subject of the verb *must run* in the dependent clause. In the second sentence *whom* is the direct object of the verb *must nominate* in the dependent clause.

The most common relative pronouns are: *who, whom, whose, which* and *that. Who* in its different forms is used to refer to persons. *Which* refers to things or animals, or to persons considered as a group. *That* may refer to inanimate objects, ideas or animals.

(The correct use of relative pronouns, especially *who* and *whom,* is treated on pages 92, 96–97, 98–100, 116–19, 122–23.)

Interrogative Pronouns

Interrogative pronouns are used in asking questions, either direct or indirect.

> *Who* was hurt in the accident? (Direct question)
> They do not know *who* was hurt. (Indirect question)

The interrogative pronouns are *who, whom, whose, which* and *what*, and they are singular or plural according to the meaning of the sentence. *Who* is the nominative form, *whom* the objective form and *whose* is the possessive.

The case of pronouns, remember, is determined altogether by the way the pronoun is used in the sentence. The most common errors are made in using *who* and *whom* incorrectly and in confusing the possessive *whose* with *who's* (*who is*). Study these sentences:

> *Whom*, then, would such a tax hurt? (Test it: The tax would hurt *who* or *whom*? *Whom* is the direct object of the verb.)
> *Who* got the assignment to get pix of the crash?
> *Who* do you think will be appointed chairman? (*Who* is correct as the subject of the dependent clause *Who will be appointed chairman*. The whole subordinate clause is the object of the predicate *do think* in the independent clause *you do think*. Use of *whom* in such a construction is a fairly common error.)
> *Whom* will the post go to? (*Whom* is correct because it is the object of the preposition *to*. This is colloquial usage of the preposition at the end of the sentence. Of course, *whom* would be correct in the more formal sentence: To *whom* will the post go?)

ADJECTIVES

Adjectives are words that modify nouns, noun equivalents or pronouns.

Adjectives either describe or limit the meaning of the words they modify. The use of adjectives enables the writer to express conceptions that nouns alone do not convey.

> The frail, 70-year-old Gerald Smathers died of malaria in the tropics. His two brothers died with him.

The descriptive adjectives *frail* and *70-year-old* give the reader a brief word picture of the man. The use of the article *the* limits the two nouns *Gerald Smathers* and *tropics*. The use of the numeral adjective *two* limits the noun *brothers*.

You can see that it would be impossible to give adequate treatment to a news story, a feature story, an editorial, or an advertisement without the judicious use of adjectives. But don't overuse them in journalistic writing.

Classes of Adjectives

The two classes of adjectives are *descriptive adjectives* and *limiting adjectives*.

Descriptive adjectives describe the nouns they modify. They include such words as: *large, small, happy, sad, pretty, beautiful, clean, exhausted*, and so on. Words like *American* and *Italian* are called *proper adjectives* and are capitalized. (Note that *American* can be a proper noun, also: That *American* speaks Greek.) *Southern* and *Western*, designating regions, are proper adjectives and are capitalized.

> A *smiling, white-haired* woman wearing a *turquoise* pantsuit was escorted into the courtroom.
>
> A *tall, rawboned* man inches up No Man's mesa in a remote part of Utah, peering intently at shrubs and rocks, making a mental picture of the place.
>
> The judge has lived 36 years in three *Western* states, but still retains her *Southern* accent.
>
> About 2,500 *American* GIs loudly applauded Bob Hope and his crew.

Limiting adjectives limit the meaning of the words they modify.

> It was *five* miles to *the* center of *the* town.

The definite article *the* and the indefinite articles *a* and *an* are sometimes classed as a separate part of speech, but most grammarians consider them limiting adjectives. However, you will find that *the, a* and *an* are treated fully as articles—not merely as limiting adjectives—in Chapter 10.

There are four *demonstrative adjectives*: *this* and *that* (singular); *these* and *those* (plural). They are limiting adjectives because they indicate which object or objects are referred to: *this* hat, *that* book, *these* hats, *those* books.

Demonstrative adjectives should cause no grammatical difficulty except when used with *kind of* and *type of*, as demonstrated here:

> INCORRECT: The animals are doing well in *these* (or *those*) *kind* (or *type*) of cages.
> CORRECT: The animals are doing well in *this* (or *that*) *kind* (or *type*) of cages.
> CORRECT: "I think members of the House and Senate want to avoid *those kinds* of disruptive actions just as much as we do," the president said.

Indefinite adjectives are used to indicate numbers of persons and objects. Errors in agreement of the subject with the predicate and with possessive pronouns sometimes result when indefinite adjectives are used. Note the following correct usages:

> *Any* newspaper, of course, *likes* to scoop *its* competitor.
> *Either* day *is* satisfactory for the meeting.
> *Each* one of the three vice presidents *has* a good chance at the presidency.

The *interrogative adjectives—whose, which, what—*are limiting adjectives used before nouns in questions. Examples: *Whose* car is that brown one? *Which* editorial won the UPI award?

Relative adjectives can often be omitted if the journalist will learn to write shorter, better constructed sentences. Note the following:

Thirty-seven Air Force cadets were caught cheating on final examinations, for *which* reason they were expelled.

Thirty-seven Air Force cadets were expelled for cheating on final examinations.

Numeral adjectives refer either to number or to numerical order. They are classified as *cardinal numerals* or *ordinal adjectives,* according to their usage. Examples follow:

one	first	forty-five (dollars)
one hundred	hundreth	one hundred and twenty
five thousand	thousandth	twenty-fourth (man)
one million	millionth	six hundredth (man)

Three days after the *second* mishap they had a *third* accident.

Comparison of Adjectives

Many errors result from a writer's failure to use the correct degree of the adjective. Adjectives have three degrees: positive, comparative and superlative. For example: tall, taller, tallest; beautiful, more beautiful, most beautiful; good, better, best. (For the correct use of the three degrees, see pages 132–35.)

Appositives, Predicate Adjectives and Objective Complements

The adjective usually precedes the noun it modifies, but it may sometimes follow it. When adjectives follow the noun and are set off by commas, they are called *appositive adjectives*. In the sentence that follows, note that reversing the normal order does give emphasis to the adjectives when used as an appositive.

The old house, *drab* and *dilapidated*, was situated squarely in the center of the tract.

When the adjective follows a linking (copulative) verb, it is called a *predicate adjective* or a subjective complement. It refers back to the subject and modifies it.

Bjorn Borg, the new tennis champion, is *handsome*.

If the adjective modifies the object of the sentence, it is called an objective complement: The potato salad made the children *sick*. The adjective *sick* modifies the direct object *children*. Writers should have no trouble with the objective complement.

ADVERBS

The journalist may find that he tends to use more adverbs than adjectives. This is to be encouraged, because the adverb is next to the verb and the noun in importance in the sentence. However, the journalist will find that adverbs, like adjectives, must not be overused. You will find that if you use action verbs—verbs in the active voice—you will not need to use modifying adverbs. For example, instead of writing that the lecturer *walked slowly* to the podium, why not make it: The lecturer *strolled.* . .? (Use of the active voice and of action verbs is discussed on pages 65–66 and 225–26.)

Most adverbs are formed by adding the suffix *ly* to the adjective: easy, easily; careless, carlessly. Not all words that end in *ly* are adverbs, however, and not all adverbs end in *ly*. For example, *friendly* and *lovely* are adjectives, and *soon* and *once* are adverbs. To determine what part of speech a word is, always test it for its use in the sentence. If the word modifies a verb, an adjective or an adverb, it is an adverb.

Classification as to Use

1. A word that modifies a verb, an adjective or an adverb is called a *simple adverb*.

> Editor Holmes read the story carefully. (*Carefully* modifies the verb *read*)
> It was a very good feature story. (*Very* modifies the adjective *good*)
> The Sunday magazine editor said that she could run it very soon. (*Very* modifies the adverb *soon*)

The simple adverb may modify a prepositional phrase.

> The climbers were *nearly* at the top of the mountain. (*Nearly* modifies the prepositional phrase *at the top*)

The simple adverb may modify a subordinate clause.

> I'll help you *just* because you are my brother. (*Just* modifies the subordinate clause *because you are my brother*)

2. Adverbs that ask questions are called *interrogative adverbs*.

> *Where* is Jim Lehrer, the producer? *When* do you expect him? He asked me *why* I was there.

3. *Sentence adverbs* modify a whole sentence or clause rather than the verb or another word: He is *undoubtedly* an able administrator.

The journalist will have no trouble with the sentence adverb used as *undoubtedly* is here. However, if such an adverb is used to introduce a sentence, the writer must know it is a parenthetical adverb that must be set off by a comma: *Undoubtedly*, he is an able administrator.

Note the punctuation of sentence adverbs used parenthetically in the following examples. Observe that such parenthetical words or phrases can be omitted without changing the essential meaning of the sentence.

> *Still*, I doubt we can get the bill passed.
> You can see, *moreover*, why we must make the effort to pass it.
> *Fortunately*, a doctor was immediately available.
> *Incidentally*, Dr. Norris Davis may be a few minutes late for the conference.

4. When the adverb *there* is used to introduce a sentence, it is called an *expletive: There* is only one reporter available to cover three simultaneous meetings.

The word *There* merely "fills in" the sentence. Notice the difference in the use of *there* in this sentence: Only one reporter was *there* to cover three simultaneous meetings. In this sentence *there* is an adverb of place modifying the verb *was*.

Journalists should use the expletive beginning sparingly, only when it makes for effective writing. (See pages 55 and 214–15 for effective use of expletives.)

5. *Conjunctive adverbs* are adverbs that are used as conjunctions to connect independent clauses. Study the example that follows.

> The president insisted that his record on carrying out promises has been adequate so far; however, a key presidential aide admits that "some of the promises in the campaign were made without the knowledge available today in the White House."

However is a conjunctive adverb that introduces the second independent clause and serves also as a connective between the two main clauses. A semicolon, not a comma, is required before such conjunctive adverbs as *however, therefore, otherwise* and *also*. Such words are not pure conjunctions, but because they are used as conjunctions, they are discussed in detail in the section on that part of speech. (See page 43.)

6. *Relative adverbs* are adverbs used to begin subordinate clauses.

> This is the town *where* Elvis Presley was born.

7. Adverbs placed at the beginning the sentence simply to introduce the sentence are called *introductory adverbs*. They are often followed by a

comma. The sentence is complete in meaning if they are omitted.

> *Well,* I believe we should interview Capote.
> *Now* that is what I call a good suggestion.

Other introductory adverbs are *why, then,* and the like. Their chief use is conversational.

8. *Flat adverbs* are adverbs that may be used correctly without the *ly* ending.

> Drive *slow*.   Talk *loud*.   Hold it *tight*.

Of course, the *ly* form also is correct in these sentences: Drive *slowly,* etc.

Classification as to Meaning

1. Some adverbs refer to *time*.

> Darwin Payne arrived *early* for the interview, but Jane Fonda was late.

Other time adverbs are *soon, then, ago, once, first,* etc.

2. Some adverbs refer to *number*. Number adverbs are used preferably without the *ly* ending: *first* rather than *firstly*.

> *First,* you should cover the plane accident; *second,* you should investigate the auto accident.

Always use *first* rather than *firstly* in such sentences as: Jones arrived *first*.

3. Some adverbs relate to *place*.

> Correspondent Ernest Conine arrived *there* an hour late.
> Police said the stolen car was being driven *north*.

Other place adverbs are *here, hither, where, aboard, east,* etc.

4. Some adverbs refer to *manner*.

> For a cub reporter, she writes *well*.
> A crowd of about 3,000 awaited *anxiously* the blast-off of Skylab 4.

Other manner adverbs are *badly, slowly, hastily, gracefully,* etc. Some manner adverbs that do not end in *ly* are *somehow, likewise, alike, wrong, fast, well*.

5. Some adverbs refer to *degree*. These include the comparative and superlative forms of the adverbs: *more, most; better, best; more easily, most easily* and the like. (For comparison of adverbs, see pages 132–35.)

6. Some adverbs refer to *result* and *reason*.

You have been late frequently; *therefore* your work has suffered. (Result)
Can you explain *why* you are late so often? (Reason)

Note that *why* may be called an interrogative adverb in the second sentence because it is used in a question. The answer to the question will supply a reason for the lateness. Other adverbs of result and reason are *hence, wherefore, consequently, accordingly*. By now you probably recognize these as conjunctive adverbs, which were discussed briefly on page 37, and which are treated thoroughly on pages 43 and 253.

7. The adverb *yes* is an adverb of *affirmation*. The adverbs *no* and *not* are adverbs of *negation*. When *yes* or *no* begins a sentence, it must be followed by a comma.

Yes, Mr. Young will continue as ambassador to the UN.
No, the board will not permit you to make a statement.

Comparison of Adverbs

Comparison of adverbs, an important topic, is treated on pages 132–35, if you wish to look ahead.

Nouns Used as Adverbs

Some nouns may be used as adverbs to refer to size, measurement, number, degree and place. They are classed as adverbs, of course, and are called *adverbial objectives*.

Neiko ran the Olympic *mile* in record time.
The premier's speech will take only twenty *minutes*.
Senator Cranston hurried *home* at the close of the session.

PREPOSITIONS

Prepositions are linking or connecting words. The preposition serves two purposes in a sentence: (1) it relates a noun or pronoun (the object) to another word in the clause or sentence; (2) it shows what relation exists between the two words.

That house *on* the hill is the home *of* the retired general.

The preposition *on* relates the noun *house* to the noun *hill*, the object of the preposition. The preposition *of* relates *home* to *general*.

Most prepositions are short words like *in, at, to* and *for*; but note such words as *between, toward, concerning*, etc.

Classes of Prepositions

There are two classes of prepositions: simple and compound.
Simple prepositions are single words.

aboard	astride	by	like	to
about	at	concerning	of	toward
above	atop	considering	on	under
across	before	down	over	underneath
after	behind	during	past	until
against	below	except	per	up
along	beneath	excepting	regarding	upon
alongside	beside	for	save	via
amid	besides	from	saving	with
among	between	in	since	within
around	beyond	inside	through	without
	but (except)	into	throughout	

The *compound prepositions,* as the name implies, contain more than one
word.

according to	in consequence of	next to
along with	in front of	on account of
because of	in reference to	on with
by means of	in regard to	up to
except for	in respect to	with reference to
from among	inside of	with regard to
	in spite of	

Prepositional Phrases

The preposition and its object make a *prepositional phrase*.

The *object of the preposition* answers the question *what?* or *whom?* after
the preposition.

The dog is *inside his kennel.*

Ask the question: inside what? The answer is *kennel:* so you know that
kennel is the object of the preposition *inside.* The prepositional phrase is
inside his kennel. It is used adverbially to modify *is.*

The letter is *from our old friend the mayor.*

The object of the preposition *from* is *friend.* The prepositional phrase is
from our old friend the mayor.

The preposition usually is the first word in the prepositional phrase, but it may follow the object, as in a question:

Whom did the police come *for*?

Whom is the object of the preposition *for*. Inverting the order of the words shows the construction: The police did come for whom? (*Whom*, not *who*, is correct, because the objective form is needed.) The object of a preposition is always in the objective case. (See pages 92 and 98–99.)

If the word has no object, it is not a preposition but an adverb.

The little boy fell *down* the hill. (Preposition)
The little boy fell *down*. (Adverb)

A prepositional phrase that modifies a noun or a pronoun is used as an adjective and is called an *adjective prepositional phrase*.

It arrived like a bolt *from the blue*.

CONJUNCTIONS

Journalists must recognize that conjunctions play a significant part in the sentence and in the punctuation of a sentence. Therefore the writer must become thoroughly familiar with the kinds of conjunctions and with their functions.

Keep in mind that conjunctions perform two functions: (1) they join words, phrases or clauses, and (2) they show or indicate the relationship between the words, phrases or clauses that they join.

Conjunctions are words that connect (join) two words or two phrases or two clauses of equal rank, or that join a dependent (subordinate) clause to a word in the independent (principal) clause. Like prepositions, conjunctions are linking words.

The two broad classes of conjunctions are the *coordinating conjunctions* and the *subordinating conjunctions*.

Coordinating Conjunctions

Coordinating conjunctions connect words or phrases or clauses of equal rank. Coordinating conjunctions are of two types: simple conjunctions and correlative conjunctions.

Although conjunctive adverbs are not true conjunctions, they are used to join independent clauses in a sentence. Therefore they are included here as another type of coordinating conjunction.

1. *Simple conjunctions* may denote addition or enumeration, contrast, choice or inference. Note the following examples.

ADDITION:

Byrd *and* Baker will confer at noon. (Joins two nouns)
Jess sent flowers to Bertha *and* to Bernice. (Joins two phrases)
John entered college *and* Jim joined the Navy. (Joins two clauses)

CONTRAST:

Schollander was tiring, *but* he held off the finishing drive of Australia's Mike
Wenden to win.
The Ghanian tired rapidly, *yet* he kept on running.

CHOICE:

The men must swim *or* drown.
We must hurry *or* we'll be late for the meeting.

INFERENCE:

He will not fail to be here, *for* he is always reliable.

The six coordinate conjunctions are easily remembered in rhyming form:

and, or, nor
but, yet, for

For may also be a subordinate conjunction.

Remember to use a comma to separate two main clauses joined by a
coordinate conjunction, except when the first clause is very short, as in this
sentence: We must hurry or we'll be late.

2. The *correlative conjunctions* are used in pairs or series. They often
connect clauses so closely related that neither clause makes complete sense
without the other. The most commonly used correlative conjunctions are:

both—and	neither—nor
either—or	not only—but also

Both Bess Ann *and* Margaret will attend the summer session.
Either he must appear before the committee *or* he must give a satisfactory excuse
for his absence.
Neither the sheriff *nor* his deputies have arrived.
Baker is guilty *not only* of hitting the child *but also* of leaving the scene of the
accident.

Did you question the use of *have* instead of *has* in the sentence: *Neither
the sheriff nor* his deputies *have* arrived? If so, you may wish to take a quick
look now at pages 153–54 to observe how to avoid errors in using correlative
conjunctions.

Other correlative conjunctions that are not used so frequently are:

although—yet	now—now	through—yet
as—as	now—then	whereas—therefore
as—so	so—as	whether—or (not)
if—then		

3. *Conjunctive adverbs* are not true conjunctions, but they often are used as coordinating conjunctions to join two independent clauses. The primary function of a conjunctive adverb, however, is to serve as a transitional device that carries the reader from one main thought to another.

The conjunctive adverbs are used to denote addition, contrast, choice, conclusion or consequence. Study the following list of most commonly used conjunctive adverbs and observe how they may be used like coordinating conjunctions in sentences.

It is most important, however, to note that a comma is not sufficient punctuation before a conjunctive adverb, as it is before a coordinating conjunction. The semicolon must be used.

ADDITION: *also, furthermore, likewise, moreover*
Estes will head the department; *also,* he will serve as general coordinator of education.

CONTRAST: *however, nevertheless, still* (meaning *but*), *yet* (meaning *however*), *notwithstanding* (meaning *although*)
"I strongly feel the possibility of an explosion or fire is nil; *however,* right now we are greatly concerned with the ecological impact of the spill."

CHOICE: *else, otherwise* (meaning *or*)
The secretary of state must recover from his illness rapidly; *otherwise* he will be unable to represent the United States at the conference.

CONCLUSION: *therefore, hence, accordingly, so, then* (meaning *so*)
Neither side will yield an inch; *therefore* the conference apparently will end in failure.

Subordinating Conjunctions

Subordinating conjunctions introduce dependent (subordinate) clauses and join the subordinate clause to the independent clause in a sentence.

Keep in mind that a subordinating conjunction joins two clauses of unequal rank; that the dependent clause may be used adverbially, adjectivally or as a noun clause; and that the subordinate clause expresses a less important idea than that expressed in the main clause.

Subordinating conjunctions that introduce adverbial clauses usually denote cause or reason, place, comparison, concession, condition and supposition, purpose, result, manner or time. Such an adverbial clause modifies a verb, an adjective or an adverb in the independent clause. Most often it modifies a verb.

For a subordinate clause used adverbially, it is essential to know when to punctuate with a comma. If the dependent clause precedes the independent clause, it is usually followed by a comma. The comma may not be necessary if the subordinate clause is very short or if the comma is not needed for clarity. Usually no comma is needed if the dependent clause follows the main clause. Note the use of punctuation in the examples in this section.

Let's take a good look now at subordinating conjunctions and how they are used to introduce *adverbial clauses*.

CAUSE OR REASON: *because, since, as*

Since and *as* have long been used as subordinating conjunctions to introduce causal clauses. But *because* now is preferred wherever the stress is on causality—meaning "for that reason"—rather than on chronological sequence—meaning "at a time in the past after or later than." It is better, then, according to such an authority as *American Heritage Dictionary*, to use *because* to introduce adverbial clauses of cause and to use *since* to introduce clauses of time. Not all authorities agree. Copperud, for one, thinks *since* is used appropriately in place of *because* in this sentence: *Since* it is raining, we had better take an umbrella. Consider the examples that follow:

> The secretary cannot attend the conference *because* he is ill. Or: *Because* the secretary is ill, he cannot attend the conference.
> *Because* the evidence was insufficient, the grand jury no-billed him. Or: The grand jury no-billed him *because* the evidence was insufficient.

The use of *because* in the foregoing sentences is considered *the* correct usage by *American Heritage Dictionary* and some other authorities. However, there are other authorities who would argue that *since* could replace *because* in some of the constructions. And *Twentieth Century Dictionary* would recommend the use of *as* instead of *because* in this sentence: *As* the evidence was insufficient, the grand jury no-billed him.

You can play it safe, of course, by following the *American Heritage* recommendation to use *because* in causal clauses and *since* in time clauses:

> Schwartz left *because* he did not receive a promotion.
> Schwartz has not received a promotion *since* he joined the firm two years ago. Or:
> *Since* he joined the firm two years ago, Schwartz has not received a promotion.
> But: *Because* (not *Since*) he has not received a promotion since he joined the firm two years ago, Schwartz resigned.
> *Since* the ambassador will arrive tonight, the conference will begin at 9 a.m. tomorrow.
> But: *Because* the ambassador is ill, he has postponed his visit to the United States.

PLACE: *where, whence, whither*
The soldier accidentally dropped his gun *where* the water was deepest.

COMPARISON: *than*

Ellis fought more daringly *than* the champion (fought).

CONCESSION: *although, though, even if*

Although nuclear-fueled power plants still enjoy an economic advantage in all but coal-producing regions, the cost of nuclear energy is far outpacing the general rate of inflation.

CONDITION: *if, unless* (referring to negative condition)

If Gen. George Armstrong Custer hadn't tangled with Sitting Bull and the Sioux nation at Little Big Horn on June 26, 1876, he may have had to tangle with the Northwest Telegraph Co. (The day Custer was killed in battle . . . was also the deadline for payment of his overdue telegraph bill.)

PURPOSE: *that, in order that, so that*

The vice president cancelled an appointment *so that* he could meet with the delegation.

RESULT: *so that, such that*

A deadly crossfire caught the platoon, *so that* not a man escaped.

MANNER: *as, as if*

He is back once more, working harder than ever, *as* he concentrates on trying to regain a lost fortune.

TIME: *before, until, when, as, since, while, after, as* (soon) *as*

Until Vance arrives in Tel Aviv, nothing can be decided.

Woodward was running wild with the football *before* he suffered the ankle injury.

Subordinate clauses that are used adjectivally may be introduced by one of the relative pronouns, such as *who, whom, whose, which,* and *that.* Study these examples:

She is the woman *whose* purse was snatched.
She quickly identified him as the youth *who* had snatched her purse.
That is the jet *that* set a transcontinental record.

In the first sentence, *whose* introduces a relative clause that modifies the predicate nominative *woman* in the main clause. In the second sentence, *who had snatched her purse* is a relative clause that modifies *youth.* And in the last sentence, the subordinate clause *that set a transcontinental record* modifies *jet.*

When the subordinate conjunction introduces a clause that is used as a noun (a substantive), it is said to have a substantive use.

Whether (or not) the U.N. secretary general will attend the meeting will be decided by his physician.

The clause *Whether the U.N. secretary general will attend the meeting* is the subject of the predicate *will be decided.*

The doctor will decide *whether* (or not) the U.N. secretary general may attend.

The clause *whether the U.N. secretary general may attend* is the direct object of the verb phrase *will decide.*

When the adverbs *how* and *why* introduce clauses that are used as nouns, they have a substantive use.

Why Bunker is going to Nicaragua is a mystery.

The clause *Why Bunker is going to Nicaragua* is the subject of the verb *is.*

We do not see *how* we can possibly get there.

The clause *how we can possibly get there* is the direct object of the verb *do see.*

Common errors in the use of conjunctions are treated on pages 152–56.

One of the best ways of varying the beginnings of sentences is to use introductory subordinate clauses. Varying the beginnings of sentences, with many examples given, is discussed on pages 211–12.

INTERJECTIONS

Interjections are exclamatory words or phrases that usually are used to express strong or sudden feeling or emotion or to attract attention. The interjection has no grammatical relation to the other words in the sentence; it is an independent, thrown-in construction.

Journalists will have little use for the interjection in news writing except in direct quotations. Interjections can be used effectively in writing features and columns.

Commonly used interjections include:

Sorry!   Stop!   Halt!   O! or Oh!   Ouch!   Good heavens!
Whew!   Hey you!

Some grammarians call such interjections as *Sorry!* an adjective in exclamation, and call *Halt!* a verb in exclamation. It does not matter how you classify such words as long as you know how to punctuate them correctly when you use them as interjections.

Because an interjection is not a real part of sentence structure, it must be separated from the remainder of the sentence with punctuation. The interjection is usually followed by an exclamation mark, and the next word is capitalized.

Hurrah! We won the game.
Good heavens! I didn't think you could make it.

If the interjection is used in close connection with what follows, however, it may be followed by a comma and the exclamation mark or point may be placed at the end of the sentence.

Oh, my aching back!
Hello, welcome home!

An order or a command may be given in the form of an interjection, in which case it is followed by an exclamation mark. Note these imperative sentences:

Forward march!   Don't touch that wire!   Right on!

There is a distinction between *O* and *Oh*. *O* is usually used with a noun or a pronoun in direct address, and it must always be capitalized. *Oh* is used to express pain, surprise, sorrow, hope, and so on.

O my lover, come back to me!
Oh, how my head hurts!

QUIZ ANSWERS

1. Whom. 2. *has*. 3. *him*, *her*. 4. *is*. 5. *who*. 6. Change *There's* to *There are*. 7. *nor* for *or*, *were* for *was*. 8. Use comma before *moreover*, to set off completely. 9. Substitute semicolon for comma or make two sentences. Change *its* to *it's*, and *her's* to *hers*. 10. No commas needed with intensive pronoun *himself*. 11. Replace *which* with *who*. 12. Replace *who's* with *whose*. 13. Need a semicolon, not comma, before a conjunctive adverb like *therefore*. Comma may follow *therefore*, but is not necessary. 14. Need comma after *teaching*. Change *its* to *it's*. Need apostrophe with *years—years'* newspaper... 15. Need comma after *Oh*. Exclamation mark at end of sentence is correct.

4

The Framework of the Sentence

> Head bone connected to the backbone,
> Backbone connected to the hip bone,
> Hip bone connected to the thigh bone . . .

You might keep the words of this spiritual in mind as you study this chapter. Up to this point you have observed that the subject and the predicate are essential in constructing a sentence. In other words, the subject and the predicate are the two main parts of the skeleton—the framework—on which the sentence is built. They may be compared to the head bone and the backbone in the human skeleton.

A simple subject and a simple predicate may be a whole sentence: Smathers died. A sentence may even be a single word, a verb with an understood subject: Run! However, most simple sentences have a third part also. So do many clauses within the other kinds of sentences. This third part may be either a direct object of the verb or a predicate nominative. Wherever this third part is used in a clause or in a simple sentence, it will be an important part of the framework of the clause or sentence, because it is essential in giving the clause or sentence real meaning.

The *direct object* of the verb and the *predicate nominative,* then, may be compared to the *legs* and the *arms* of the human skeleton.

Until you can identify these parts of the sentence without hesitation, and until you can recognize the three kinds of verbs—transitive, intransitive and linking—you will find yourself making errors that a journalist simply should not make.

You may ask, "Why do I need a review of transitive, in linking verbs?" This is a fair question, one that you can be yourself by testing your knowledge.

In each of the following 15 sentences, ask yourself which c parentheses is the correct one to use—and why.

QUIZ

1. The senator said he really did not feel too (*badly*, *bad*) about his defeat.
2. The skunk smelled (*bad*, *badly*).
3. The U.N. delegation arrived (*safe*, *safely*) in Zaire.
4. One out of ten soldiers (*lays*, *lies*) dead on the beach. (TV broadcast)
5. The Alabama quarterback (*laid*, *lay*) flat on his back on the Orange Bowl turf.
6. He would never let the baby (*lay*, *lie*) still.
7. A foul flag was thrown at the prone figures of two Packers (*lying*, *laying*) in the end zone.
8. The grandmother tried to (*set*, *sit*) the cups on the shelf.
9. The desk (*set*, *sat*) in the far corner of the room.
10. The wounded Marine had (*laid*, *lain*) on the battlefield for seven hours.
11. McEarchen (*lay*, *laid*) the ball squarely into Jackson's outstretched hands.
12. It was (*he*, *him*) who made the error.
13. The prime minister (*sat*, *set*) (*erect*, *erectly*) across the room.
14. (*Who*, *Whom*) do you think the judges will select as Miss Teen-Ager?
15. It is (*she*, *her*) (*who*, *whom*) must deliver the keynote speech.

If in the first sentence you selected the word *badly*, you need not feel too *bad*, because you committed one of the most common errors in English grammar. *Bad* is correct because it is a predicate adjective following a linking verb and refers back to the subject, which it modifies. Use of the adverb *badly* would give the sentence an entirely different meaning, implying that the senator's sense of touch is impaired. *Webster's Third New International Dictionary* and some other authorities now approve the use of *badly* in such a construction. Some editors also would accept it, especially since it is used colloquially here in an indirect quote. However, most newspaper editors and the press associations do not approve the use of *badly* as an adjective.

The journalist, then, should use *bad* as a predicate adjective, except possibly in quoting someone. *Badly* should be used only when it actually modifies the verb rather than the subject, as it does in this sentence: "The committee feels *badly* (intensely) the need for much more data on the subject."

Unless you can recognize *feels* as a linking verb, rather than as a transitive or intransitive verb, you will make this error—and others like it. In sentence

2 you should be able to recognize that *bad* is a predicate adjective following the linking verb *smelled,* and that use of the adverb *badly* would imply that the skunk's sense of smell is not up to par. In sentence 3 the same rule applies: The correct word is the predicate adjective *safe,* which follows the linking verb *arrived* and refers to the subject delegation.

In sentences 4, 5, 6, 7, 8, 9, 10, 11, 12 and 13, the correct words, respectively, are: *lies, lay, lie, lying, set, sat, lain, laid, he, sat, erect.* If you missed a single one of these, you need to review transitive and intransitive verbs. Even if you got all the words correct but could not tell *why* you selected these words, you need a review of transitive and intransitive verbs to make sure that you can select correct words unerringly. A journalist should not have to guess why *bad* instead of *badly* or *lying* instead of *laying* is correct in a certain sentence. He should know why it is correct, and be able to prove it.

In sentence 14 in the quiz, *Whom* is correct, and in sentence 15, *she* and *who* are correct.

TRANSITIVE, INTRANSITIVE AND LINKING VERBS

Verbs are classified, according to their use, as transitive verbs, intransitive verbs and linking verbs.

Transitive Verbs

A *transitive verb* is a verb that takes a direct object to complete its meaning.

The mother *laid* the doll on the bed.

Ask: The mother laid what? The answer is *doll;* so you know that *doll* is the direct object of the verb *laid,* and that use of the intransitive verb *lay* would be incorrect.

She finally *invited* Ann and me (not I).

It is obvious that *Ann and me* is the compound direct object of the transitive verb *invited.* Therefore the objective personal pronoun *me,* instead of the nominative *I,* has to be correct. However, the use of *I* for *me* is one of the most common errors heard on the air and seen in print today. Most editors will accept such usage only if the writer is quoting someone.

When a transitive verb is used in the passive form, there is no direct object, but the subject receives the action of the verb. The transitive passive verb is always a verb phrase made up of some form of the verb *be* plus the past participle of the transitive verb. You should have no trouble with the transitive passive.

The game *was canceled* because of rain.

A transitive verb, then, is in the active voice if its subject performs the action. It is in the passive voice if its subject is the receiver of the action. Use the active voice in preference to the passive in your writing.

Intransitive Verbs

Intransitive verbs do not take direct objects. In other words, an intransitive verb is one in which the action ends; the action is not carried across to some person or object.

The gunman *turned* quickly.
The policeman *sat* on his prisoner.

The adverb *quickly* modifies the verb *turned*. The prepositional phrase *on his prisoner* modifies the verb *sat*. Neither verb has a direct object.

You will not make errors in the use of intransitive and transitive verbs if you remember to ask Who? or What? after the verb. You can see that *set* would be incorrect in the second sentence because *set* would need an object to complete its meaning. Set what? There is no object of the verb; *prisoner* is the object of the preposition *on*.

Remember, then, that three parts—the subject plus the predicate plus a direct object or a predicate nominative—make up the essential framework of a majority of the simple sentences and of many clauses within the other kinds of sentences which the journalist will write. All other words are simply modifiers of these three parts, added to make the meaning clearer. Note these sentences, in which the essential words are italicized:

The *explosion shattered* the *cafe*.
An *explosion shattered* a crowded *cafe* in this southeastern Utah uranium mining town last night, killing 15 and injuring about 50 diners.
Jerry Rodgers is manager of the cafe.
The *explosion was terrific*, according to Fire Chief Robert F. Bryan, *who will begin* an *investigation* today to determine the cause.

In the first two sentences, *cafe* is the direct object of the verb (predicate) *shattered*. This direct object is necessary to complete the meaning of the sentence.

In the third sentence, *manager* is a predicate nominative. It follows the linking verb *is* and refers back to the subject, *Jerry Rodgers*. It means the same thing as the subject.

The predicate nominative may be a noun, a pronoun or an adjective. Here's an example of a predicate pronoun: The manager is *he*.

In the fourth sentence *terrific* is a predicate adjective, and predicate adjectives may be classed as predicate nominatives. Like a predicate noun or pronoun, the predicate adjective follows the verb and refers back to the subject. However, instead of meaning the same thing as the subject, the predicate adjective modifies (describes) the subject. Here *terrific* refers back to *explosion*.

In the four sentences you will find that all words and phrases which are not italicized are modifiers of one or more of the essential three parts. The second half of the fourth sentence—*who will begin an investigation today to determine the cause*—is a subordinate clause used as a modifier. It is a relative clause used adjectivally to modify *Fire Chief Robert F. Bryan*.

Remember that some nouns can be used as adverbs when they refer to size, measurement, number, degree and place. Don't let these nouns fool you into thinking that they are direct objects. Example: The wounded soldier had been *lying* (or *laying*) there an *hour*. *Hour* is a noun used adverbially. It modifies the verb and answers the question: How long? It cannot possibly be a direct object; therefore the intransitive verb *lying* is correct.

Linking Verbs

A *linking* or *copulative verb* is one that links or couples the subject to an equivalent word in the sentence. As has been pointed out, the equivalent word may be a noun or pronoun or an adjective, and it is called a predicate noun or predicate pronoun or predicate adjective. It answers who? or what? following the verb and refers back to the subject.

There are two kinds of linking verbs. The forms of the verb *be*, such as *is, are, was, were*, may be used as linking verbs. The other kind of linking verb, often called a copulative verb, is really an intransitive verb used in a weakened sense, such as *seem, smell, appear, feel* and *look*. When these verbs are followed by predicate nominatives, they are copulative or linking verbs.

The main point to remember in identifying linking verbs is that the predicate noun or predicate pronoun must mean the same thing as the subject. The predicate noun or predicate pronoun simply completes the predicate and refers back to the subject, meaning the same as the subject. The predicate adjective also completes the predicate and refers back to the subject, but it does not mean the same thing as the subject; it simply modifies (describes) the subject.

Remember that the predicate nominative must always be in the nominative case; otherwise, you are likely to use incorrect forms of the pronoun, such as: It is *me* who must do it. *I* is correct.

The captain of the team is her *brother*. (Predicate noun)
The victim of the robbery was *he* (not *him*). (Predicate pronoun)
That yellow rose smells *sweet*. (Predicate adjective)

Test the first example above: *captain* (subject) *is* (verb) *what* or *whom?* *Brother* answers the question *what*. It refers back to the subject and means the same thing as the subject. Therefore, *brother* is a predicate noun following the linking verb *is*.

The second and third examples illustrate why you need to recognize linking verbs if you are to avoid making common errors. In the second sentence the pronoun follows the linking verb *was* and is identical with the subject, the noun *victim*. *He* (not *him*) is correct since predicate nominatives must always be in the nominative case. In the third example the adjective *sweet*, not the adverb *sweetly*, is correct, because it is a predicate adjective referring back to—and modifying (describing)—the subject *rose*.

The verbs *lie* and *sit* sometimes function as linking verbs. Most errors occur in using the past tense of *lie*, which is *lay*. The transitive verb *lay* has the past tense of *laid*.

The beautiful blonde actress *lay* motionless on the bed.
Her mother *sat* erect in a chair near the door.

Do not use the adverbs *motionlessly* and *erectly* in these sentences. *Motionless* in the first sentence is a predicate adjective that refers to the subject *actress*. *Erect* in the second sentence is a predicate adjective modifying *mother*.

In the following sentence the adjective *bad* (not the adverb *badly*) is correct. Here *look* is a linking verb, linking the subject *woman* to the predicate adjective *bad*, which describes the subject.

The woman in Room 207 looks *bad*.

Bad is a predicate adjective modifying the subject *woman*. If you said, "The woman looks *badly*," you would be referring to her eyesight, not to her general appearance. (Refer to pages 49–50.)

The most common linking verbs are *be, appear, become, feel, get, grow, lie, sit, look, prove, remain, seem, smell, sound, taste* and *turn*.

Remember that many verbs, such as *turn*, may be transitive, intransitive or linking according to use in a sentence.

The milk *turned* sour. (Linking)
He *turned* the pages quickly. (Transitive)
The gunman *turned* quickly. (Intransitive)

SUBJECTS, DIRECT OBJECTS AND PREDICATE NOMINATIVES
Subject of the Sentence

Next to the verb, the subject usually is the most important part of the sentence. A simple subject and a simple predicate can make a complete sentence: Smathers died.

The subject of the sentence answers the question *What?* or *Who?* placed before the verb. The simple subject may be any one of the following.

1. A noun: The *issues* are to be discussed thoroughly.
2. A pronoun: *He* limped painfully along the road.
3. An infinitive: *To play* bridge well requires concentration.
4. A gerund: *Making* a lot of money is not his aim in life.
5. A noun clause: *That the bond issue would be approved* was evident.

Object of the Verb

The *direct object* of the verb is the word that receives the action of the verb. The simple object is found by asking *What?* or *Whom?* after the verb. Only transitive verbs take direct objects.

> They evacuated *residents* living within a seven-mile area.
> The foreman scolded John and *me* (not *I*) for our error.

The direct object of the verb may be any one of the following:

1. A noun: He had delivered the *will* to Mormon Church headquarters shortly after Hughes' death.
2. A pronoun: Dick West interviewed Holbrook and *me* (not *I*).
3. An infinitive: Does Otha Spencer plan *to write* a novel?
4. A gerund: He abhors *drinking* and *dancing*.
5. A noun clause: The mayor thinks *that the bond issue will be approved*. They will offer *whatever he demands*.

(See pages 102–112 for detailed treatment of case.)

Predicate Nominatives

A *predicate nominative*, remember, is a word or group of words that means the same thing as the subject or that modifies the subject. Predicate nominatives are used after linking verbs. They may be predicate nouns, predicate pronouns, or predicate adjectives. Because they refer to the subject, predicate nouns and pronouns are always in the nominative case.

The following may be used as predicate nominatives:

1. A noun: David Eisenhower is his *son-in-law*.
2. A pronoun: It was *he* and *I* (not *me*) who made the error.
3. An infinitive: The secretary's job is *to collect* the fees.
4. A gerund: His only recreation is *swimming*.
5. A noun clause: The mayor's hope is *that the bond issue will be approved*.

POSITION OF PARTS IN THE SENTENCE

The regular order of the essential parts of the sentence is subject—predicate—direct object or predicate nominative. In interrogative sentences, however, the object often comes first:

Whom will they nominate for president?

Whom is the object of *will nominate*.

Although journalists may start a majority of their sentences with the subject, they need to give readers a variety of sentence beginnings. You may begin with prepositions, participles, infinitives, noun clauses, adjectives, adverbs, nominative absolutes and with many kind of subordinate clauses. You may even begin with conjunctions such as *and* and *but*.

You know, too, that you can begin some sentences with the expletives *it* or *there*. However, you are warned to be sparing in use of expletives. Some editors will even advise you to avoid their use altogether. But when you find you can use the expletive beginning effectively, do it. Note the effective use of an expletive during the 1977 World Series: There's no Wednesday for the Los Angeles Dodgers.

Learning to give your sentences interesting beginnings is a most important way to improve your writing. (Varying the beginnings of sentences, including leads, is thoroughly treated on pages 207–15.)

5

Verbs Are Most Important

About half the grammatical errors made in writing are mistakes in the use of verbs. The purpose of this chapter, then, is to give you a review of the most powerful but also most troublesome part of speech—the verb.

You need, then, to test yourself on use of the verb. This is the most comprehensive quiz you will have in any of the chapters.

QUIZ

1. The sophomore quarterback led his receiver and (*laid, lay*) the ball into the hands of Granger for a go-ahead touchdown.
2. The man paused in his work, (*lay, laid*) down the heavy shovel and wiped away the perspiration.
3. The Marines just (*lay, laid*) there in their hastily dug foxholes.
4. Part of the marijuana was (*lying, laying*) on the kitchen table.
5. As the enemy force approached, we just (*set, sat*) there.
6. He carefully (*set, sat*) the rifle on the floor.
7. He had (*laid, lain*) there unconscious for three hours.
8. The child saw him (*set, sit*) the bottle on the shelf.
9. The river was slowly (*rising, raising*).
10. The little girl was trying to (*sit, set*) her baby sister on the stool.
11. Her hat (*set, sat*) jauntily upon her head.
12. Either the two sisters or the mother (*are, is*) to be there.
13. The mob (*dragged, drug*) the screaming man from his cell and (*hung, hanged*) him from an oak tree in the town square. His body (*hanged, hung*) there for almost an hour before it was removed.

14. Schmidt (*swam, swum*) out, (*dove, dived*) to the bottom and (*drug, dragged*) the (*drowned, drownded*) child from the creek.
15. The coach's selection of a starting quarterback (*paid, payed*) big dividends, because Kramer (*lead, led*) the nation in passing for the season.

Do you find anything wrong with the following sentences?

16. Grasp the ball firmly; then it is released with a quick twist of the wrist.
17. The dean objected strenuously to us breaking the rule. *okay*
18. If I was in his place, I would ask for a conference. *would have*
19. If Haywood were involved in the swindle, he probably has left Syracuse by now.
20. The 42-year-old housewife was beaten severely about the face, and all four of her abductors raped her.

To see how well you did on this test, see the end of the chapter.

REGULAR AND IRREGULAR VERBS

Verbs are classified according to form as regular verbs and irregular verbs.

A *regular verb* is one that forms its principal parts by adding *d* or *ed* to the present tense to form the past tense and the past participle.

walk, walked, walked
prove, proved, proved

An *irregular verb* is one that forms its past tense and past participle by changing the form of the present tense.

grow, grew, grown   swim, swam, swum

Tense

The noun *tense* means "time." The tense of a verb shows the time of the action or being of the verb.

1. The *present tense* denotes present time.

I *am* late.   I *see* him.

2. The *past tense* denotes past time.

I *was* late Friday.   I *saw* him yesterday.

3. The *future tense* denotes future time.

I probably *will/shall be* late.   I *will/shall see* him tomorrow.

(*Will* is now preferred to *shall* in first-person constructions to express the simple future, but *shall* is still correct. However, *shall* is used now largely to express determination in all three persons. See page 79 for discussion of *shall/will*.)

4. The *present perfect tense* is used to show that the action expressed by the verb is perfected, that is, completed, but that the action is still important at the present time. It is formed by using *has* or *have* with the past participle.

> I *have been* late three times this week.
> I *have seen* him only once today.
> Mary *has lost* her purse.

5. The *past perfect tense* is used to show that the action expressed by the verb occurred in the past and that the action was important at some time in the more recent past. It is formed by using *had* with the past participle.

> I *had been* late several times before that.
> I *had seen* the editor before you arrived.
> Mary *had lost* her purse before she met me.

6. The *future perfect tense* is used to show that the action of the verb will be perfected, or completed, at some time in the future. It is formed by using *shall* or *will* plus *have* and the past participle.

> We *will/shall have seen* him before you arrive.
> The president *will have been traveling* to three continents in nine days.

Most tense errors result from using wrong forms of the irregular verbs. If you learn the principal parts of the verbs given in this chapter, you should not make mistakes.

There are also *progressive forms* of the verb, but the journalist will have little trouble with these if he knows the tenses discussed above and learns the principal parts of verbs.

> I *will/shall be living* well in another year.
> She was *lying* (not *laying*) down.

You should keep in mind that the present tense form is the first one of the principal parts, and that it is used also with certain *auxiliary verbs* to form verb phrases:

> General Guthrie said he *could leave* next week.
> The general indicated that he *may* (*might*) *retire* next year.

(The correct use of tense is discussed in detail on pages 73–81.)

Auxiliaries

Some verbs are called *auxiliary verbs* because they are helping verbs. They are added to a main verb to make a verb phrase: *will go, may see.*

1. Forms of *be* help make the passive and progressive forms of other verbs.

> The rewrite *was done* in only ten minutes.
> I *am helping* Jeri with the review of "Star Wars."

2. Forms of *do* help to ask questions, help to emphasize and help to make negative statements.

> *Do* you *expect* to meet him at the airport?
> I *do* not *like* the way he said that.

3. *Have, has* and *had,* and *shall* and *will* help to make the tenses.

> The reporter covering city hall *has had* a hard day.
> They *will fly* on the Concorde to London.

4. *Can, could, may, might, must, should* and *would* help express mood.

> The president *might hold* a press conference Wednesday morning.
> You *must report* for duty by 8 a.m. tomorrow.
> We had hoped that he *could have been* here.

The foregoing examples are in the indicative, the imperative and the subjunctive mood, respectively. (Mood of the verb is discussed on pages 66—67 and 73.)

If the predicate is a one-word verb, it is not an auxiliary verb. Always look to see if one of the verbs listed above is used with another verb.

To avoid many errors made in use of tense, you should be sure never to use *past tense* forms in verb phrases. The past tense is *never* used with auxiliary verbs. Example: I *had swam* past him.

The *past participle* is always used with an auxiliary verb to form a verb phrase. Examples: I *have swum* the river. I *had swum* the river before.

Never use the past participle alone as a verb. Examples: I *swum* the river yesterday. The teacher *rung* the bell.

PRINCIPAL PARTS OF VERBS

To use the tense forms correctly, you must know the *principal parts* of verbs. These are the present tense form, the past tense form and the past participle of the verb.

The *present tense* form is the root form of the verb. It is the same as the *present infinitive* form: to break, to shave.

The *past tense* form is made by adding *d* or *ed* to the present tense form if the verb is regular. It has a different form from the present tense form in the irregular verbs.

The *past participle* is the same as the past tense form in many regular verbs, but it has a different form in most irregular verbs. This form is used with *have, has* and *had:* have *eaten*, had *drunk*.

The following list contains most of the verbs with which you may have trouble at times. As you study the list, a useful mental exercise will be to use each part in a sentence in which an adverb is included to indicate the time, or tense. For example: *Every day* I swim here. *Yesterday* I swam here. *Many times* I have (had) swum here. Another good mental exercise is to identify the tense which you have used in the sentence. Verbs that most often give students difficulty are marked with an asterisk (*). Consult the dictionary for verbs not in this list.

PRINCIPAL PARTS OF VERBS

PRESENT	PAST	PAST PARTICIPLE
awake	awoke *or* awaked	awaked *or* awoke
be—am, is, are	was, were	been
bear	bore	borne (born—passive voice)
beat	beat	beaten *or* beat
begin	began	begun
bid	bade *or* bid	bidden *or* bid
bind	bound	bound
bite	bit	bitten *or* bit
blow	blew	blown
break	broke	broken
broadcast	broadcast *or* broadcasted	broadcast *or* broadcasted (in radio)
burst	burst	burst
choose	chose	chosen
come	came	come
creep	crept	crept
deal	dealt	dealt
dive	dived *or* dove[1]	dived
do	did	done
*drag	dragged	dragged
draw	drew	drawn
drink	drank	drunk
drive	drove	driven
drown	drowned (*not* drownded)	drowned
drug	drugged	drugged (to administer a drug to)

[1]*Dove* is colloquial. Press associations forbid its use, but it is acceptable for broadcast usage.

PRESENT	PAST	PAST PARTICIPLE
eat	ate	eaten
fall	fell	fallen
flee	fled	fled
flow	flowed	flowed
fly	flew	flown
forbid	forbade *or* forbad	forbidden
forget	forgot	forgotten *or* forgot
freeze	froze	frozen
get	got	got *or* gotten[2]
give	gave	given
go	went	gone
grow	grew	grown
*hang (to suspend something)	hung	hung
*hang (to put to death)	hanged	hanged
hide	hid	hidden *or* hid
hurt	hurt	hurt
know	knew	known
*lay	laid	laid
*lead	led (*not* lead)	led
leap	leaped *or* leapt	leaped *or* leapt
lend	lent	lent
*lie	lay	lain
light	lighted *or* lit	lighted *or* lit
loan	loaned	loaned
*loose (to free)	loosed	loosed
*lose (to part with)	lost	lost
marshal	marshaled *or* marshalled	marshaled *or* marshalled
mow	mowed	mowed *or* mown
pay	paid (*not* payed)	paid
prove	proved	proved (*not* proven)[3]
*raise	raised	raised
rend	rent	rent
rid	rid	rid
ride	rode	ridden
ring	rang	rung
*rise (*intransitive*)	rose	risen
run	ran	run
saw (to cut)	sawed	sawed *or* sawn

[2]*Got* is preferred, but *gotten* is still popular in the United States.
[3]Use *proven* only as an adjective. Example: a *proven* remedy.

PRESENT	PAST	PAST PARTICIPLE
see	saw	seen
seek	sought	sought
*set	set	set
sew	sewed	sewed *or* sewn
shake	shook	shaken
shave	shaved	shaved *or* shaven
shed	shed	shed
shine (to emit light)	shone	shone
shine (to polish)	shined	shined
show	showed	shown *or* showed
shrink	shrank *or* shrunk	shrunk *or* shrunken
sing	sang *or* sung[4]	sung
sink	sank *or* sunk	sunk
*sit	sat	sat
slay	slew	slain
slink	slunk	slunk
smell	smelled *or* smelt	smelled *or* smelt
smite	smote	smitten *or* smote
sow (to plant)	sowed	sown *or* sowed
speak	spoke	spoken
speed	sped *or* speeded	sped *or* speeded
spell	spelled *or* spelt	spelled
spill	spilled *or* spilt	spilled *or* spilt
spin	spun	spun
spit	spit *or* spat	spit *or* spat
spoil	spoiled *or* spoilt	spoiled *or* spoilt
spring	sprang *or* sprung	sprung
steal	stole	stolen
sting	stung	stung
stink	stank *or* stunk	stunk
strew	strewed	strewed *or* strewn
string	strung	strung
strive	strove *or* strived	striven
swear	swore	sworn
sweat	sweat *or* sweated	sweat *or* sweated
sweep	swept	swept
swell	swelled	swelled *or* swollen
swim	swam	swum
take	took	taken
tear	tore	torn
tie	tied (*not* tyed)	tied (tying, pr. part.)

[4]Recent usage strongly favors *sang*.

PRESENT	PAST	PAST PARTICIPLE
thrive	throve *or* thrived	thriven *or* thrived
tread	trod	trod *or* trodden
use	used (*not* use to live)	used
wake (*intransitive*)	waked *or* woke	waked (*woken* rarely used)
wring	wrung	wrung
write	wrote	written

Some Troublesome Verbs

The following pairs of verbs often give trouble. To avoid using the wrong verb, you need to do only two things: (1) learn the principal parts of these verbs; (2) learn to identify the verbs as being either transitive or intransitive. Before using one of these verbs in a sentence, first check to see whether it does or does not take an object. It's as simple as that! Carefully study the following sections.

1. The verbs *lay* and *lie* are often confused.

Lay and its tense forms—*lay, laid, laid*—are transitive. They always take an object. *Laid* is the form for both the past tense and the past participle, and *laying* is the present participle. Some examples follow:

> Please *lay* the book on the table. (The object of *lay* is *book*.)
> He paused in his work and *laid* down the heavy shovel. (The object of *laid* is *shovel*.)
> Bob *laid* the book on the table.
> He said he *had laid* the book on the table.
> Bob is *laying* the book on the table.

Lie and its tense forms—*lie, lay, lain*—are intransitive. These forms may be modified by an adverb or a prepositional phrase, but they never take objects. They are intransitive verbs that refer to a state of reclining in a horizontal position. Study the following examples:

> Her Bible always *lies* on the bedside table. (There is no direct object; *table* is the object of the preposition *on*.)
> She *lay* down on the couch an hour ago. (Couch is the object of *on*, not of the verb *lay*.)
> The soldiers just *lay* there in their foxholes. (*Lay has no object.*)
> Marie *lay* on the beach for three hours. She said she *had lain* in the sun too long.
> Police found the stolen car *lying* in a ditch; it was overturned and wrecked.

2. The verbs *sit* and *set* are sometimes confused.

Sit and its tense forms—*sit, sat, sat*—are intransitive. They never take an object. Examples follow:

Beth always *sits* here. She *sat* up front at the concert, however. She had *sat* there before.

Sit down, Brown. Brown's buddy was *sitting* on the steps.

Set, which does not change form in the past tense and the past participle, is transitive. It takes an object. Note these examples:

Please *set* the table, Nano. "I *have* already *set* it," she replied.

Where *is* the errand boy *setting* the box? He *set* it in the utility room.

But note two exceptions in which *set* is intransitive:

The sun will *set* at 5:56 p.m.

The hens *are setting* (on the eggs).

3. The verbs *rise* and *raise* have different meanings.

Rise—rose—risen is intransitive. It does not have an object.

Please *rise* when the judge enters.

James *rose* to the occasion.

The plane *had risen* from the ground safely.

Prices were *rising* sharply as the first quarter ended.

Raise—raised—raised is transitive. It takes an object.

Charles Mayhew *raises* Hereford cattle at his San Saba ranch.

The man slowly *raised* himself from the bed. (Reflexive object)

The safe *has been raised* to the fifth-story window. (Subject is acted upon)

4. The verbs *drag* and *drug* should not be confused.

Drag—dragged—dragged is transitive and takes an object, the thing or person that is pulled along by force.

The men *dragged* (not *drug*) the lifeless body into the camp house.

The verb *drug—drugged—drugged* means "to administer drugs to."

Police said the two men *had drugged* the kidnapped boy.

5. The verb *hang* has two forms, according to whether it refers to an act performed on a person or on an object.

Hang—hung—hung refers to objects.

He *hung* the mirror over the sideboard.

The Fords' portraits were *hung* in the White House.

Hang—hanged—hanged refers to executions or suicides.

They *hanged* the murderer at dawn.

They found the farmer *hanging* from a rafter in the barn.

VOICE OF THE VERB

Voice is the form of transitive verb that shows whether the subject acts or is acted upon.

A verb is in the *active voice* when it shows that the subject acts or does something.

> Sheriff Decker *shot* the robber.

The subject *Sheriff Decker* performs the action of the verb *shot*. The direct object is *robber;* it is acted upon.

A verb is in the *passive voice* when the subject of the verb is acted upon.

> The robber *was shot* by Sheriff Decker.

The passive voice is formed by using some form of the verb *be* with the past participle of the action verb: *is shot, was shot, has been shot, had been shot, may be shot, will be shot.* The passive voice is regarded by journalists as the weaker voice, and they use whenever possible the more direct and more vigorous active voice.

The passive voice, however, is often used by copyreaders in writing headlines. For example: Energy program stalled/As new deadline nears.

And reporters certainly should use the passive voice in sentences in which the person or thing receiving the action is more important than the person who is doing the acting. For example, the passive voice is right in the following lead:

> Herbert Noble, "The Cat," was blown to bits by unidentified gangsters Friday.

The fact that Noble, who had escaped so many attempts on his life, was finally killed, was more important than who killed him.

On the other hand, consider this example:

> Governor Ferguson shot and wounded a burglar who entered the governor's mansion Friday.

The active voice is needed here because the readers are more interested in the governor and what he did than they are in the unidentified burglar. (How the active voice—and other devices—may be used to obtain emphasis in the sentence is discussed on page 201.)

Be especially careful to avoid using the passive voice when it would make the sentence sound awkward or affected, as in the following:

> Casper's eyes twinkled as he declared, "That lesson was learned early in life by me."

Perhaps Casper's modesty led him to avoid using the pronoun *I*, but the sentence would sound better if it read: I learned that lesson early in life.

Avoid shifting from one voice to the other, and especially shifting from the active to the passive. Notice this error in the following:

> Frances McCartney, who will portray Gigi's mother Andree, *majored* in music at SMU, *acted* for Arden Club and *was employed* by WFAA—TV.

After using the two active verbs *majored* and *acted*, the writer should have written: and *worked* for WFAA—TV. This keeps all three verbs in the active voice. (Unnecessary shifting of voice in the sentence is treated further on page 193.)

MOOD OF THE VERB

The *mood* of the verb refers to the manner in which the action or the being or the state of being of the verb is stated.

In English there are three moods: the indicative, the imperative and the subjunctive.

1. The *indicative mood* states a fact or asks a question.

> Italian police *arrested* 11 suspects. (Action)
> *Is* Harold his only son? (Being)
> No, he *is* the second oldest of three sons. (Being)
> He *was* anxious about getting into a good college. (State of being)

2. The *imperative mood* expresses a command or makes a request or an entreaty. The subject of a verb in the imperative mood is always *you* and is usually omitted. *You* is then said to be an understood subject.

> You there! Stand aside!
> Amanda, please close the door.
> Help me please!

Note that the exclamation mark is used after a command if it is given as an exclamation. And it may also be used to punctuate an entreaty.

3. Use of the *subjunctive mood*—largely the use of *were* for *was* and *would* for *will*—is no longer considered necessary by some grammarians. However, most editors and the press associations insist that certain forms of the subjunctive mood continue to be recognized by writers.

Use the subjunctive mood to express a condition or a supposition that is contrary to fact or that is highly improbable. Also use it for expressions of doubts, wishes, uncertainties, regrets or desires. Study the examples that follow.

> If she *were* (not *was*) my sister, I would take her on the trip. (Contrary to fact)

McIntyre doubts that increasing the appropriations *would* (not *will*) be the answer. (Expresses doubt)

Matt wishes he *were* old enough to enlist. (Impossible wish)

He acts *as if* he *were* president of the company. (Contrary to fact)

The subjunctive forms most often are introduced by conjunctions of concession, condition, contingency, possibility and so on. The most common ones are *if, as if* and *as though*. (Note the first of the foregoing examples: *If she were...*) It is most important, though, for the journalist to note that these conjunctions are often used with the *indicative* forms. Certainly any reporter would consider it better to write *If he is not here by Thursday,* ... than to say *If he be not* ... . Writers must always use the indicative in stating merely a condition, as in this sentence: If the ex-convict *was* involved in the affair, he probably has left the city.

The Associated Press Stylebook makes it clear when to use the subjunctive and when to use the indicative mood. Sentences that express a contingency or a hypothesis may use either the subjunctive or the indicative mood, depending on the context. In general, use the subjunctive if there is little likelihood that a contingency might come true.

If I *were* to marry a millionaire, I *wouldn't* have to worry about money.

If the bill *should* overcome the opposition against it, it *would* provide extensive tax relief.

But:

If I marry my millionaire beau, I *won't* (*will not*) have to worry about money.

If the bill passes as expected, it *will* provide an immediate tax cut.

Here's an example the author found recently in a wire service story. Do you agree that the indicative *was* should have been used instead of the subjunctive *were*?

The controversy over Marston's ouster centers on whether President Carter or Bell *were* aware of the investigation of Eilberg when he was urging they replace the Philadelphia prosecutor last year.

PERSON AND NUMBER OF VERBS

The verb must always agree with its subject in *person* and *number*. The only special form occurs in the third person singular of the present tense. The verb adds an *s* after *he* or *she* or *it* in the present tense: He *rides*. She *walks*. It *falls*.

The exceptions are a few irregular verbs: I *have,* he *has;* I *am,* she *is,* etc.

A compound subject composed of two nouns and/or pronouns connected by *and* is plural, and it takes a plural verb. A compound subject consisting of nouns and/or pronouns connected by *or* is either singular or plural, depending on whether the nouns and/or pronouns are singular or plural. If the nouns and/or pronouns joined by *or* differ in number, the verb agrees in number *with the noun or pronoun nearest the verb*.

> The father and the mother *are* meeting him tomorrow.
> You and I *are* meeting him tomorrow.
> Either the mother or the two sisters *are* coming.
> Either the two sisters or the mother *is* to be there.
> Either you or he *is* supposed to cover the speech.
> Either Hunter or you *are* supposed to cover the speech.

Journalism students seem to have more trouble observing the grammatical principle of agreement than any other. Most students, then, will need to spend plenty of time on Chapters 7, 8 and 9. (Chapter 8 is devoted entirely to a review of agreement of subject and predicate in person and number. And in Chapter 9, Using Pronouns Correctly, agreement of the pronoun with its antecedent is covered fully on pages 119–22.)

THE VERBALS: PARTICIPLES, INFINITIVES AND GERUNDS

Three special forms of the verb are called the verbals; some grammarians call them verbal phrases. They are the participle, the infinitive and the gerund. The verbals have certain characteristics of the verb but they cannot be used as predicates. The participle is used as an adjective; the gerund is used as a noun; and the infinitive is used as a noun, an adjective or an adverb.

1. The participles of a verb may be used as adjectives and as parts of verb phrases used adjectivally. The *present participle* is formed by adding *ing* to the simple form of the verb: falling, writing, raising. The *past participle* is the third principal part of the verb: fallen, written, seen, forbidden, lost, depressed. The *perfect participle* consists of *having* or *having been* plus the past participle: having fallen, having walked, having flown, having been beaten.
Used as an adjective:

> The children watched the *escaping* water. (Modifies noun *water*)
> The *fallen* tree was removed from the road. (Modifies noun *tree*)
> *Trembling*, he approached the vicious dog. (Modifies the pronoun *he*)

Used in an adjectival phrase:

> *Raising his hand*, the man asked to speak. (Modifies noun *man*)
> *Depressed in spirit*, I went home. (Modifies pronoun *I*)
> The tree, *fallen across the road*, was removed. (Modifies noun *tree*)
> *Having been injured*, King forefeited the match. (Modifies *King*)

Always be careful not to have a participle "dangle." For example, someone might say: Climbing through the barbed-wire fence, his coat was torn. Surely it was a person who climbed through the fence, not his coat. Correct: Climbing through the fence, the hunter tore his coat.

2. The *infinitive* is the simple form of the verb preceded by *to,* either expressed or understood. *To* is usually omitted if it would make the sentence awkward or stilted: Bid him *go.*

The infinitive is usually used as a noun, an adjective or an adverb.

As a noun:

> *To fight* was foolish. (Subject of verb *was*)
> He plans *to fight* if necessary. (Object of verb *plans*)
> His plan is *to fight*. (Predicate nominative)

As an adjective:

> This is the way *to fight* him. (Modifies noun *way*)

As an adverb:

> He is ready *to fight*. (Modifies the adjective *ready*)

3. The present participle form of the verb, ending in *ing,* is called a *gerund* when it is used as a noun. It is also called a verb-noun. Unlike a noun, however, a gerund retains some of the characteristics of a verb and may take an object. It requires the possessive case of any noun or pronoun used with it. Note the following examples of gerunds:

> The constant *pounding* of the waves weakened the rocks. (Subject of verb *weakened*)
> *Complaining* about it will not help you. (Subject of verb *will help*)
> I don't like your *going* to that meeting. (Object of verb *like*)

Note the possessive *your* with the gerund *going* in the last sentence. Failure to use the possessive form with the gerund when necessary, is a common error. (See pages 100–01 for guidelines on such usage.)

QUIZ ANSWERS

1. laid. 2. laid. 3. lay. 4. lying. 5. sat. 6. set. 7. lain. 8. set. 9. rising. 10. set. 11. sat. 12. is. 13. dragged, hanged, hung. 14. swam, dived or dove (dove is colloquial, but acceptable broadcast usage), dragged, drowned. 15. paid, led.

Sentences 16-20 should read as follows: 16. Grasp the ball firmly; then release it with... 17. Change *us* to *our*. 18. If I were in his place... 19. If Haywood was involved... 20. The 42-year-old housewife was beaten severely about the face and was raped by all four of her abductors.

6

Using Verbs and Verbals Correctly

This is a "roundup" chapter with three main purposes: (1) to treat in more detail certain verb usages which have been called to your attention in previous chapters; (2) to present uses of verbs and verbals not already covered; (3) to provide further drill on correct verb usage.

In the quiz that follows, you may test yourself on the correct usage of verbs and verbals. Included in the quiz are examples of unnecessary splitting of verb phrases and infinitive phrases; incorrect use of mood; incorrect use of tense; and incorrect usage of future tense verbs such as *shall* and *will* and of other auxiliary verbs such as *may* and *can*. You may find some sentences to be correct.

QUIZ

1. The mayor attempted without any fanfare to get the facts.
2. Johnson reiterated that the opposition would early in the campaign attempt to disprove all six charges.
3. He had never been able to find a discrepancy in Stinson's books.
4. You should read many books on feature writing, study the markets and then you ought to write, write, write.
5. We expected to have seen you at the Marquette-Xavier game.
6. They handed the new man a camera, showed him how to operate it, and he started down Main Street snapping pictures.
7. Until enlightened in today's session, Commissioner Jercks was displaying muddled thinking on the use of the new voting machines.

8. George Washington was said to be the originator of the first cherry pie.
9. Gradually Craig Morton learned to more skillfully conceal the ball, to feint with great deceptiveness and passing accurately to either left or right.
10. She has sung for many years and always will in the Lakeside Baptist Church choir.
11. Mayor Johnson says he shall open the meeting promptly at 7:30 p.m.
12. Up to now he was floundering for a solution.
13. Griffin asked Jercks. "Shall you resign if the plan fails to pass?" Jercks replied, "I shall not resign, come hell or high water."
14. If Griffin can slightly revise the plans for a municipal center and could persuade James and Peterson to reverse their stand, he can be in position to get the board's approval.
15. Penny Dean told the reporters, "I can swim the English channel in record time." A majority of the reporters agreed that she may do it.

Turn to the end of this chapter to see how well you did with this important quiz.

VERB PHRASES

Most newspaper editors frown upon the practice of needlessly separating the parts of the verb phrase. Adverbs and phrases used adverbially are sometimes placed between the words that make up the predicate for the sake of smoothness, but ordinarily these adverbs could have other positions in the sentence.

No editor can object to the use of the adverb *not* when it separates the words of the predicate.

The weatherman does *not* see any signs of rain for tomorrow.

It would be impossible to place *not* in any other place than between *does* and *see*.

Of course the verb phrase must be split in asking a question: How could he possibly vote against the treaty?

Most editors do not object to splitting the predicate with the adverb *never*.

Coach Schwartzwalder had *never* anticipated having three star quarterbacks in one season.

Not many editors would prefer to have the sentence read: *never had anticipated*.

Most grammarians today say that the normal place for the adverb is between the auxiliary verb and the rest of the compound verb or after the first auxiliary verb if there are two auxiliaries.

The session was *needlessly* prolonged.
The delegation must *definitely* be pledged to support our man.
The city budget was *tentatively* approved.

But the use of an adverbial phrase or a prepostional phrase or a subordinate clause to split the predicate is condemned by most editors.

INCORRECT: He predicted that the Lions would in the first quarter score two touchdowns.
He predicted that the Lions would before the first quarter ended score two touchdowns.
CORRECT: He predicted that the Lions would score two touchdowns *in the first quarter*.
Or:... before the first quarter ended.

Both the prepositional phrase and the subordinate clause can be placed correctly at the end of the sentence, and the sentence reads more easily then.

Variety in expression is important in journalistic writing, but readability is even more desirable. The position of the phrase or clause may be changed to the first part of the sentence, but in general it is best to keep the adverbial modifier close to the predicate.

Before the first quarter ends, he predicts, the Lions will score two touchdowns.
BETTER: The Lions will score two touchdowns before the first quarter ends, he predicts.

INFINITIVES

Newspaper tradition is strong against the splitting of the infinitive. However, as H. W. Fowler points out in his *Dictionary of Modern English,* example after example of the split infinitive may be found today in newspapers of high repute. Note these examples:

It will be found possible to *considerably* improve the miners' working conditions, the commissioner believes.
He seems to *still* be allowed to speak at Black Panther meetings.

The use of a single adverb to separate the infinitive, as in the examples above, may get by the copy editor, and a certain amount of emphasis is obtained by it; but most American editors would blue-pencil such constructions as *to carefully use* and *to soon return*.

Splitting the infinitive with several words or phrases is inexcusable.

INCORRECT: He will attempt to within the course of this year's campaign cover all 50 states.

The infinitive *to cover* should be kept intact.

CORRECT: Within the course of this year's campaign, he will attempt to cover all 50 states.

The safe rule to follow is to split the infinitive only if this makes the meaning clearer and keeps your writing from sounding artificial and awkward.

Summer internships are provided *to better equip* students for newspaper work.

It sounds artificial to say: *to equip students better....*
In the following sentence the split infinitive is objectionable because it sounds awkward.

The city manager urged the council *to immediately enact* the zoning ordinance.

The adverb *immediately* fits easily at the end of the sentence.

CORRECT USE OF MOOD

The verbs in a sentence should not shift from one mood to the other.

POOR: The police captain told the youth, "Just sit there for an hour and think of the worry you have caused your parents; then you should think about mending your ways."

The verbs *sit* and *think* are imperative; the verb phrase *should think* is in the indicative mood.

CORRECT: The police captain told the youth, "Just *sit* there for an hour and *think* of the worry you have caused your parents; then *think* about mending your ways." (All verbs are now imperative.)

CORRECT USE OF TENSE

The verbs in a sentence should all be in the same tense unless there is some good reason for their differing.

1. The general rule is that the tense of the predicate verb in the independent clause determines the tense of the predicate verb in the dependent clause. Very often the tense is the same in both clauses, as in the following correct sentences.

Her friends *came* to comfort her when they *heard* of her misfortune.
Her friends *had come* to comfort her after they *had heard* of her misfortune.
The opposition *would react* vehemently if we *should change* our tactics without warning.
Had it not *been* for their foul tactics, we *would have had* a tighter contest.

2. Unless you are quoting someone who is deficient in grammar, avoid the use of the present tense to express past actions.

INCORRECT: He raced fifteen yards to his left, then stops dead in his tracks.
Foster makes a difficult one-handed catch and then threw cleanly to home plate to catch Cash.

The verbs *stops* and *makes* should be past tense to agree with *raced* and *threw*.

CORRECT: He *raced* fifteen yards to his left, then *stopped* dead in his tracks.
Foster *made* a difficult one-handed catch and then *threw* cleanly to home plate to catch Cash.

3. The present tense may be used occasionally to refer to future action. Most editors would advise using the future tense in such cases, however.

The president *flies* (*will fly*) to California tomorrow.

This use is called the *historical present tense* and its use in newspaper headlines is standard practice.

4. Many journalism students puzzle over whether to use the present-tense form *is said, is reported,* etc., or the past-tense form *was said, was reported,* etc., in writing about past action. Most editors consider the present-tense form correct.

Yesterday the governor *is reported* to have told Californians...
The Secretary of the Interior left the train at Chicago, it *is said*.

5. It is also correct to use the present tense in referring to a universal truth or a permanent fact, within a dependent clause.

He reminded his audience that slums *breed* (not *bred*) criminals.
He recalled that the two countries *are* not in the same hemisphere.

However, there is a strong trend toward using the past tense form in a dependent clause following the use of the past tense in the independent clause.

The lost girl told police that she *lived* in South Evanston.
Their experiments proved that yellow fever *was* transmitted by the bite of a mosquito.

Be sure, however, to use the past tense in the independent clause in referring to a universal truth.

Pasteur's discovery *was* (not *is*) of great economic value.

6. There is some controversy over the tense to be used in direct quotations

and indirect quotations, but in general the following rule is accepted: In an indirect quotation that follows a verb in the past tense, keep the present tense in the subordinate clause unless the past tense was used in the original quotation. In other words, retain the tense used in the original quotation in the indirect quotation.

The senator declared that the fear of Communists *is* a real fear.

However, many journalists use the past tense in both clauses:

The senator declared that the fear of Communists *was* a real fear.

7. Many errors are made in using the perfect tenses. Recall the forms of the perfect tenses in the active and passive voice, and of the progressive forms of the verbs.

PRESENT PERFECT

ACTIVE	PASSIVE
I have beaten	I have been beaten
you have beaten	you have been beaten
he, she, it has beaten	he, she, it has been beaten
we have beaten	we have been beaten
you have beaten	you have been beaten
they have beaten	they have been beaten

PAST PERFECT

ACTIVE	PASSIVE
I had beaten, etc.	I had been beaten, etc.

FUTURE PERFECT

ACTIVE	PASSIVE
I shall/will have beaten	I shall/will have been beaten
you will have beaten	you will have been beaten
he, she, it will have beaten	he, she, it will have been beaten
we shall/will have beaten	we shall/will have been beaten
you will have beaten	you will have been beaten
they will have beaten	they will have been beaten

PROGRESSIVE FORMS

I am beating, I had been beating, I shall/will have been beating.

a. The *future perfect tense* must be used to indicate an action that **will have** been completed before some expressed time in the future.

By next year he *will have been* with the company 25 years.

Will be would be incorrect in this sentence. Avoid incorrect use of the future tense for the future perfect.

b. The *present perfect tense,* not the past tense, is used to refer to action that began at some indefinite time in the past and is continuing in the present; or to refer to some action that has been completed when the statement is made; or to refer to actions that happen frequently or continuously.

> Up to now, he *has been floundering* (not *was floundering*) for a solution.
> In her first month on the newspaper she *has learned* to turn out good copy.
> The team *has been playing* well all season.

c. The *past perfect tense* refers to some action completed before the past time of the verb in the other clause.

> He *had married* (not *married*) Irene before he got his inheritance.
> After the deputy *had warned* the prisoner, he locked him in.
> Because he *had turned* (not *turned*) in the story late, it missed the first edition.

You will note that in these sentences the past perfect refers to action definitely completed in the past, and that this past time preceded the other past event mentioned in the sentence.

You will not make errors in using verbs if you strive to be consistent in the use of tenses. Always remember to avoid needless shifting from one tense to another.

8. The *infinitive* used after a verb in the past or past perfect tense very often causes trouble unnecessarily when the writer tries to force the infinitive into the past tense. The infinitive is usually present tense, and the writer must guard against making the common error of letting the infinitive be attracted into the perfect tense.

> The president intended *to present* the matter earlier.

The president intended to do what? He intended *to present* the matter. It would be incorrect to say "to have presented."

This error is made most often in using the perfect infinitive instead of the present infinitive after the past perfect subjunctive of such verbs as *like, intend, hope, desire, wish, want* and the like. Consider the examples that follow.

> The chairman would have liked *to obtain* (not *to have obtained*) a negative vote on the question.
> Shawhan had hoped *to leave* (not *to have left*) Des Moines last week.
> The vice president had wanted *to resign* (not *to have resigned*) yesterday.

The perfect infinitive may be used after a verb not in the past perfect tense, of course, but the present infinitive is preferred by many writers in such constructions as these:

He *was* the first ever *to win* (or *ever to have won*) the governorship without a runoff.

He intended *to submit* (or *to have submitted*) his resignation by yesterday.

The *present perfect infinitive* is used, however, if the action was completed at the time indicated by the predicate.

Benjamin Harris is said *to have been* one of the most militant editors in the history of the press.

That book was said *to have been published* in the eighteenth century.

Also, the perfect infinitive is used with a verb in either the past tense or the past perfect tense when the verb expresses hope or desire that was not realized.

Krueger hoped *to have introduced* his bill three days earlier. (It was not introduced then.)

9. Participles also give trouble sometimes.

The *present participle* is used when the action it refers to has the same time as the main verb in the sentence.

Being first in line, he *is* the winner of a complimentary ticket.

The *past participle* is used when it refers to action that came before the time of the main verb in the sentence.

Having been (not *Being*) first in line, he *was given* a free ticket.

Check particularly the tense of a participle that follows a verb. In the following sentence, the main verb is in the present tense, but the action of the participle occurred before that time; therefore the past participle is used.

This *is* his most prized cup, *having been given* (not *being given*) him for winning the National Open Tournament.

Whether to use the present participle or the perfect participle can present a problem sometimes. For example, consider this sentence: Testing the springboard a few times, he dived into the pool. Should the sentence have read: *Having tested* the springboard a few times, he dived into the pool. Bernstein advises use of the perfect participle only if there is a significant interval between the two actions or events. Because there is no significant interval here, he would advise using: *Testing* the springboard a few times, he dived into the pool.

10. Watch closely the tenses of compound verb phrases and of verbs used in compound and complex sentences. If the principal verb changes its

spelling in its use later in the sentence, it must be repeated, not left to be understood.

> She *has sung* for many years and always *will sing* (not *will*) in the Lakeside Baptist Church choir.

Sing must be given after *will*, since this future tense form differs in spelling from *sung* in *has sung*, which is in the perfect tense.

11. When two or more predicates in a sentence have different tenses, the subject must be repeated with each verb.

> *He installed* the split-T system at the university in 1959; *he has used* it every year since; and *he* probably *will continue* to use it as long as he coaches.

12. Predicates used in clauses of equal rank, as in two or more independent clauses or in two or more dependent clauses, should agree in tense and in every other possible way. The predicates should have the same subjects unless retaining the same subject is impossible or extremely awkward. This is called using parallel construction. The following sentences illustrate parallel construction:

> Tarkenton *fakes* the ball well and *he passes* (not *is passing*) superbly.
> If *he can perfect* his left jab and *can put* (not *could put*) on more weight, *he may go* on to take the championship.

Awkward errors may result from failure to keep parallel construction, especially when equivalent clauses are joined by the coordinate conjunctions *and, but* or *or* in compound sentences.

> AWKWARD: The quarterback sidestepped the charging tackle and the ball *was snapped* to wingback Johnson.
> CORRECT: The quarterback sidestepped the charging tackle and *snapped* the ball to wingback Jackson.

The awkward compound sentence above has been converted into a simple sentence with a compound predicate.

> AWKWARD: Burgin *committed* two goal-line fumbles, but they *could not score*.
> CORRECT: Burgin *committed* two goal-line fumbles, but the opposition *failed* to make a touchdown.

Note also in the following sentence that parallel construction forbids mixing of infinitives and participles or gerunds as equivalents within the same complete predicate.

> WRONG: He tried *charging* the line fast and *to get* through the guard and tackle.
> CORRECT: He tried *charging* the line fast and *getting* through the guard and tackle.
> *Or:* He tried *to charge*... and *to get* through...

TROUBLESOME VERBS
Shall and Will

No longer does a writer have to puzzle over whether to use *shall* or *will* in the future tense.

The old formula, you may recall, was to use *shall* with the first person and *will* with the second and third persons to express the simple future: I *shall* leave early. You (or *They*) *will* leave early.

To express determination, resolution, emphatic assurance, command, promise, obligation and the like, the old formula was reversed, with *will* to be used with the first person and *shall* with the second and third persons.

But today the old rules no longer apply. *Will* has replaced *shall* for the most part. However, the journalist must recognize that *shall* is not extinct.

Shall now is used to express determination. This reverses the old rule, which required *will* with the first person. Winston Churchill, you know, violated the old rule in 1940 with a superb example of using *shall*, rather than *will*, to express determination: "We *shall* not flag or fail. We *shall* go on to the end. We *shall* fight in France, we *shall* fight on the seas and oceans...."

Note the effective use of *shall* in an AP story: "*Shall* we support and give confidence to those in the Middle East who work for moderation and peace?" Carter wrote. "Or *shall* we turn them aside, shattering their confidence in us and serving the cause of radicalism?"

The modern, simple new rules to follow in using *shall* and *will* are succinctly stated in The Associated Press Stylebook:

Use *shall* to express determination: We *shall* overcome. You and he *shall* stay.

Either *shall* or *will* may be used in first-person constructions that do not emphasize determination: We *shall* hold a meeting. We *will* hold a meeting.

For second and third-person constructions, use *will* unless determination is stressed: You *will* like it. She *will* not be pleased.

In addition to following the foregoing rules, the journalist will continue to use *shall* in first-person questions where it is used idiomatically, as a rhetorical question: *Shall* we dance?

Should and Would

Should has largely followed the same fate as *shall*, and it is no longer necessary to differentiate between *should* and *would* except in these instances: *Should* is generally used now in the sense of *ought to*, expressing obligation. We *should* vote for the resolution or resign from the board.

Also, use *should* in expressing a condition in the future tense. If they *should* respond by Wednesday, let us know immediately. But use *would* in the main clause following a conditional clause in a past tense: If Sanders *had not had* an injured ankle, Thomas *would* not have been in the lineup.

Use *would* also to express a customary action: Margerum *would* always arrive at his office about 9 a.m.

Can and Could

Present tense *can* and past tense *could* ordinarily express ability, power, and so on.

> Nolan Ryan *can* (or Walter Johnson *could*) throw the fastest ball in the majors.
> He *can* fire you, remember. He said he *could* fire you.

May and Might

Present tense *may* and past tense *might* express permission or possibility. Don't misuse *can* for *may*.

> *May* I take this assignment? You *may* (not *can*).
> The instructor told the pupils that they *might* (not *could*) leave.
> It is possible that I *may* be able to join you in London.

Also, it is necessary to use *might*—the subjunctive form—to express a condition contrary to fact: If the board had obtained the data needed, it *might* (not *may*) have accepted the proposal.

Must and Ought

The auxiliary verb *must* is used in the present tense to express obligation, necessity, etc.

> The message *must* (not *should*) be delivered by seven o'clock.
> Soldiers *must* obey the orders of their commanders.

The auxiliary verb *ought* is sometimes used to express duty or responsibility in the present tense. It is a stronger form than *should*.

> You *ought* to keep an accurate set of books.
> Gordon McLendon *ought* to run for Congress.

Miscellaneous Uses

1. As you have seen, the auxiliaries *shall, will, may* and *can* ordinarily are

used in the subordinate clause if the governing verb in the independent clause is in the present tense. The auxiliaries *should, would, might* and *could* are used if the governing verb is in the past tense. However, *would* may now be used in place of *should*. Observe the following examples:

> The captain *tells* us that we *may get* a ten-day leave.
> The captain *told* us that we *might get* a ten-day leave.
> The captain *told* us that we *would* get a ten-day leave.
> The chairman *said* (that) he *would call* (not *will call*) a special meeting Tuesday to consider the petition.
> If Detroit *had* not *committed* four errors, the Tigers *might have won* the game.
> If Detroit *had* not *committed* four errors, the Tigers probably *would have won* the game.

After a verb in the present perfect tense in an independent clause, *may* should be used in the dependent clause. After a verb in the past perfect, *might* is correct.

> The captain *has said* that we *may take* a ten-day leave.
> The captain *had said* that we *might take* a ten-day leave.

2. The auxiliary verb *do* is used in what is called the *emphatic form* of the verb. *Do, does* and *did* add emphasis to the main verb.

> He *does intend* to come, doesn't he?
> I *did do* the exercise, I tell you.
> They really *did mean* what they said.

Do, does and *did* may be used in place of the main verb, as in this sentence:

> They know that Jenks stole the money, although he maintains that he *didn't* (steal it).

3. Keep in mind the fact that *has* and *have* are used as main verbs as well as auxiliary verbs.

> The company *has* (*has obtained*) a franchise.

Avoid using *has* or *have* with *got*.

> I *have* (not *have got*) two classes tomorrow.

Below, *has* is an auxiliary in the present perfect tense. Also, the use of *has got* is more emphatic.

> The FBI *has* finally *got* Public Enemy No. 1.

QUIZ ANSWERS

1. Place *without any fanfare* either first or last in sentence. 2. Place *early in the campaign* last. 3. Correct. 4. Delete *you ought to*. 5. We expected to see you . . . 6. They handed the new man . . . and started him down . . . 7. Change *was displaying* to *had been displaying*. 8. George Washington is said to have been the originator . . . 9. Gradually Craig Morton learned to conceal the ball more skillfully, to feint with great deceptiveness and to pass accurately . . . 10. Needs *sing* after *will*. 11. Change *shall* to *will*. 12. Change *was floundering* to *has been floundering*. 13. Change first *shall* to *will;* second *shall* is now considered correct, to express determination. 14. Change *could* to *can*. 15. Change *may* to *could* or *can* or *might*.

7
Properties of Nouns and Pronouns

In most of the remaining chapters you will find yourself concerned with proper usage of the parts of speech in writing correct sentences. Before proceeding to a study of errors commonly made in the use of the subject and the predicate together, it is logical that you first have further review of *nouns* and words and constructions used as nouns—and of *pronouns*.

Test your knowledge of nouns and pronouns—and their correct use—by taking the following quiz. If you have difficulty with the quiz, you need further study of the properties of nouns and pronouns, particularly of *case* and *number*.

QUIZ

Correct any errors in the following:

1. The dog is lying on it's back, but I cant tell whether its dead or not.
2. Baker's dithering has enraged the anti's and worried the pro's.
3. The Buccaneers, like anyone in their position, would make a deal for Campbell if it was sufficiently significant, but remember last year when everybody talked about them trading their choice and they kept it and drafted Leroy Selmon.
4. The two Mexican's faces looked familiar.
5. Her lady's hats are famous throughout the nation.
6. That is the Ellis' house.
7. Father sent for the children—Lillian, Curtis and I.

Select the correct word in the following:

8. They asked for Reese and (I, me).

9. If I were (he, him), I would resign.
10. (Who, Whom) will be nominated in 1972?
11. Between you and (I, me), I think she is guilty.
12. Most of these people, like (us, we) Americans, have the free ballot.
13. (Whom, Who) do the experts think will win the Orange Bowl game?
14. Could it have been (him, he) (who, whom) was injured?
15. Mrs. Castleberry will serve as (chairperson, chairwoman) and Mr. Hitt will be the (spokesman, spokesperson).
16. Do you remember (who, whom) it was (who, whom, that) we invited first?
17. (Who, Whom) do the police suspect?
18. They declared the winners to be Jane, Joe and (I, myself, me).
19. It looks as if no one except (myself, me, I) can be there early.
20. The captain ordered John and (I, me, myself) to clean our rifles.

Refer to the end of the chapter to see how many errors you missed.

Briefly review the discussion of nouns and pronouns in Chapter 3. Recall that nouns are words used to name persons and things, and that there are four kinds of nouns: common, proper, abstract and collective. And, recall that a pronoun is a word used in place of a noun.

Nouns and pronouns have four properties: gender, number, person and case.

GENDER AND SEX (SEXISM)

Gender is purely a grammatical term and is not synonymous with *sex*. Today's journalists must be largely concerned with sexism. They must especially avoid discrimination against women.

It is still necessary for writers to recognize the four genders: *feminine* (woman, actress, cow); *masculine* (man, actor, bull); *neuter* (implies no sex, like house); and *common gender*, which implies that the person or animal may be masculine or feminine, but the gender is not stated, such as *child* or *dog*.

But the main problem today is to see that women receive the same treatment as men in all areas of coverage.

In compiling the 1977 AP-UPI Stylebook, the editors had difficulty adopting a "uniform" style in the use of courtesy titles for women.

The press associations prohibit the use of courtesy titles (Miss, Mr., Mrs., or Ms.) on first reference. The first and last names of the person should be used: Betty Ford, James Schlesinger. On sports wires, AP does not permit the use of courtesy titles *in any reference* unless needed to distinguish among persons of the same last name. For example, it would be Martina Navratilova on first reference and only Navratilova on subsequent references. On news wires, AP uses courtesy titles for women on second reference, following the woman's preference.

The unisex advocates suffered a setback in the new style. AP calls for avoiding the use of coined words such as *chairperson* or *spokesperson* in regular text. Instead, the terms *chairman, chairwoman, spokesman* and *spokeswoman* are recommended. Or, if applicable, use a neutral word such as *leader* or *representative*, advises AP. *Chairperson* or similar coinage should be used only in direct quotations or when it is the formal description of an office, according to the new stylebooks.

Copperud calls the use of *newsperson* for *reporter* "the most obnoxious of these obsequious terms," and he wonders if it is possible that *personkind* will replace *mankind* as meaning *human being*. It has even been suggested that since *personkind* contains the masculine *son*, possibly both *personkind* and *perdaughterkind* may be necessary.

NUMBER OF NOUNS AND PRONOUNS

The *number* of a noun or a pronoun indicates whether it is *singular,* indicating a single person or thing, or *plural,* indicating more than one person or thing. A few exceptions are nouns that may be either singular or plural: fish, deer.

Journalism students must know the following rules for forming the plurals of nouns if they are to write correct sentences in which the verb and its subject agree in number. Also, remember that it is necessary to know plural forms in order to use the possessive case correctly. Study these rules:

1. Most nouns form their plurals by adding *s* to the singular.

boy, boys   hat, hats   relation, relations

2. If a noun ends in a sibilant (*s, x, sh* or *z* sound) it forms its plural by adding *es* to the singular.

dish, dishes   box, boxes   bush, bushes   buzz, buzzes.

3. Some nouns change the stem root vowel to form the plural.

woman, women   man, men   mouse, mice   foot, feet

4. Some nouns add *en* to form the plural.

ox, oxen   child, children

5. Some nouns have the same form for singular and plural.

deer, deer   fish, fish[1]   sheep, sheep

---

[1] Note that the dictionary gives the plural *fishes* as also correct when referring to different species.

6. Most nouns ending in *f* or *fe* form the plural by adding *s*, but some nouns change the *f* to *v* before adding *s* or *es*.

    chief, chiefs   leaf, leaves   belief, beliefs   wife, wives

7. Nouns that end in *y* preceded by a vowel add *s* to form the plural. If the *y* is preceded by a consonant, the *y* is changed to *i* before *es* is added. Watch this type of noun!

    boy, boys   lady, ladies   sky, skies
    relay, relays   city, cities   party, parties

8. Proper names that end in *y* do not change the *y* to *i* before adding *s* or *es* to form the plural.

    Mary   the two Marys

9. *The* usually precedes the plural of a proper name; the Astors, the Thomases (referring usually to families). Be particularly careful in forming the plural of proper names ending in *s*.

    the Thomases   the Holmeses   the Joneses

10. Most nouns ending in *o* add *s* to form the plural.

    alto, altos   Eskimo, Eskimos   folio, folios
    cello, cellos   cameo, cameos   radio, radios
    piano, pianos   curio, curios

Some nouns that end in *o* preceded by a consonant add *es* to form the plural, however.

    echo, echoes   tomato, tomatoes   potato, potatoes   hero, heroes

Some nouns ending in *o* may add either *s* or *es* to form the plural. The dictionary will show which form is preferred.

    halo, halos *or* haloes   tornado, tornados *or* tornadoes
    motto, mottoes *or* mottos   volcano, volcanoes *or* volcanos
    cargo, cargos *or* cargoes   mosquito, mosquitos *or* mosquitoes

11. Most nouns ending in *i* form the plural by adding *s*.

    alibi, alibis   rabbi, rabbis

12. Some foreign nouns, particularly Latin-root words, retain the foreign plural.

    alumnus, alumni   addendum, addenda   crisis, crises
    datum, data   stratum, strata   thesis, theses

Most foreign words are now used correctly in either the foreign plural or the English plural, which simply calls for an *s* or *es* ending. There is a trend toward use of the English plural. Consult the dictionary or the stylebook when in doubt. The following list, with the plural form preferred by Webster listed first, should be helpful.

analysis, analyses	index, indexes, indices
antenna, antennae, antennas	medium, mediums, media (if referring to
appendix, appendixes, appendices	mass communications)
basis, bases	memorandum, memorandums, memoranda
beau, beaux, beaus	phenomenon, phenomena, phenomenons
curriculum, curricula, curriculums	radius, radii, radiuses
formula, formulas, formulae	stadium, stadia, stadiums
hypothesis, hypotheses	tableau, tableaux, tableaus

(Agreement of foreign plural subjects with the verb is treated in Chapter 8.)

13. Some words, like *day, foot, head, hour, mile, dozen, score,* etc., may be used as plurals without pluralizing them in form. This may be done only when the word is used together with a numerical adjective, especially to form a hyphenated adjective which modifies a noun that follows, as: There was a *three-hour* delay. No hyphens are required in a construction that follows the verb.

a three-day session	He won't reach three score and ten.
a 24-foot jump	He owns 75 head of cattle.
a two-mile race	She bought four dozen cookies.

14. Some nouns that are plural in form are singular in meaning and use. They require singular predicates.

Mathematics is a difficult course for the student.
Your *news is* most interesting.
Measles is a painful disease of childhood.

Other nouns in this category include the following. Always consult the dictionary to find how to use a word correctly if you are in doubt.

acoustics	checkers	dynamics	mumps	physics
aeronautics	dominoes or	economics	optics	tactics
ballistics	dominos	molasses	phonetics	

Some of these nouns have a singular or a plural meaning according to the use made of them. For example, *checkers* and *dominoes* are regarded as singular nouns when they refer to a game. *Statistics* is singular when you refer to a body of facts, but it is plural when you designate separate facts that are grouped together. Similarly, *athletics* is singular to refer to a system of physical training; it is plural when it refers to two or more sports. For example: Athletics has transformed him from a weakling into an Olympic star; but: Intercollegiate athletics have been abandoned by the college.

15. Most compound words make the last word plural in forming the plural of the noun. Nouns that are called *solid compounds*—those that do not have a hyphen—usually follow the regular rules for plurals. Note carefully the solid compounds ending in *-ful*.

airship, airships	cupful, cupfuls
bookkeeper, bookkeepers	handful, handfuls
textbook, textbooks	spoonful, spoonfuls

Compound nouns that are hyphenated form the plural by adding *s* to the main word in the compound.

by-line, by-lines *or*	father-in-law, fathers-in-law
byline, bylines[1]	great-grandmother,
passer-by, passers-by	great-grandmothers
hanger-on, hangers-on	maid-of-honor, maids-of-honor

Compound words that consist of two words used without a hyphen make both words plural in some cases, and make only the main word plural in other cases.

chargé d'affaires, chargés d'affaires
attorney general, attorneys general
notary public, notaries public

16. The plural of letters, figures and symbols, and of specifically designated words and phrases is usually formed by adding an apostrophe and *s* (*'s*).

two i's and three s's	too many and's
6's and 7's	the ABC's

There is a trend to omit the apostrophe when the words are used with a special meaning: pros and cons, the whys and the wherefores, 14 noes, etc.

PERSON AND NUMBER OF NOUNS AND PRONOUNS

Person and *number* of nouns and personal pronouns was discussed briefly on pages 29–31. For agreement of the pronoun with its antecedent in person and number, see pages 119–22, and for unnecessary shifting of pronouns in person and number, see page 194.

[1] Associated Press does not hyphenate *byline*.

CASE OF NOUNS AND PRONOUNS

One of the most common faults of writers is the incorrect use of case. *Case* indicates the relationship of a noun or a pronoun to other words in the sentence. There are three cases: nominative, objective and possessive.

Most important for the writer to remember is that the case of a noun or a pronoun is always determined by its use in the sentence or clause.

Note this sentence: *She* borrowed *her* sister's car to visit *him. (She,* the subject, is the nominative case form; *her* and *sister's* are in the possessive case since *her* modifies *sister's,* and *sister's* shows possession of the car; and the objective case form *him* is correct as the object of the infinitive *to visit.)*

Nouns show a case change only in the possessive form. Because nouns do not change form in the nominative and the objective cases, they will cause the writer little trouble. However, the writer does need to recognize the use of the nominative and objective cases as descriptive words that help to explain such grammatical terms as *predicate nominative, nominative absolute, nominative by exclamation, objective complement* and *adverbial objective.*

It is certain pronouns that cause difficulty in use of the proper case. Most of the personal pronouns and the relative and/or interrogative pronouns *who* and *whom* have different forms for the objective. Journalists, therefore, must take care to use the correct case of the personal pronouns: *I* or *me; we* or *us; he* or *him; she* or *her;* and *they* or *them.*

The relative and/or interrogative pronouns *who* and/or *whom* and *whoever* and/or *whomever* prove most troublesome for many writers. The journalist, then, simply must never forget that the case of these pronouns—and of all pronouns, in fact—is determined altogether by the way the pronoun is used in the clause that the pronoun introduces.

The writer should have no trouble with the personal pronouns *you* and *it* and the relative pronouns *which* and *that* because they retain the same forms in the nominative and the objective cases. And, of course, the relative pronoun *whose* is in the possessive case.

Nominative Case

A noun or a pronoun or a substantive, such as a gerund or an infinitive used as a noun, is in the nominative case when it is used in one of the following ways.

1. The *subject* of a verb or verb phrase is in the nominative case. The verb, remember, makes an assertion about the subject and completes a statement. A verb must agree with the subject in person and number and usually in tense.

Sheriff Bill Decker (or *He*) shot the fleeing robber.

The *bodies* of Elvis Presley and his mother were moved today for reburial at Graceland Mansion.

John Tower is the man *who* has the closest race for reelection. (*Who* is the subject of the relative clause.)

To win without a runoff is his objective. (*To win without a runoff*, an infinitive phrase, is the subject of the predicate *is*.)

Jogging is his favorite exercise. (The subject *jogging* is a gerund.)

2. A noun or a pronoun used as a *predicate nominative* is always in the nominative case. Since the predicate nominative completes the meaning of the predicate and denotes the same person or thing as the subject, it is also called a *subjective complement*.

Charles P. Player is his top-ranking *deputy sheriff*.

It is *he* (not *him*) who captured the man who escaped jail this morning.

His objective is *to win* without a runoff. (The infinitive phrase completes the predicate and denotes the same thing as the subject, *objective*.)

His favorite exercise is *jogging*. (The gerund *jogging* refers back to *exercise*, the subject.)

3. A noun or pronoun used in addressing a person is called a *nominative of address*. If if is used in an exclamatory sense, it is sometimes called a *nominative by exclamation*: Fire! Fire!

Judge Atwell, I object to his question.

You there! You are not listening to me.

4. The *nominative absolute*, usually consisting of a noun followed by a participle, expressed or understood, is used as a grammatically independent expression in the sentence.

Although the construction is not grammatically related to any word in the sentence, it is related to the thought of the sentence and is in effect usually an adverbial modifier because the participle ordinarily expresses time, cause, circumstance, condition, etc.

The nominative absolute is not a construction that the journalist will use often, but any writer will find occasional use for it.

The nominative absolute is used most often at the beginning of a sentence, but it may be placed in the middle of a sentence or at the end. And because the nominative absolute is an independent element of the sentence, it must be set off from the rest of the sentence by a comma or by commas.

Study the examples that follow:

The bow having been rammed, the ship began to sink.

The flaming, sulphide gas-well fire (being) extinguished, families in the area were allowed to return home.

The battery having gone dead, he was forced to abandon the stolen car.

Avoid using a pronoun in the nominative absolute at the beginning of a sentence. Such a construction is usually awkward: *She being an excellent teacher*, the school board regretted to accept her resignation. Better: *Because she is an excellent teacher*, the school board regretted....

Journalists may find occasional use for the nominative absolute to begin a lead. It can be used effectively to play up human interest description or to give antecedent circumstances. (See page 213 for an excellent example.)

5. An *appositive* is a substantive—a word, a phrase or a clause used as a noun—that is parallel to and explains or identifies another substantive, usually a noun or a noun equivalent.

Appositives are inserted loosely into the sentence and are usually set off by commas or dashes. The exceptions are single-word appositives: his brother *John*. Such appositives are called *restrictive appositives* because they are essential to the meaning of the sentence.

The appositive agrees in case with the substantive that it explains or identifies. The journalist, therefore, must be careful to use the right case for a pronoun that is in apposition with a noun or another pronoun. Study the examples that follow.

> They live east of the city on a 550-acre ranch, *Rancho Rio*.
> Felix McKnight, *the editor*, called us into his office.
> That is Felix McKnight, *the editor*.
> Police told him that his brother *John* was injured. (No commas needed)
> The two brothers, *John and James*, were both injured severely in the wreck.
> Swimming and bicycling, *exercises highly recommended by doctors*, are popular in this area.

The appositive usually is placed immediately after the word with which it is in apposition, but it can have other positions and it can be set off by dashes rather than by commas.

> Father sent for the children—*Hazel, Delores and me (not I)*. (Because the appositive refers back to *children*, which is the object of the preposition *for*, the use of *me* in the objective case is correct.)
> There is one course I never liked—mathematics. (*Mathematics* is in apposition with the noun *course*.)
> The expert pointed out Hughes had a unique way of crossing his t's and dotting his i's—*a trait that appears in the disputed will*. (The appositive, effectively set off by a dash instead of a comma, refers back to *way*.

An appositive does not always have to be a substantive. Here's an adjectival modifier used as an appositive: The mansion, *huge and rambling*, overlooked the lake.

Objective Case

The objective case is used in the following ways.

1. The *direct object* of the verb is in the objective case.

> Shuford blocked *Tucker* and *him* (not he) on the two-yard line.
> The committee will send Black, Jones and *me* (not *I*) to Mexico City.
> *Whom* (not *Who*) will the committee send to Mexico City?

In these sentences note that pronouns such as *him, me* and *whom* are in the objective case because they are objects of verbs. To test the interrogative sentence, turn it around: The committee will send *whom* to Mexico City? *Whom* is the object of *will send*.

2. The *object of the preposition* is in the objective case.

> The choice is between *Sharp* and *me*.
> For *him* there is no other choice.
> Take it to the person for *whom* it was bought.

3. The *indirect object* of a verb is in the objective case.

> Street handed *Gilbert* the ball.
> Johnson told *him* and *me* (not *he* and *I*) the very same story.
> Braniff sent Blankenship and *me* (not *I*) plane tickets to London.

Note that you can find the indirect object by inserting *to:* handed the ball *to* Gilbert; told the story to *him* and *me*; sent plane tickets *to* Blankenship and *me*.

4. The *subject of an infinitive*—as well as the *object of an infinitive*—is always in the objective case. Study some examples:

> Jack asked Dorris and *me* (not *I*) to go to Underground Atlanta.
> The chairman urged *her* and *me* (not *she* and *I*) to attend the meeting.

The compound *Dorris and me* is the subject of the infinitive *to go,* and the compound *her and me* is the subject of *to attend.* Let's analyze three more examples:

> The reporter asked *them* to answer a few questions. (The whole group of words *them to answer a few questions* is the object of the verb *asked*, and *them* is the subject of the infinitive *to answer*.)
> The postman took *her* to be *me* (not *I*). (*Her* is the subject of the infinitive *to be*, and *me* is the *object* of the infinitive.)
> The tennis coach let my sister and *me* (not *I*) play first.

A verb, such as *play*, with *to* understood, is always considered to be an infinitive following the verb *let*. Also, when *let* is used in the imperative to introduce a request or a proposal, the following pronoun or pronouns must be in the objective case: "Let's you and *me* (not I) play on through," Trevino suggested.

5. *The object or the complement of any verbal*—including gerunds and participles as well as infinitives—must be in the objective case. Be careful to use the objective forms of personal pronouns in such constructions.

> The captain wants to see *you* and *me* (not *I*). (*You* and *me* are objects of the infinitive *to see*.)
>
> Reprimanding *Jerry* and *her* does little good. (*Jerry* and *her* are objects of the gerund *Reprimanding*.)
>
> In this situation, Glenn and I surely would like to be *them* (not *they*). (*Them* is a predicate complement—a predicate pronoun. It is the object of the infinitive *to be*.)
>
> Having recognized *him* instantly, the officer gave chase. (*Him* is the object of the participle phrase *Having recognized*. Writers should have no difficulty in using the correct case of the personal pronoun in this kind of construction.)

6. Two kinds of objects—the retained object and the objective complement—should give the writer no trouble. The *retained object* is the object of a passive verb: Coach Bear Bryant was given an *auto*.

The *objective complement* or predicate objective is either a noun or an adjective that follows a direct object and explains it or means the same thing as the object. Examples: The committee appointed her *chairman*. They named the ranch *Bourbon Branch*.

7. The *adverbial objective*—a noun used as an adverb to modify a verb, an adjective or an adverb—should give the writer no grammatical trouble, but you might note how it is used.

> Neiko ran the Olympic *mile* in record-breaking time.
>
> Because Frani returned *home* a *day* early, her mother left this *morning*. (*Home* and *day* are adverbial objectives that modify the verb *returned* and the adverb *early*, respectively; *day* modifies the adverb *early*; and *morning* modifies the verb *left*.)

8. In an *elliptical clause*, one in which the verb is omitted, and which is introduced by *than* or *as*, the pronoun should be in the case called for in a complete clause. It is a good idea to complete the clause mentally to determine the case of the pronoun. Journalists should use the objective forms (*me, him, her*) only colloquially.

> Jack Taylor is taller than *I* (than *I* am).
>
> Carlton, you are as good an accountant as *she* (is). (Not as *her*)
>
> > But: The boss likes him better than (he likes) *me*. (Here the pronoun has to be in the objective case.)

9. *Who* and *whom,* used as interrogative pronouns, are likely to cause trouble in selecting the nominative or objective case. See page 116 for help with this problem.

Possessive Case

The *possessive case* indicates the person or thing that possesses something. Most errors are made in placing the apostrophe. Make sure that you know how to indicate singular and plural possessives of nouns.

Nouns indicate possessive case in three ways:

1. By use of the *apostrophe*

Have you seen *Marie's* new office?
The *children's* toys must be put away.
Five *boys'* hats are in the hall.

2. By use of the preposition *of,* making a prepositional phrase

The point *of the pen* is broken.
The man is a pal *of that hoodlum.*

3. By use of both the apostrophe and the preposition *of*

Are you a friend *of John's?*

Pronouns indicate possession in two ways:

1. By *inflection,* a change of form

She left *her* coat.   That copy is *mine.*
That coat is *hers.*   The dog lost *its* collar.
Which hat is *his?*   They launched *their* boat today.

The possessive pronouns do not require an apostrophe to show possession. Note *hers* and *its* in the examples above.

2. By use of the preposition *of* with the possessive pronoun forms

The Temple fans were thrilled by that run of *his.*
Aaron Spelling is a graduate *of mine.*

FORMING POSSESSIVES OF NOUNS

The author is convinced that journalism students would have little difficulty with possessives of nouns if they would learn the correct plurals of nouns. If you are not sure of the plurals of nouns, you should turn back to pages 85–87 before proceeding with this section.

Singular Possessives

You will not make errors if you follow these steps in forming the singular possessives of nouns:
1. Make sure that you have written the whole *singular* word.
2. Check to see if the singular noun ends in *s*.
3. If the singular noun does not end in *s*, add *'s*.

John's hat	the horse's stall	the church's needs
the woman's briefcase	the ship's route	the VIP's seat

4. If it is a singular common noun ending in *s*, add *'s* unless the next word begins with *s*.

the hostess's invitation	*But*: the hostess' seat
the witness's answer	*But*: the witness' story

5. If it is a singular proper name ending in *s*, use only an apostrophe.

Burns' poems	Kansas' schools	Jesus' life
Moses' law	Descartes' theories	

This is the style followed by newspapers and the press associations. But many magazine editors, book editors and others require the use of *'s* for proper nouns of one syllable (Burns's poems).
6. Only the apostrophe is used in possessives before the word *sake*:

for goodness' sake	for conscience' sake	for appearance' sake

Plural Possessives

Follow these three steps in forming the plural possessives of nouns:
1. Write the correct plural of the word. (Refer to pages 85–87.)
2. If a plural noun does *not* end in *s*, form the possessive by adding *'s*.

the men's suits	the children's toys
women's rights	the alumni's support

3. If a plural noun ends in *s*, form the possessive by adding only an apostrophe.

the girls' toys	the Joneses' house	the churches' needs	states' rights

Miscellaneous Uses of the Possessive

Study these further rules for correct form of the possessive.

1. If joint ownership is to be shown, use the *'s* with the last name only. But if separate ownership is to be shown, use the *'s* with each name.

> Cullum and Boren's store   Jane and Betty's sister
> Jane's and Betty's clothes

2. Most compound nouns form the singular possessive by adding *'s*. The possessive of plural compound nouns is best indicated by using an *of* phrase.

> her son-in-law's home   the homes of her sons-in-law
> the passer-by's comment   the comments of the passers-by

3. To show possession by an inanimate object, follow the usual rules in use of the apostrophe: a *day's* pay; a *hair's* breadth; a *two-weeks'* vacation. It might be better journalistic style to use the hyphenated form: *two-week* vacation.

Usually it is best to use an *of* phrase to indicate possession by an inanimate object: the roof *of* the barn; the wheels *of* the car; the noise *of* the trains.

There is no rule against using a possessive form for an inanimate object such as a *day's pay* or your *money's worth*. However, you are advised to avoid excessive personalization of inanimate objects. There's nothing wrong with using *death's call* or the *wind's sigh*, but you certainly go too far to write: *Cancer's death toll* has been declining. Use an *of* phrase: The death toll *of* cancer has been declining.

Remember, however, there are many phrases which are considered correct and which "sound right." You are advised to use these as acceptable journalistic writing: a *minute's* time, the *sun's* course, the *ship's* side, the *earth's* crust and so forth.

4. Do not add an apostrophe to a word ending in *s* when it is used primarily in a descriptive sense: citizens band radio; a teachers college, a writers magazine.

5. Some governmental, corporate and institutional organizations with a descriptive word in their names use an apostrophe; some do not: Diners Club, The Ladies' Home Journal, Actors Equity, the National Governors' Conference, the Veterans Administration. Check such names in the stylebook or in an almanac.

CORRECT USE OF NOMINATIVE CASE

A thorough study of the rules that follow will enable you to avoid making the most common errors in use of the nominative case.

1. Always remember that the subject and the predicate nominative of a

clause or a sentence must be in the nominative case. Watch *inverted sentences* particularly, where the subject follows the predicate, as it often does in interrogative sentences.

Who (not *whom*) was elected? (*Who* is the subject.)
Who (not *whom*) shall it be? (*Who* is the predicate nominatve. It shall be *who?*)

2. Watch closely any clauses and sentences in which the subject precedes the predicate but in which several words or phrases or a thrown-in clause comes between them.

Who (not *whom*) do you think will be elected?

Who is the subject of the verb *will be elected*. *You do think* is a thrown-in clause.

3. Be careful to use the relative pronouns *who* and *whom* correctly. Most important to remember is that the case of a relative pronoun is determined by exactly how it is used in the dependent clause. A relative pronoun used as the subject of a dependent clause must be in the nominative case. It is also in the nominative case if it is used as a predicate pronoun.

The witness *who* was to appear today is ill.

The pronoun *who* is the subject of the predicate *was to appear* in the dependent (relative) clause.

Senator Kerr, *who* they predicted would lose, won the election.

The clause *who would lose* is the object of the verb *predicted* in the relative clause. In this clause, *who* is the subject of the verb *would lose*.

To the question of *who* would run, the senator named two men.

Although *who* follows the preposition *of* in this sentence, it is not the object of the preposition. The entire clause *who would run* is the object of the preposition *of*, and *who* is the subject of the verb *would run*.

Do they know *who* he is?

The pronoun *who* is a predicate nominative in the clause *who he is* (He is *who?*). The relative clause *who he is* is the direct object of the predicate *do know* in the other clause.

They asked him *whom* he would name.

In this sentence, *whom* is the object of the verb *would name*.
Always determine how the pronoun is used in the sentence to know which word, *who* or *whom,* is correct.

4. Nouns and pronouns that are connected by a form of the verb *be* are usually in the same case.

It is *I*.

The subject *It* and the predicate pronoun *I* are both in the nominative case.

This rule is considered controversial by some editors. They accept "It is me" as correct, especially in quoting a person, but the use of *me* in this case is colloquial and should not occur in formal writing.

CORRECT USE OF OBJECTIVE CASE

By now you know that nouns and pronouns used as objects of verbs, of prepositions or of participles, gerunds or infinitives, or as subjects of infinitives, are in the objective case. This, then, is a quick review of the correct use of the objective case, with emphasis placed on a few of the more troublesome problems.

Here again, remember that the use of the word determines its case.

1. Pronouns used as objects of verbs and prepositions must be in the objective case. The chief errors are made when the object is compound.

Between *you* and *me*, I think the award should go to Mary and *her*.

You and *me* are objects of the proposition *between; her* is part of the compound object of the preposition *to*.

The policeman arrested both *him* and *me*.

Him and me is the compound object of the verb *arrested*.

The most common grammatical error heard on TV today probably is the use of *I* for *me* as an object. The use of *me* for *I* as a predicate nominative (It is *me*) is listed now in Webster's as standard usage and it is largely accepted in colloquial speech. However, the use of *I* for *me* as the object of a verb or of a preposition (between *you* and *I*) should be avoided in formal writing as being affected, if not as substandard usage. A reporter certainly will not use *I* for *me* except in quoting someone exactly.

Here are just a few misusages of *I* for *me* heard on television fairly recently, and the first one was by one of the top newscasters in the nation:

He phoned the attorney general and *I*.
The increase in fuel cost will be passed on to you and *I*.
He was sitting beside O. J. Simpson and *I*.
For you and *I*, the result will be unreasonable prices for poultry.

2. The relative and the interrogative pronouns *who* and *whom* often give trouble. Their case is determined by their use in the sentence.

It was Woodward *whom* the coach praised so highly.

Whom is the object of the verb *praised* in the subordinate clause.

   Whom are you going with?

Whom is the object of the preposition *with*. You will see the construction if you turn the sentence around: With whom are you going? *or* You are going with whom?

   If there is an extra clause in an interrogative sentence, you must check the construction carefully to know whether *who* or *whom* is correct.

   Who do you suppose will be our next president?

Do you suppose is a parenthetical clause that is inserted between the subject and the predicate. If you leave out *do you suppose*, you see at once that *who* is the subject of the verb *will be*.

   3. A pronoun used as an appositive agrees in case with the word with which it is in apposition.

   The chairman selected two men, *you* and *me*.

You and *me* are in the objective case; they are in apposition with *men*, object of the verb *selected*.

   The chairman called on three men—Goodman, Todd and *me*.

The antecedent of the appositive is *men*, object of the preposition *on*.

   Mrs. Art Goering had a card party for *us* girls.

Us, a restrictive pronoun appositive, must be in the same case as the noun which it explains, *girls,* which is the object of the preposition *for*. Compare with the following sentence, which shows the correct use of the nominative form, *we*.

   We girls—Amelia, Catherine, Natalie and I—were asked to serve.

   In the preceding example, note that, to achieve clarity, the writer used dashes instead of commas to set off the appositive.

   4. The subject of an infinitive is always in the objective case. Also, a predicate nominative that completes an infinitive must be in the objective case.

   The captain ordered John and *me* to hurry.

   The whole group of words—*John and me to hurry*—is the object of *ordered*. *John and me* is the compound subject of the infinitive *to hurry*; therefore *me* is the correct usage.

   They declared the winners to be John and *me*(not *I*).

John and me is the compound predicate nominative. It refers back to *winners* and completes the infinitive *to be*. The pronoun has to be in the objective case.

Although you recognize, of course, that the *object* of an infinitive is always in the objective case, you may need to watch out when writing a question such as: *Whom* (not *who*) do you wish to appoint? Test it: You do wish to appoint *whom*? *Whom* is the object of the infinitive *to appoint*.

CORRECT USE OF POSSESSIVE CASE

1. What used to be considered a common error made by writers—failure to use the possessive case of the noun or pronoun with the gerund—is now accepted as informal and colloquial usage. And grammarians agree that the fused participle, as the possessive gerund has been called, is correct usage in some instances.

In a *fused participle*, as Copperud explains, the subject of a gerund is in the objective, rather than the possessive, case. He gives as an example of the fused participle "I object to *him* being appointed." The correct form has long been considered to be "I object to *his* being appointed." The principle has applied to nouns as well as to pronouns: "She resented *John's* ringing the doorbell."

Journalists will find that the possessive form is preferred in formal writing, particularly when the subject of the gerund is a pronoun (*his* being appointed). But the objective form may be used when the subject is emphatic: The mother was proud of *him* doing it. Or, it may be used when emphasis comes from contrasting the subjects: We seem to think nothing of *a boy smoking*, but resent *a girl smoking*.

And certainly it is obvious that the possessive cannot be used in this construction cited by Bernstein: *Women having* the vote reduces men's political power. The subject is neither *Women* nor *having*, but a compound notion formed by fusion of the noun *Women* with *having*, which is actually used here as a gerund instead of as a participle.

Tacking an *'s* onto a noun is not always the way to avoid a fused participle, Bernstein points out. He gives these examples:

> This would result in *many's* having to go into lodgings.
> The eggs were shipped without *one's* being broken.

Journalists, then, must exercise discretion in using the possessive case of the noun or the pronoun with the gerund. Note, for example, how the use of the *'s* gives a different meaning to this sentence: The audience did not approve of the *man's speaking* first. (Did the audience object to *his speaking* or to the *man* who was speaking?)

You probably would agree that use of the possessive with a pronoun is correct in this sentence: The sergeant said he didn't mind *your* (not *you*) asking. And do you agree that the magazine writer would have done better to use *his* instead of *him* in this sentence: "I'm going to the American people and tell them I've goofed (on the Bay of Pigs disaster) and pledge that I'll do better in the future,'' his aides remember *him* saying.

2. Pronouns in the possessive case do not require an apostrophe. The most common errors are in the use of *its* and *it's*. *Its* is the possessive pronoun. *It's* is the contraction of *it is*.

> The cat licked *its* paws.
> *It's* time to start for the office.

3. Take care not to confuse the possessive pronoun *whose* with the contraction *who's*, which means *who is*.

> *Whose* car is that out front?
> She's a girl *who's* always willing to help.

4. Be careful not to confuse the possessive pronoun *your* with the contraction *you're*, which means *you are*.

> When *your* car arrives, we'll be ready.
> If *you're* going downtown, I'll go along with you.

5. Avoid the use of possessive nouns in appositive expressions. It is better to use a prepositional phrase with *of*.

> AWKWARD: University of Iowa coach Hayden Fry's car was wrecked.
> BETTER: The car of the University of Iowa coach, Hayden Fry, was wrecked.

6. Avoid awkward expressions arising from the use of double possessives.

> AWKWARD: President Chapman's son's car was wrecked.
> CORRECT: The car of President Chapman's son was wrecked.

USING REFLEXIVE AND INTENSIVE PRONOUNS

For correct usage of reflexive and intensive pronouns, see pages 112—13.

QUIZ ANSWERS

Sentences 1-7 should be corrected as follows: 1. The dog is lying on its back, but I can't tell whether it's dead or not. 2. *Baker's dithering* is correct. There is a trend toward omitting the apostrophe when words are used with a special meaning: pros and cons or antis, 14 noes, the whys and wherefores, etc. But it is still correct to use the apostrophe. Check with the editor. 3. Substitute the possessive gerund *their* for *them*. 4. The two Mexicans' faces . . . 5. Her *ladies'* hats are . . . 6. That is the *Ellises'* house. 7. Change *I* to *me*.

Correct words in sentences 8-20 are: 8. me. 9. he. 10. Who. 11. me. 12. us. 13. Who. 14. he, who. 15. Chairwoman, spokesman. 16. who, whom. 17. Whom. 18. Me; the object or the complement of an infinitive is in the objective case. 19. me. 20. me; the subject of an infinitive is in the objective case.

8

Agreement of Subjects and Predicates

Failure to recognize the grammatical principle of *agreement* results in far too many errors. Journalism students commit this type of error almost as often as all other errors in grammar, and the error is found repeatedly in newspapers.

This chapter reviews the agreement of subject and predicate. A verb must agree with its subject in number and person. Certain types of construction may give writers difficulty in following this rule.

Before we take a look at the most common errors in agreement of subjects and predicates, suppose you test yourself on this most important subject by taking the following quiz.

QUIZ

Select the correct word in each sentence.

1. There (are, is) only one minute and twenty seconds left to play, the sportscaster reported.
2. Intramural athletics (is, are) stressed at Duquesne.
3. A number of political bigwigs (was, were) gathering at the courthouse.
4. Dr. Hal Dewlitt, city health director, stated that measles in adults (are, is) dangerous.
5. Not only the Cubs' manager but also the players (were, was) blamed for the slump.
6. The store with all its contents (were, was) damaged.

7. Among the dead (was, were) Herbert Asbell of Brooklyn, John Mooney of Toledo and Horace Apfelbaum of Dallas.
8. Where (is, are) the data you gathered?
9. About 600 Eskimos (was, were) examined.
10. Fire Marshal Lawrence said there (has, have) been three losses, none of which (have, has) exceeded $50.
11. The mayor, as well as half the councilmen, (were, was) late for the meeting.
12. Neither the twins nor Mr. Howard (intend, intends) to do a complete "fade-out."
13. The couple (was, were) arrested last night in a Milwaukee cafe.
14. This season there (is, are) John Moore, Ron Baxter and Jim Krivacs who are setting a surprising fast pace.
15. Neither the Warriors coach nor the players (were, was) downcast.
16. There (was, were) one Dalmation, four Toy Bostons and eight Poodles in the dog show.
17. Many a man and woman in American universities (is, are) in need of financial assistance.
18. Hiding in the brush (were, was) a covey of quail.
19. This brand of bluejeans (are, is) in most demand today.
20. Every one of the players we have named (enjoy, enjoys) football for what it is—a great sport.
21. The depth of the drainage ditches (vary, varies) no more than a foot.
22. The heart of the newspaper (is, are) the editorials.
23. The emcee asked, "Now, (what's, what are) their names?"
24. None of the advertising agency's clients (were, was) lost.
25. None of the teachers (was, were) willing to sign contracts.

To see how well you did on this most important quiz, see the end of the chapter.

EIGHTEEN RULES FOR AGREEMENT

1. The *compound subject* made up of two or more parts connected by *and* requires a plural verb.

She and her son Bob *have gone* fishing in Canada.
The fishing and the hunting in Arizona *were* good that year.

The compound subject made up of more than two parts joined by *and* sometimes leads to an error. Also watch the agreement carefully in inverted sentences in which the subject follows the verb.

Rain, hail and wind *have caused* an estimated $22,000,000 damage to crops and livestock.
Among the injured *were* Harold Bell of Brooklyn and John Boone of Toledo and his son.

The error of using *has caused* and *was* in these two sentences might be overlooked in conversational English, but good reporters will not use them in their writing.

Be especially careful to use the correct number of the verb when it precedes the subject in an interrogative sentence. This error was found in a leading journal for journalists: Where *has* Nader and his raiders been for the last few years?

When a sentence starts with the expletive *there*, remember that the expletive is *not* the subject of the verb. *There* is just a fill-in introductory word. The subject follows the verb, and the verb must agree in number with the subject.

> *There are* some fine backfield performers returning next season—Lam Jones, Ham Jones and Randy McEachern.

The subject is *performers*; the plural verb *are* is correct. However, writers often slip up when the contraction *There's* is used, as in this example: There's outfielder Page and two pitchers, Dave Guisti and Doc Medich, involved in the trade. Note that the true subject is *Page and two pitchers*, a *compound* subject; therefore the plural verb *are* is needed: *There are* outfielder Page... .

You have been advised to use the expletive *There* sparingly. Remember that it is simply a filler that you can use to change the word order of the sentence, usually with the purpose of placing emphasis on what follows. Recall this example given earlier: *There's* no Wednesday for the Los Angeles Dodgers. (In the 1977 World Series.)

(See pages 214–15 for the use of expletives for variety of sentence beginnings.)

When a compound subject that follows the verb consists of two or more nouns that are mixed in number, the singular verb may be used if the first subject—the noun nearest the verb—is singular.

> There *was* one Dalmatian, four Toy Bostons and eight Poodles entered at the dog show.

Consult your editor or your publication's stylebook in regard to this usage.

There are three *exceptions* to this rule:

a. It is correct to use a singular verb with certain compound expressions that have come to be thought of as a unit.

> This ice cream and cake *is* good.
> Ham and eggs *is* a good breakfast.
> Bread and butter *makes* a tasty snack.

b. It is correct to use a singular verb when the two nouns in the compound subject refer to the same person or thing. If two persons are meant, the verb must be plural and the article *the* should be inserted.

> The secretary and treasurer *is* absent. (One person)
> The secretary and the treasurer *are* both away. (Two persons)

c. Compound subjects modified by *each, every* and *many a* require a singular verb.

> Every boy and every girl in this room *is* entitled to a copy.

The meaning is: Every boy is entitled and every girl is entitled.

> Many a man and woman in this community *finds* himself or herself in need.

Without knowing the rule, you might make two errors in this sentence by writing: Many a man and woman . . . *find themselves* . . . The verb must be the singular *finds* and the reflexive pronoun should be the singular *himself* or *herself*.

2. When the parts of a compound subject are joined by *or, nor, either . . . or* or *neither . . . nor, not only . . . but also,* the verb must agree with the subject nearest to the verb. This is a foolproof rule to follow.

> Neither the Kansas players nor the coach *was* overconfident.
> Neither the Kansas coach nor the players *were confident of victory.*

3. When an affirmative expression and a negative expression are joined to make a compound subject, the verb agrees with the *affirmative* subject.

> The *teacher*, not the students, *was* wrong.
> The *students*, not the teacher, *were* wrong.

4. Collective nouns, which often give journalists "agreement trouble," were discussed briefly on page 29. Here we take a futher look at how a collective noun—such as *jury* or *team* or *committee*—when used as a subject, must agree with the predicate and with a possessive pronoun if one is used.

If the action of the collective noun is performed by the group as a whole, acting as a unit, the singular number must be used.

> The anti-crime committee *makes* its report tomorrow.
> Stewart, Burgess, Morris & George (a law firm) *has announced* a new policy.
> The city council *is meeting* to set *its* agenda. (Note that the pronoun, as well as the verb, is singular.)
> Hiding in the brush *was* a covey of quail. (When the predicate precedes a collective noun as it does here, be especially careful to use the singular number.)

If the members of the group are reported as acting separately, the collective noun subject takes a plural verb.

The committee *have returned* to their homes.

Since the plural verb in sentences like this may sound awkward, it is often best to make the sentence read: The grand jury members (*or* members of the grand jury) have returned. . .

To decide whether to use a singular or a plural verb with such nouns as group, herd, class, breed, type, species and variety, test the subject and decide what idea it conveys. If the subject refers definitely to a number of individuals acting as a unit, a singular verb is required. If the persons or animals or things that make up the group named in the subject are acting individually, the plural must be used.

That *group* (or *platoon* or *squad*) of soldiers *is* a top-notch fighting unit.
That *group* (or *platoon* or *squad*) of soldiers *have* the best ratings of individual performance.
That *herd* of cows and calves *is* the healthiest the farm has had in some time.
The *herd* of cows and calves *are moving* toward the sheds by twos and threes.

Awkwardness could be avoided in these examples by recasting the sentences:

Soldiers in that squad have the best individual performance ratings.
Cows and calves in the herd are moving toward the sheds by twos and threes.

5. Nouns that designate an amount of money, a period of time, a unit of measure, and the like, although plural in form, are regarded as referring to a unit and take a singular verb. This is an important rule for the journalist to remember.

The treasurer thought that sixty-five dollars ($65) *was* not too much to ask.
Six months *is* too short a time, General Westmoreland warned.
Three miles *was* too long a distance for Freedman to run.
Five hours *is* needed to complete the outline.

The meaning in the last sentence is: Five hours is the time needed.

6. If the subject is modified by a phrase which begins with such an expression as *along with, as well as, in addition to, together with*, the verb must agree with the *simple subject*, which is not changed by the expression.

The *father*, as well as his sons, *is* going to enroll.
Bill, together with his sisters, *was* hurt in the accident.
The *truck* along with all its contents *was* destroyed.
The *barn*, in addition to the house, *was* burned.

Note that it is often better to set off the phrase with commas.

7. The verb agrees with the *true* subject, remember—not with a noun which comes between the subject and the predicate, such as a noun that is the object of a prepositional phrase which modifies the subject. Watch this construction especially in the case of *compound* subjects modified by an *of* phrase.

> A *committee* of five men and three women *is* to consider the matter.
> The *series* of three games *was* completed quickly.
> The increasing *rate* of births in India *is* viewed with alarm.

However, when the complete subject—including a modifying *of* phrase—strongly conveys the idea of *individuals*, a plural verb should be used, even though the simple subject is singular. Study the following sentences:

> An *average* of 25 persons *apply* each month.
> An *average* of 25 applications a month *is* not unusual.
> A *majority* of the town's younger men *are* moving to the city.
> A *majority* of three votes to one *was* recorded.

8. A verb must agree in number with its subject, not with any predicate nominative used in the sentence.

> The strongest unit in the Panther team *was* the tackles.

The subject is *unit*, a singular noun. The verb agrees with *unit*, not with the predicate noun *tackles*.

> Long study and constant practice *are* the secret of Beverly Sills' success as a
>   singer.
> The bellows of the bull *were* the only sound that reached his ears.

To avoid awkwardness in such sentences it is sometimes better to change the construction of the sentences, thus:

> The Panther team *is* strongest at the tackle positions.

9. Certain nouns that are plural in form but singular in meaning take singular verbs, such as: All the news is bad today.

> Mumps *is* contagious.
> What *is* his politics?
> Short-sighted politics *causes* long-term effect.

Some nouns, however, may take either a singular or a plural verb, depending on the exact meaning of the word in the sentence.

> *Athletics* (a system of training) *has transformed* him from a weakling into a star.
> Intercollegiate *athletics* (all intercollegiate sports) *have been* discontinued at that
>   university.

10. Titles of books, poems, movies and so on require a singular verb, even if the title has a plural form.

Twice Told Tales is a good book for children.

11. Such nouns as *abundance, half, part, plenty, rest* and *variety* take a singular verb or a plural verb according to the number of the noun in the *of* phrase which modifies the noun. The same rule applies to fractions used as subjects.

Plenty of apples *are* on the market now.
Two-thirds of the business district *was* destroyed.
Half of the members *are* absent today.

12. The word *number*, when modified by *the*, takes a singular verb; when modified by *a*, it takes a plural verb.

The number of students who failed *was* small.
A number of the workers *have* failed to get by the picket lines.

13. Foreign plurals usually require plural verbs.

The Vassar alumni were getting ready for homecoming.
Are the criteria for California teachers too high?

The plurals of many foreign nouns, including Latin-root words, have been naturalized; that is, they have assumed the regular English -*s* or -*es* ending: *memoranda* or *memorandums*; *termini* or *terminuses*; *fungi* or *funguses*; *octopuses* instead of *octopi; curricula* or *curriculums; candelabra* or *candelabrums; phenomenons* instead of *phenomena*, etc. This does make it easy for the writer to select a plural verb to agree with the foreign plural noun.

Remember, however, that when the foreign plural is regarded as a unit—a collective noun—it requires a singular verb.

The data *was presented* by Senator Proxmire.
The data *is* sound. *But:* The data (individual items) have been carefully collected.

Reporters might note that the word *agenda* no longer means "things to be done" but means "a list or plan of things to be done." It requires a singular verb then. *Agenda* even has its own English plural now—*agendas*.

The agenda for Monday night's meeting *was* approved by the school board president.
The agendas of the two committees *were* adopted by the board.

14. The nouns *all* and *most* and the pronouns *none, any* and *such* are ordinarily considered singular when they refer to quantity, but they are

regarded as plural when they refer to number. A safe way is to regard them as collective nouns: If they refer to units, use a singular verb; if they refer to individuals, use a plural verb.

> *Most* of the money *was* recovered by Deputy Player. (Quantity)
> *Most* of the members *were* there. (Number)
> *All* (of the cargo) *was* lost. (Quantity)
> *All* (of the crew) *were* saved. (Number)

The pronoun *none* causes a great deal of trouble. Some authorities say that it means *no one* or *not one* and must take a singular verb. Others regard it as either singular or plural according to the meaning of the sentence. A majority of editors prefer the use of a singular verb with *none*, but there is a strong trend toward the use of a plural verb with it. The safest rule may be: Use a singular verb if *none* means *no one* or *not one*; in all other uses of *none*, you either may follow your newspaper's stylebook or determine the correct number by context, that is, according to the meaning to be conveyed.

The Associated Press Stylebook possibly offers the safest rule to follow: *None* usually means no single one. When used in this sense, it always takes singular verbs and pronouns: None of the seats *was* in *its* right place.

Use a plural verb only if the sense is no two or no amount: None of the consultants *agree* on the same approach. None of the taxes *have* been paid.

Here are some other examples:

> None (Not one) of the company's clients *was* lost.
> None but the best *were* accepted.
> None of the cars *was* (or *were*) wrecked.

You can play safe by writing: No cars were wrecked *or* Not a single car was wrecked.

15. The nouns *kind* and *sort* should be modified by the singular demonstrative adjectives *this* and *that* even when the noun in the *of* phrase is plural. Do not say: *these kind* of errors or *those sort* of actions. The plural forms—*these* kinds and *those* kinds—are correct, or course. This is a common error that journalists should avoid making. Examples: The team can't expect to win its division if the players continue to make *those kind* of errors. They were told not to answer *those type* of questions.

Note how the president was correct in his usage in this sentence: ''I think members of the House and Senate want to avoid *those kinds* of disruptive actions just as much as we do,'' the president said. More examples of correct usage follow:

> He prefers *that kind* of pens.
> Where can I buy *this sort* of shrubs?
> *This kind* of sheets is selling well.

It is considered correct sometimes to use a singular noun in the *of* phrase after *these kinds*.

> *These kinds of apple* are delicious.

Never say, "This kind of a. . . ." The aritcle *a* or *an* is not needed.

16. The plural forms *kinds of* and *brands of* and so on may have a singular or a plural noun as the object of the preposition, according to the meaning to be conveyed.

> Six brands of *paper* were tested.
> Two kinds of *oil* were found in the area.
> Six brands of *cans* were ordered.

17. In general, you should keep the same number throughout a sentence.

> POOR: Buy some ordinary fishing corks, cover each one with cellophane, and attach sequins to them with short pins.
> BETTER: Buy some ordinary fishing *corks,* cover *them* with cellophane. . . .

However, some sentences may use a singular noun with a plural possessive to make the meaning clear, thus:

> The two pilots plunged to *their death*.
> The publisher knew most of them by *their first name*.

18. A *gerund* used as a subject requires a singular verb.

> *Increasing* their wages *has raised* the crew's morale.

QUIZ ANSWERS

1. is. 2. are. 3. were. 4. is. 5. were. 6. was. 7. were. 8. is. 9. were. 10. have, has. 11. was. 12. intends. 13. was. 14. are. 15. were. 16. were or was. 17. is. 18. was. 19. is. 20. enjoys. 21. varies. 22. is. 23. what are. 24. *Was* is preferred by newspaper editors but there's a strong trend toward use of the plural. 25. same as 24.

9

Using Pronouns Correctly

Journalists may encounter "agreement" trouble in using pronouns correctly, particularly in the agreement of the subject with the predicate and in agreement with the antecedent.

In this chapter we consider the correct way to use each class of pronouns—personal pronouns, demonstrative pronouns, indefinite pronouns, distributive pronouns, interrogative pronouns and relative pronouns.

Test your knowledge of the correct use of pronouns by taking the following quiz.

QUIZ

1. Each of the committeemen interviewed qualified (their, his) remarks to some extent.
2. The plane (that, which) is just outside the hangar is Shawhan's.
3. The Fightin' Hoosiers won (their, its) opening game.
4. The Utah State team won (its, their) first game of the season.
5. The Oregon State University president spoke to the Chamber of Commerce at (their, its) annual election banquet Friday night.
6. He promised to support (whoever, whomever) of the prospects was chosen.
7. The Asian flu has struck 26 persons, 11 of (which, whom) have died.
8. We knew it would be Dr. David Clarke (who, whom) would be selected as journalism director.
9. McKissack is the only one of the three candidates who (have, has) conducted a hard campaign.

10. "We will nominate (whoever, whomever) you believe can make the strongest campaign," Rich declared.
11. Harlan Wetz is only one of many players on the team who (have, has) shown a top brand of sportsmanship on the gridiron this fall.
12. He declared that everybody must play (their, his) part.
13. Two nephews survive him. Neither (live, lives) in Montana.
14. The practice of setting low bail bonds is one of many evils which (tend, tends) to perpetuate (itself, themselves) under the present system.

What's wrong with the following sentences?

15. We hope that you will not be too disappointed about our failure to show up for your birthday, which we hope won't happen again.
16. Lewis told his brother that his car had been stolen.
17. Criminals pass in and out of jails as if they were equipped with revolving doors.
18. He thought it was necessary that it be given further study.
19. The future is bright for anyone, whether he is a high school graduate or a college graduate, who has the ability to better themselves.
20. To call defensive signals, the coach selected Jenkins, which the majority of the players did not like.

See end of chapter to find how well you did on this most important quiz.

PERSONAL PRONOUNS

Personal pronouns do not usually give the writer much trouble in agreement in number. You must, however, be careful to see that a personal pronoun agrees in number with a collective-noun antecedent: The jury has reached *its* (not *their*) verdict. (Refer to pages 105–06.)

Also, in using personal pronouns, remember these rules:

1. The pronoun *you*, even when singular, always takes a plural verb.

You, and only you, *are* to blame, he told the clerk.

2. The pronouns *he, she* and *it* should not be used with *don't*, the contraction of *do not*. *Does* is the third person singular form of *do*.

The mayor *does* look tired and drawn, *doesn't* he?
It *doesn't* (not *don't*) hurt to try out for Cowboys cheerleader.

3. The *reflexive pronouns* often give the journalist trouble. They are formed by adding *self* or *selves* to some of the personal pronouns.

Reflexive pronouns should not be used as part of a compound subject or compound object of a verb or preposition. This is one of the most common errors made on television and radio today. Note some examples:

The committee chairman and *myself* will confer today on the proposed bill.
The speaker praised the chairman and *myself* for our work on the bill.
He agreed with the speaker and *myself* that the bill should not be introduced now.

It certainly should be obvious that only *I* can be correct as part of a compound subject in the first sentence, and that *me* is correct as the object of the verb in the second sentence and as object of the preposition *with* in the third sentence.

4. The reflexive pronouns may be used for emphasis, however, and are then called *intensive pronouns*.

Mayor Koch himself will conduct the arbitration sessions.
They expect to do the work *themselves*.

Note that the second sentence can also be written: *They themselves* expect to do the work. It is usually best to place the intensive pronoun close to the noun or pronoun it refers to. In the first sentence following it should be apparent that *itself* is misplaced:

INCORRECT: Any one of the books is a thorough treatment of the subject by *itself*.
CORRECT: Any one of the books by *itself* is. . . .

Be careful not to use intensive pronouns unnecessarily. One intensive pronoun may be needed for emphasis, but the use of a second one in the sentence is often incorrect, as in this sentence:

The Hanoi bureau chief himself should have interviewed the premier and should have turned in the story himself.

The second *himself* is unnecessary.
And of course you know that there are no such words as "hisself," "theirself" or "theirselves." Use the objective forms of the personal pronouns in forming the reflexive pronouns.

DEMONSTRATIVE PRONOUNS

The *demonstrative pronouns* are *this* and *that* in the singular, and *these* and *those* in the plural. They are the pronouns that point out persons and things. These pronouns should give no trouble.

That is not the book I wanted; *this* is the one.
These will be used rather than *those* over there.

Remember that *this, that, these* and *those* are adjectives if they are used with nouns: Those apples are winesaps.

INDEFINITE PRONOUNS

Indefinite pronouns, which make a general rather than a specific reference, were listed on page 32. They may give trouble in agreement in number because some of them are singular, some are plural and some may be either singular or plural.

1. The following indefinite pronouns always take a singular verb and also a singular pronoun if there is one:

one	everyone	no one	nobody	another	other	everything
each	anyone	everybody	someone	anything	either	
neither	many a	somebody				

Everyone in the three communities *is* expected to do *his* or *her* share in the drive.

Remember that when one of these words is used to modify a substantive, it becomes an *indefinite adjective*. (Indefinite adjectives were treated on page 34.)

Every member of the board *was* expected to attend and to cast *his* vote.

2. The following indefinite pronouns always take a plural verb:

both   few   many   several
Both are expected to compete in the meet.
Few are expected to enter the meet.

3. The following indefinite pronouns may be either singular or plural: *all*, *some*, *none*.

These pronouns are singular when they refer to a quantity. They are plural when they refer to a number. However, many editors require the use of the singular verb with *none* referring to number.

All his money *is* gone. (Quantity)
All have arrived by now. (Number)
None (of the money) *is* left. (Quantity)
None (of the members) *have left* yet. (Number)
or None of the members *has left*. (Number)
Some (of the money) *is* left. (Quantity)
Some (of the members) *are* still here. (Number)

4. Most errors in the use of the indefinite pronouns occur when the writer fails to make a pronoun which comes later in the sentence agree in number with its indefinite pronoun antecedent.

Anyone (Anybody) in the club may compete if *he* or *she* registers by May 15.

It would be an error to say "if they register." *He* and *she* must agree in number with their antecedent *Anyone* (or *Anybody*).

5. Be careful to distinguish the difference between *anyone* and *any one*, *everyone* and *every one*, and *someone* and *some one*. Notice these sentences:

> At this point he will hire *anyone* who can type.
> He will hire *any one* of the applicants who can type.
> *Someone* must stand guard.
> *Some one* of the soldiers must stand guard.

DISTRIBUTIVE PRONOUNS

The *distributive pronouns* are *each, either* and *neither*. They are always singular, and they are used to single out an individual from some group. Make sure that any other pronoun in the sentence is singular if its antecedent is the distributive pronoun.

> *Either* (or *Neither*) of the two players *is* eligible.
> *Each* of the members *was* in *his* seat when the session began.

Errors can be avoided if the adjective is used instead of the distributive pronoun, thus: *Each member* was in his seat. Another method is to use a plural subject and omit *each*, thus: *All members* were in their seats.

> INCORRECT:
> *Each* of the three Minnesota quarterbacks *are* good runners, passers and kickers.
> Baylor and Arkansas *each have won* six games and lost two.
> CORRECT:
> *Each* of the Minnesota quarterbacks *is* a good runner, passer and kicker.
> *All* three Minnesota quarterbacks *are* good runners, passers and kickers.
> *Both* Baylor and Arkansas *have won* six games and lost two.
> *Baylor and Arkansas have won* six games and lost two *each*.

It is considered good grammar to use *each other* and *either* in referring to two, and *one another* and *any one* in referring to more than two.

> The two brothers no longer admire *one another*.
> All members of the Crosby family admire *one another*.
> Executive Editor Tom Simmons said he would hire *either* of the two applicants.
> The editor said he would hire *any one* of the three women.

Note here the difference between *any one* and *anyone*. *Anyone* means the same as *anybody*, whereas *any one* refers to a single person or thing.

> The foreman said he would hire *anyone* (*anybody*) who applies. (*Everyone* and *someone* are similar to *anyone* in usage.)

INTERROGATIVE PRONOUNS

Interrogative pronouns and their usage were treated earlier. Review page 33.

RELATIVE PRONOUNS

The common *relative pronouns* are *who, whom, whose, which* and *that*. *Who* and *whom* refer to persons; *whose* refers to persons, animals and sometimes to things; *which* refers to things, animals and to persons considered as a group; and *that* may refer to inanimate objects, places, ideas and animals.

To avoid incorrect usage of relative pronouns, you must remember these main points about them.

1. A relative pronoun introduces a subordinate clause, called also a relative clause, which is usually used adjectivally to modify an antecedent.

> Jerry Brown is the man (or *the one*) *who* has the best chance to be nominated, the experts predicted.
> Most of the stockholders had heard nothing about the plan *that* was presented Friday.
> The material in *Berkeley Barb, which* is largely exposé and counter-culture, is all staff-written.

2. Keep in mind that the word the relative pronoun refers to is outside the subordinate (relative) clause and usually immediately precedes the clause. In the three foregoing sentences, the antecedents of *who, that* and *which* are *man, plan* and *Berkeley Barb*. The relative clauses are used adjectivally to modify their respective antecedents.

Study some other examples:

> Police identified him as the man *whom* they saw in the area yesterday. *(Whom* introduces a restrictive relative clause referring to a person, *man*.)
> The car *that* was stolen yesterday was recovered last night. *(That* introduces a restrictive clause referring to a thing. *Which* could be used instead of *that*, but *that* is now preferred in a restrictive clause—a clause that is not set off by a comma or by commas.)

Grammarians still argue over whether to use *that* or *which* to introduce a restrictive clause that refers to things, ideas or animals.

In choosing whether *that* or *which* is the proper pronoun to introduce a relative clause, writers first must clearly recognize the distinctions between the restrictive (essential) clause and the non-restrictive (non-essential) clause. The essential clause is a limiting or defining clause that modifies an antecedent in the independent clause. The restrictive (essential) clause, therefore, cannot be eliminated without changing the meaning of the sentence. If omission of the clause would leave the noun it modifies incomplete or would materially alter the sense of what is being said, you may be sure the clause is restrictive (essential). Its absence from the sentence would lead to a substantially different interpretation of what the writer meant.

The non-restrictive clause is not essential to the meaning of the sentence. It may be information that is helpful to the reader, but it is parenthetical and can be eliminated without altering the basic meaning of the sentence.

That is the preferred pronoun to introduce restrictive (essential) clauses that refer to inanimate objects, places, ideas and animals. The literary *which* may be used to introduce such a restrictive clause, but it has been largely replaced by *that*, which sounds much more natural than *which*.

Use *which* to introduce the non-restrictive clause, which is non-defining and parenthetical. *Which* also may be used occasionally to avoid repetition of *that* in a sentence: *That* is the same proposal *which* (not *that*) has been voted down before.

Study the examples that follow.

> An automobile tire *that develops blisters* is extremely dangerous, the ombudsman pointed out. (Try leaving out the restrictive clause and see what an absurd statement you have: An automobile tire is extremely dangerous.
>
> The river *that* flows slowly from Fort Worth to the Gulf of Mexico is the much-publicized Trinity.
>
> The Trinity River, *which* flows slowly from Fort Worth to the Gulf of Mexico, is still being considered as a possible inland waterway for barges.
>
> The jet *that* crashed in San Diego Monday in the nation's worst air disaster was a Boeing 727.
>
> The plane *that* is just outside the hangar belongs to Shawhan.
>
> Apollo-Saturn 16, *which* was crewed by Eugene A. Seman and Harrison H. Schmidtt, made the sixth manned lunar landing and had a record stay of 75 hours.
>
> Carter's export promotion program, *which* has been on the drawing boards for months, is expected to be formally announced Tuesday.

Be assured, then, that you will be using *that* and *which* correctly if you follow this modern rule: *That* now is usually used to introduce a restrictive clause, and *which* is used to introduce a non-restrictive clause.

Remember that a restrictive clause is essential in making a sentence and is not set off by commas. A non-restrictive clause must be set off.

Note the usage of relative pronouns in the sentences that follow.

> It was General Clay *who* organized the Berlin Airlift in World War II. (*Who* introduces a restrictive clause. The antecedent is General Clay.)
>
> Clay, *who* died Monday at the age of 80, organized the airlift. . . . (*Who* introduces a non-restrictive clause that is set off by commas.)

It was Lucius D. Clay *whom* the people of West Germany mourned today as the architect of the Berlin Airlift. (*Whom* introduces the relative clause, which is restrictive. *Whom*, not *who*, is correct because it is the object of the verb *mourned*.)

"For my citizens and me, General Clay is the man *whose* name is linked with our existence in freedom," Lord Mayor Dietrich Stobbe said. (*Whose* introduces a restrictive relative clause. The antecedent is *man*, a predicate nominative in the independent clause.)

Because far too many errors are made in the use of *who* and *whom*, we will review next in some detail the main principles to follow in avoiding misuse of this difficult pair.

3. The relative pronoun may be subject, object or predicate nominative in the clause in which it occurs.

Ask for the person *who* directs the company's PR program.
Is Wright the person *whom* the school board wants as president?
Few of the stockholders know *who* he is.

Who is the subject of the verb *directs* in the relative clause in the first sentence. *Whom* is the object of the verb *wants* in the relative clause in the second sentence. Test the clause by reversing the order: The school board wants *whom* as president. The relative clause is used adjectivally to modify *person*. In the third sentence *who* is the predicate nominative. The normal order of the clause would be *he is who*, with *he* as the subject. The whole relative clause is the direct object of the verb *know* in the main clause.

4. The use of the relative pronoun *within its clause*—the subordinate clause—determines its case. A relative pronoun does agree with its antecedent in person, number and gender—but does not agree in case. Failure to recognize this principle results in many errors in using *who* and *whom*. Study these examples:

a. He is the player *who probably will play shortstop.*
b. He is the player *who was bought early in the season.*
c. He is the player *whom the Yanks bought this spring.*
d. Is he the player *for whom they paid a bonus?*
e. The manager already knows *who his best pitcher is.*

Note the use of the nominative *who* within the italicized relative clauses in (a), (b) and (e). In (a) *who* is the subject of *will play*. In (b) *who* is the subject of *was bought*. Many writers would mistakenly use *whom* in this sentence, thinking that since the subject is acted upon, the objective form is called for. But remember that *was bought* is a transitive passive verb, which means that the subject—not an object—receives the action. Therefore, *who* is correct.

In (*e*) *who* is a predicate nominative. This is easily seen by revising the clause thus:. . . his best *pitcher* is *who*.

Note that the objective *whom* is correct in (*c*) and (*d*) because it is the object of the verb *bought* in (*c*) and the object of the preposition *for* in (*d*). To see this clearly, revise the order of the clauses: the Yanks *bought whom* this spring. . . ; they paid a bonus *for whom*. . . .

Note in (*e*) that there is no specific word in the independent clause to which the pronoun *who* may refer. In other words, there is no antecedent. In such constructions as this the pronoun often is called an *indefinite* relative pronoun, and the subordinate clause is regarded as a noun clause rather than as an adjectival clause. In (*e*) *who his best pitcher is* becomes the direct object of the verb *knows* in the independent clause. It answers the question: The manager knows what?

Analyze one more example: Sheriff White shot his deputy, *whom* he mistook for a burglar. Here *whom* introduces a non-restrictive relative clause that is set off by a comma. The clause is used adjectivally to modify *deputy*, a direct object in the independent clause. However, the objective form *whom* is not used because its antecedent is an object, but because it is the object of the verb *mistook* within the relative clause. Test it: He *mistook whom* for the burglar.

5. The relative pronoun *whose* and the contraction *who's*—for *who is*—should not be confused.

He's the man *whose* daughter is missing.

Whose introduces the subordinate clause *whose daughter is missing*, shows possession of *daughter*, and has the antecedent *man* in the independent clause.

AGREEMENT OF PRONOUNS WITH ANTECEDENTS

A pronoun agrees with its antecedent in number, person and gender. Its case, however, depends on the use of the pronoun in the clause or phrase in which it occurs. The *antecedent* of the pronoun is the word to which it refers.

Several constructions need to be watched closely to avoid errors in agreement of pronouns with antecedents, and in agreement in number of a relative pronoun with its verb.

1. Prepositional phrases which come between the pronoun and its antecedent often cause "false agreement" trouble.

Keyes is the only *one* of the players *who has* learned all the plays.

The antecedent of *who* is not *players* but *one*, which is definitely a singular pronoun here. Note that it is modified by *the only* (one). Therefore the singular verb *has* is correct.

> Keyes is one of the few *players who have* learned all the plays.

Here the antecedent of *who* is *players*, a plural noun.

> Wells is one of those editors *who* always *take* (not takes) a leading role in *their* (not *his*) community.

In this sentence two errors in agreement, instead of one, could have been made. The antecedent of *who* is not *one*, but *editors* in the prepositional phrase. Therefore the plural verb *take* and the plural possessive pronoun *their* are correct.

2. The reflexive pronoun used after a relative pronoun must agree with the antecedent.

> Dictatorship is one of the many *evils which* tend (*not* tends) to perpetuate *themselves*.

The antecedent of both *which* and *themselves* is *evils*; therefore both *which* and *themselves* are plural.

Note that if *the* is used before *one* in a sentence like the following, then *one*, which is a noun here, becomes the *antecedent* of the relative and reflexive pronouns that follow; so, the pronouns are singular.

> Selfishness is *the one* of her many faults *which* defeats *itself*.

3. When the pronouns *anyone, everyone, everybody, no one, nobody,* etc., are used as antecedents, the pronouns referring to them must be singular.

> On the Boy Scout hike *everybody* was told by the scoutmaster to bring *his* own drinking water.
> "Does *anyone* think *he* may be unable to attend?" the mayor asked.

4. Similarly, pronouns referring to *either* and *neither* are singular.

> *Neither* of the women has brought *her* certificate.

5. A pronoun referring to a plural noun and a singular noun connected by *or* or *nor* sounds better in the plural form.

> Neither the members of the cabinet nor the President will reveal *their* plans.

The plural possessive is preferred because the plans are being made by all the persons mentioned.

The rule for the agreement in number of the verb with the subject is followed for the possessive pronouns in other cases of reference to an antecedent. If the antecedent is composed of two singular nouns connected by *either. . . or* or *neither. . . nor*, the pronoun is singular. If the two nouns are plural, the pronoun is plural.

Either John or James, who are twins, has left *his* sweater.
Neither the twins nor their cousins have finished *their* courses.

6. Before the important issue of sexism was raised, most writers followed these two rules: If the antecedent of the pronoun may be either masculine or feminine in gender, the masculine pronoun is used. If the antecedent is a compound of a masculine and a feminine noun, it is considered correct to use a masculine pronoun. For example: *Everyone* is asked to do *his* part. *Every man and woman* is asked to contribute *his* share.

Today, however, women receive the same treatment as men in all areas of news coverage. The old rules have been junked, and today the reporter knows to make it read: Vance told *reporters*—not *newsmen*—that he would leave Friday morning for Tel Aviv. And, to use the plural wherever necessary: The *taxpayers* (not The *taxpayer*) complain that *they* (not *he*) cannot pay the higher taxes.

In some cases, both the masculine and the feminine pronoun may strictly be required, as in this sentence: *Every boy and every girl* is called upon to do *his* or *her* part. However, why not simply use the plural: *All boys and girls* are called upon to do *their* part.

7. If the antecedent is a collective noun, the pronoun is singular if the noun refers to a unit, but it is plural if the noun refers to the individuals making up the collection.

The basketball *team* lost *its* first play-off game. (Unit)
The defeated *team* hung *their* heads in shame. (Individuals)

Awkwardness could be avoided by rewriting the second sentence:

The defeated team members hung their heads in shame.

8. Special care must be taken when reflexive pronouns are used. The relative pronoun or personal pronoun and the reflexive pronoun must agree with the antecedent in number.

No manager should do for his *staff* what *they* can do for *themselves*.

Because the collective noun *staff* is considered as made up of individuals, the plural pronouns *they* and *themselves* are correct.

9. A personal pronoun is used correctly to refer to the antecedent *one*. Repetition of *one* now sounds stilted.

If *one* considers the plan carefully, *he* will find many flaws in it.

10. The antecedent of a pronoun must be made clear by the agreement of

the pronoun with the antecedent. In the following sentences, for example, there is no clear antecedent of *This*:

> POOR: Abolishment of the progressive income tax, complete revamping of the social security system and elimination of four cabinet posts are three proposals. *This* is the main part of the platform of the new party.

The sentences can be combined to omit *This* in a better construction.

> BETTER: Abolishment of the progressive income tax, complete revamping. . . and elimination of four cabinet posts *are the main planks* in the platform of the new party.

11. When successive pronouns refer to the same antecedent in the sentence, the pronouns must all have the same gender.

> The dog scratched *his* ear, shook *himself* and fell over on *his* back.

Do not say "fell over on *its* back" after using *his* and *himself* to refer to *dog*.

CONSTRUCTIONS TO BE WATCHED

In using pronouns, especially relative pronouns, there are some constructions which must be watched closely to avoid making errors.

1. Parenthetical clauses which come between the pronoun and its verb do not affect the case of the pronoun. Such confusing expressions or thrown-in statements, which may or may not be set off by commas, are: *they believe, they thought, it is believed, it is thought, he says,* etc.

> The child who (not *whom*) *we thought* was lost was found in the next block.

We thought is a parenthetical phrase and has no effect on the construction of the clause *who was lost*. *Who* is the subject of the verb *was* in the dependent (relative) clause.

> The woman *who* (not *whom*) *police believed took the jewels* was cleared.

The main clause is *The woman was cleared*. Note that the parenthetical expression *police believed* in the subordinate clause does not affect the case of *who*. *Who* is the subject of the verb *took*.

Note two more examples of this kind:

> They hope to bring from Korea the man *who* (not *whom*) *the prosecutor says* can give incriminating evidence. (*Who* is the subject of *can give*.)
>
> The youth *who* (not *whom*) *they said* was the most advanced in the group did prove to be the leader. (*Who* is the subject of *was*.)

2. The case of the relative pronoun depends on its use in the subordinate clause, as you have seen. Note these sentences also:

The man *whom they arrested* confessed to the crime.

Whom is the object of the predicate *arrested* in the subordinate (relative) clause. Test it: They (subject) arrested *whom*?

That is a woman *who may be president of the company some day*.

Who is the subject of the verb *may be* in the dependent clause.

Although the foregoing example is grammatically correct, it is not good writing; it is redundant. You could simply write: She may be president of the company some day. However, the strongest construction could be obtained simply by substituting the definite article *the* for the indefinite article *a* in the original sentence, thus giving emphasis to *the one woman* as the antecedent of *who*: That is *the* (*one*) woman who may be president. . . .

Members of the club do not know *who it will be*.

Who is a predicate nominative after *will be*. (It will be who?)

He promised to support *whoever* (not *whomever*) *of the Republican prospects was chosen*.

Whoever is the subject of *was chosen*. In this construction the entire relative clause, not just the pronoun alone, is the object of the infinitive *to support* in the independent clause.

3. Some of the most glaring errors appearing in newspapers and magazines result from careless misplacement of the relative clause. The relative clause should be placed near the word it modifies. Or, if possible, change the clause to a word or phrase.

WRONG: The waif held a doughnut in his hand which was coated with chocolate.
CORRECT: The waif held in his hand a doughnut which was coated with chocolate.
In his hand the waif held a chocolate-coated doughnut.
WRONG: He showed the silver dollars to his friends which he found lying on the floor.
CORRECT: He showed his friends the silver dollars which he had found on the floor.

4. Be sure that pronouns like *he* and *it* do refer to a specific word—a clearly recognizable antecedent. Failure of a writer to keep his pronouns referring to the same person or thing throughout a sentence may lead to misunderstanding.

UNCLEAR: The governor promised Tompkins that he would hold his job if he won.
CORRECT: The governor promised Tompkins that he would hold his job if the governor won.
UNCLEAR: Cabbage contains this vitamin, and it is essential to sound teeth. (Does *it* refer to cabbage or vitamin?)
CORRECT: Cabbages contain this vitamin, and it is essential to sound teeth.
BETTER: Cabbage contains this vitamin, which is essential to sound teeth.

5. Change an indirect quotation to a direct quotation if that will make the statement clearer and avoid the use of several pronouns.

The governor promised Tompkins that he would hold his job if he should win again.
Governor Black told Tompkins yesterday, "You will keep your job if I win."

6. A pronoun should refer to the substantive which is central or uppermost in the writer's mind.

INCORRECT: The senator's *theory* of politics on the local level is interesting, and many citizens agree with *him*.
CORRECT: The senator's *theory* of politics on the local level is interesting, and many citizens agree with *it*.

The *theory* is the thing with which the citizens agree, not the *senator*. An even better way to express this would be to use two sentences.

BETTER: The senator's theory of politics is interesting. Many citizens agree with it.

Be sure to see that the pronoun *it* has a clearly recognized antecedent. Avoid writing sentences like those below.

Mr. and Mrs. Perkins have been generous contributors, and they will be recognized for *it*.
The girls will dance for the veterans; *it* will cheer them up.

The sentences could be recast as follows: Mr. and Mrs. Perkins have been generous contributors, and they will be recognized for their generosity. To cheer up the veterans, the girls will dance for them.

7. The antecedent of the pronoun should not be a possessive. In number 6 above, the first illustration given is incorrect for the wrong reference of *him* to *senator's*, as well as for reference to the wrong noun.

8. The indefinite use of the pronoun *they* is not good usage.

POOR: Down in Texas they are noted for the telling of tall tales.
BETTER: Down in Texas the citizens are noted for the telling of tall tales.
Texans are noted for telling tall tales.
POOR: They say that it may be a hard winter.
BETTER: The prediction is that the winter will be a hard one.
Meteorologists predict a hard winter.

If you use *they* in a sentence, ask yourself, "Who are *they*?" If the meaning is not clear, rewrite the sentence.

However, the use of *they* with an obscure antecedent is frequent in broadcast journalism. Even the use of *they* in referring to a singular antecedent, although grammatically incorrect, is common broadcast usage: The city placed a barrier across the street. *They* want to reduce traffic in the neighborhood.

Most news directors will accept such usage in broadcast writing because they believe it helps to achieve the conversational (colloquial) tone they feel is essential to that form.

9. The expletive *it* and the pronoun *it* should not be used in the same sentence.

> POOR: It is best to keep the soap on hand for a few weeks so that it will shrink slightly before it is used for sculpturing.
> BETTER: If possible, keep the soap on hand. . . .

10. Do not use a pronoun with a double reference, that is, reference to more than one antecedent in the same sentence.

> INCORRECT: Beth telephoned Helen that *she* would be on the committee.
> CORRECT: Beth telephoned Helen, "You will be on the committee."
> Beth telephoned Helen, "I will be on the committee." Beth telephoned Helen that she, Helen, would be on the committee.
> INCORRECT: He sent for Pollard and told him that when Edwards was added to the staff, *he* would serve as chief agent.
> CORRECT: He sent for Pollard and told him that. . . Pollard would serve as chief agent (*or* Edwards would serve). . . .

11. Do not fail to have an antecedent for any pronoun you use.

> INCORRECT: It was Amateur Night, and the program was presented by them.
> CORRECT: Amateurs presented the entire program on Amateur Night.

In the first sentence, there is no antecedent for the pronoun *them*.

> INCORRECT: Dr. Laura Casey has spent 13 years in these areas in Africa and knows what their customs are.
> CORRECT: Dr. Laura Casey has spent 13 years in these areas in Africa and knows what the customs of the natives are.

In the first sentence *their* apparently refers to *areas*, but areas do not have customs.

12. Construct sentences so that *which* and *that* will have definite antecedents to refer to.

> POOR: Burkett was given the leading role in the play, which the other members of the cast did not like.

Which does not refer to the nearest noun *play*, or to *role* or to *Burkett*. It is best to completely recast such sentences, as shown below.

> Selection of Burkett as the leading man in the play displeased the rest of the cast.
> Burkett's being given the leading role displeased the rest of the cast.
> The cast was displeased when Burkett was given the leading male role.

13. Do not use a coordinating conjunction before a relative pronoun unless a similar pronoun is used earlier in the sentence.

> INCORRECT: Sutton, a squad member for three years, keeps training rules and practices hard but who simply does not have the knack for playing the game well.
> CORRECT: Sutton, who has been a squad member for three years and who keeps training rules and practices hard, simply does not have the knack for playing the game well.
> Sutton has been a squad member for three years, and he keeps training rules and practices hard; but he simply does not have the knack for playing well.

14. Be consistent in the use of the person of the pronouns throughout the sentence.

> If *any student* turns in *his* assignments late, *he* (not *they* or *you*) will get poor grades.
> If *any students* turn in *their* assignments late, *they* will get poor grades.

15. Subjects, predicate nominatives, appositives, etc., should be consistent throughout the sentence.

> POOR: Because *she* arrived early, *it* was easy for her to get the interview with the general.
> CORRECT: Because *she* arrived early, *she* found it easy to get the interview with the general.

The subject *she* in the dependent clause and the expletive *it* in the independent clause of the first sentence are not consistent. It would be still better in the revision to avoid the use of *it* by saying *she easily got the interview*.

> POOR: Shuford is now a full professor, a rank that he has worked hard to obtain.
> CORRECT: Shuford now holds a full professorship, a rank. . .

Rank, as an appositive, is incorrect in referring to *full professor*.

QUIZ ANSWERS

In sentences 1-14 the correct words are: 1. his. 2. *that* is correct in a restrictive clause. 3. their. 4. its. 5. its. 6. whoever. 7. whom. 8. who. 9. has. 10. whoever. 11. have. 12. his *or* his or her. 13. lives. 14. tend, themselves. Correct sentences 15-20 as follows: 15. Make a sentence out of the misplaced phrase, to read something like this: We hope we won't ever miss another of your birthday parties. 16. Lewis told his brother, "Your (or *My*) car has been stolen." 17. Criminals pass in and out of jails as if the jails were equipped. . . . 18. He thought it was necessary that the plan be given further study. 19. The future is bright for. . . who has the ability to better himself. 20. To call defensive signals, the coach selected Jenkins. The majority of the players did not like the coach's choice.

10

Using Adjectives and Adverbs Correctly

To put flesh on the skeleton, the framework of the sentence, the writer uses modifiers. Human skeletons look pretty much alike. But, except for identical twins, all persons look different. It is the flesh added to the skeleton which makes it possible to distinguish one human being from another. Just as flesh added to the skeleton gives a person an observably different appearance from that of his fellows, so do modifiers added to the skeleton of a sentence give individuality to that particular construction.

The modifiers—adjectives and adverbs—are important grammatical tools which the journalist must learn to use with deftness. Verbs, nouns and pronouns are the important parts of speech that make the sense of the sentence, but try to imagine how flat the journalist's writing would be if he had to use them without any modifying elements.

Adjectives and adverbs are essential parts of speech because they present the reader with definite word pictures of the persons, things and actions named in the sentence. Through the use of adjectives and adverbs the journalist can present facts and ideas in more specific, concrete form. Such words are indispensable in stating exactly what the writer desires to say. For example, if the word *pear* is used, how much clearer your conception of it is if the writer uses one or more of the following adjectives with it: *ripe, green, yellow, bitter, sweet, luscious, juicy, large, Bartlett, dew-covered*. Similarly, a verb like *turned* conveys more meaning if it is modified by some such adverb as: *slowly, quickly, jerkily, painfully, hesitatingly, apprehensively, expectantly*.

128

The expert use of adjectives and adverbs will give color to your writing. It is not always possible to write colorfully in handling routine news stories, to be sure, but any journalist worth his salary strives to turn out colorful writing.

Do not confuse *colorful* writing with *colored* writing. Colored writing is biased material, writing that is slanted to fit the editorial policy. Most editors and publishers do not condone or require writing that fits any one policy. But they do approve of *colorful* writing, writing that presents vivid pictures to the reader.

To produce colorful writing you first of all must learn to use specific, concrete nouns and concrete, active verbs and verbals. Next, you need to learn how to use adjectives and adverbs expertly. Observe how adverbs, as well as adjectives, are used effectively by a metropolitan newspaper reporter covering a sanity hearing. A psychiatrist had just agreed that the woman involved needed psychiatric treatment. Here's what the reporter wrote:

> But when a *smiling, white-haired* woman took the stand, she *calmly, coherently, believably* denied the traffic violations and denied having diabetes. Asked if she needed a psychiatrist, she replied, "I *definitely* don't. I resent that." (The judge committed her to a local hospital's psychiatric unit for observation.)

(Using specific, concrete words is discussed on pages 225–26 if you would like to take a look ahead.)

Since modifiers are such important tools for the journalist, he or she must be able to use them correctly. Before you take up the sections in this chapter, review pages 33—39 and make sure that you can identify the classes of adjectives and adverbs and recognize their various uses as modifiers.

Recall, too, that many adjectives and adverbs may be compared to show degree, and that many errors in the use of adjectives and adverbs result from lack of knowledge of the three degrees of comparison.

Test your knowledge of correct usage of adjectives and adverbs by taking the following quiz.

QUIZ

1. Baker made a very strong appeal to freshmen senators Friday.
2. When the police entered the room, an hysterical, thinly-clad woman rushed out a rear door.
3. Palmer only allowed three hits as he pitched the 50th shutout of his very distinguished career Saturday, beating the Oakland A's 1–0.
4. He is more efficient at the free-throw line than anybody on the Lincoln University team. Cashing in on free shots very consistently, the coach pointed out, is one of the toughest, if not the most difficult, chore that a basketball player is called upon to perform.

5. He's an excellent prospect, and his passing is the more effective of all the backs, but surely he cannot hardly ever hope to equal the incomparable Sammy Baugh.

6. He began to run toward her, and he scarcely had covered half the distance between them than she recognized him.

7. The advantages and the disadvantages tend to almost offset each other.

8. Walker executed most all of his college football feats in the Cotton Bowl.

9. "Alright, I agree that every member of the starting freshmen quintet are good shot-makers," said Coach Prewitt, "but I think Phillips and Berg will prove to be the better sharp-shooters."

10. This kind of old-fashion mountings are some different than the type your mother's ring is set in. The medium-size mounting is as attractive, if not more so, than the larger size.

11. He said he was hitting the ball as good as he has ever hit it, both with his irons and off the tee.

12. Mayor Mayhew feels very badly about the proposed railroad through his ranch.

13. Parton received a M.S. degree Monday and promptly told his father, "That is the kind of a car I want as a graduation present."

14. Doyle Dane Bernbach's copywriting techniques are the most effective of all advertising men in the United States.

15. The largest of the two bream barely weighed a half a pound.

How many did you miss? Turn to pages 142–43 to find out.

THE ARTICLES

1. The indefinite article *a* is used before words that begin with a consonant or a consonant sound.

a table	a future year
a man	a historical novel

The *h* in *historical* is pronounced.

In the following words, the vowel *o* is sounded like the consonant *w,* and the vowel *u* is sounded like *you.*

a one-armed bandit	a union
a used automobile	a unique ring

2. The indefinite article *an* is used before words that begin with a vowel or a vowel sound, or with a silent *h,* as in *honor.*

an arrow	an illegal arrest	an heir
an orange	an airy manner	an hour

The h in heir and hour is silent; the words begin with a vowel sound.

3. Be careful to apply rules 1 and 2 in the case of *abbreviations* used in newspapers and magazines. Some abbreviations are read as letters and some are read as words. You may determine how the reader will use them by pronouncing the words to yourself.

> It was *a* MS of 350 pages.
> He received *an* M.S. degree in June.

The average reader will read MS as *manuscript,* but probably will read M.S. as letters rather than as *Master of Science.*

The same rule applies to figures used before nouns.

> *a* $10,000 loss   *a* 10-ton load
> *a* $50,000,000 deficit   *an* 11-man team

4. If two or more nouns in a compound subject or object refer to different persons or things, the article must be repeated before each noun. If the nouns refer to the same person or thing, the article is used before the first noun only.

> They met *the* general manager and *the* editor. ((Two persons)
> Wells is the general manager and editor. (One person)
> *The* feature article and *the* short story are somewhat similar.

The exception to this rule is the compound subject or object that names two or more nouns which constitute a unit. A single article is used then: A horse and buggy appeared around the bend.

5. Only one *the* is necessary before two adjectives modifying a plural noun. If *the* is repeated, the noun must be singular.

> The Irwin-Keasler and Socony-Mobil buildings were destroyed in an early morning fire.
> *The* fifth and eighth chapters have been completed.
> *The* fifth and *the* eighth chapter have been completed.

6. If adjectives in a series modify the same noun, the article is used only before the first adjective when the noun denotes one item; the article is repeated before the second adjective when the noun denotes two or more items.

> He bought *a* rayon and nylon shirt. (One shirt)
> He bought *a* rayon and *a* nylon shirt. (Two shirts)

Of course only one article is needed in: *a* tall, heavy-set, dark-complexioned man.

7. Use *the Rev.* before a minister's name on first reference: the Rev. Billy Graham. Substitute Monsignor before the name of a Catholic priest who has received this honor. For second reference, consult a stylebook.

8. Be sure to include the article when it is part of the official title of a newspaper, a magazine, a book, a poem, etc.

> The Dallas *Times Herald*
> *The Reader's Digest*
> "The Art of Readable Writing"

The article does not have to be capitalized in mid-sentence when it is the first word in the official name of a publication.

9. The article is repeated sometimes for *emphasis*.

> *The* wealth and *the* riches of this land shall be yours.

10. Journalists must learn to avoid the use of superfluous articles. Omission of the article is common practice in the following cases, and such omission saves precious space.

> Directors of the First National Bank voted to declare a dividend.
> Johnson was gone only a half-hour.
> The children have chicken pox.

Do not say *The directors* or *a half an hour* or *the chicken pox*.

11. Do not use *a* or *an* after *kind of* or *sort of*.

> Jenkins invented a new *sort of* zipper.
> That is the kind of (not kind of *a*) car I want.

12. On the other hand, be careful to use the article if it is necessary for clarity. Note how the meaning is changed in the following sentence if the article *a* is omitted.

> He found *a little comfort* in the message.
> He found *little comfort* in the message.

DEGREES OF COMPARISON

Many errors in the use of adjectives and adverbs result from failure to use the correct degree of the modifier. The degrees of quality or quantity are shown by means of the positive, comparative and superlative forms of adjectives and adverbs.

Remember that the *comparative degree* is used when two persons or things are compared, and the *superlative degree* is used when three or more are compared.

1. Most adjectives of one or two syllables form the comparative and superlative degrees by adding *er* and *est* to the positive degree.

> high, higher, highest
> pretty, prettier, prettiest

A few adverbs are compared in the same way.

fast, faster, fastest
slow, slower, slowest
soon, sooner, soonest

Most adjectives of more than two syllables and most adverbs form the comparative and superlative degrees by using *more* and *most* or *less* and *least* before the positive degree.

ADJECTIVES: beautiful, more beautiful, most beautiful
kind-hearted, less kind-hearted, least kind-hearted

ADVERBS: carefully, less carefully, least carefully
easily, more easily, most easily

Some adjectives and adverbs are compared irregularly. They are called *irregular comparatives*.

ADJECTIVES: good, better, best
bad, worse, worst
little, less, least

ADVERBS: much, more, most
far, farther, farthest
well, better, best

Many of these words may be used both as adjectives and as adverbs.

Many degree adverbs, such as *most, very, less, somewhat, almost, rather, about, altogether* and *much*, can be used as other parts of speech. For example, *most* may be either an adverb or a pronoun or part of a degree adverb.

The director was *most* cordial. (Adverb of degree modifying adjective *cordial*)
He received us *most* cordially. (Adverb of degree modifying adverb *cordially*)
Most of the chaperones are young. (Pronoun, subject of verb *are*)

2. The words *farther* and *further* have always given writers trouble. Within the next fifty years there probably will be no distinction between *farther* and *further*. *Further* likely will drive out *farther*. However, until this occurs, the journalist will do well to observe these two rules: (1) *Farther* is usually an adverb and *further* an adjective, but it is not safe to assume that this is always the case. (2) Use *farther* to refer to distance and space; use *further* to refer to time, quantity or degree.

The retired judge lives on the farther side of the hill. (Adjective)
Fran Tarkenton can throw the ball farther than Hart. (Adverb)

Further study of the committee's report is needed. (Adjective)
The committee will discuss the matter *further*. (Adverb)
Foreign exchange traders saw the dollar slip further. (Adverb)

3. There is now more permissiveness in using *last, latest* and *past.* Some grammarians still insist that *last* can only mean *final*, and that *past* must be used for immediately preceding, as in *during the past week* or *the past year*. However, *during the last week* or *the last year*, used in the sense of *just past*, are now accepted.

You cannot be wrong if you still follow the old rules observed by many editors. Use *last* in referring to an object or person that follows all others. Use *latest* in referring to that which is nearest the present time.

Note the usage of *last* twice in this short sentence from a story about the sentencing of two men for the murder of reporter Don Bolles: The *last* execution in the United States was in Utah *last* January. Other examples follow:

He is the *last* living member of the Hunt family.
The *last* edition of the *last* afternoon newspaper in Chicago began rolling off the presses at 3 a.m. March 4.
The article appears in the *latest* issue of *Editor & Publisher*.
The *latest* (not *last*) announcement was made at noon today.

To avoid redundancy, do not use the word *last* with the name of a month or a day.

PREFERRED: It happened Monday. It happened in May.
BUT: It happened *last* week. It happened *last* month.

4. Be careful not to compare anything with itself. Use *any other* and *anything else* to designate the other items in the comparison.

The Mississippi is larger than *any other river* in the United States.
His story on the hospital fire is better than *anything else* he has turned in.

It would be incorrect to say: larger than *any river* or better than *anything*.

5. Use the word *all* in the superlative degree to express comparison of a person, a place or a thing with the rest of its class.

Edwin Moses, Olympic champion, may develop into the fastest of *all* hurdlers in track history.

6. Be sure to compare things *within the same class*.

INCORRECT: Doyle Dane Bernbach's copywriting techniques are the most effective of all advertising men in the United States.
CORRECT: Doyle Dane Bernbach's copywriting techniques are the most effective of all those used by advertising men in the United States.

7. Do not confuse *as* and *than* in making comparisons. Always state the comparison fully before you add the qualifying expression. Be sure to use a second *as*.

> INCORRECT: Theismann may be *as good,* if not better, *than* Kilmer (is) in the quarterback position.
> CORRECT: Theismann may be *as good* in the quarterback position *as* Kilmer, if not better (than Kilmer is).

8. In comparisons, avoid using a singular noun that confuses the reader as to number.

> INCORRECT: Supplying the city with sufficient water is one of the most difficult, if not the most difficult, *problem* that the city council has faced.

The singular noun *problem* is used incorrectly.

> CORRECT: Supplying the city with sufficient water is one of the most difficult problems that the city council has faced, if not the most difficult.

9. Some adjectives and adverbs should not be compared. Such words as *unique, perfect, perfectly, square, round, absolute, absolutely,* and **supreme** represent a superlative degree in themselves; so one should not say "**more** perfect," "more unique" and so on. Avoid such expressions as: "the most perfect diamond," "the most perfectly executed play" and the like. To express degree with these words, use "most nearly perfect," etc.

> Example: Stuart has one of the most nearly perfect swings in baseball.

USING MODIFIERS PROPERLY

To round out your review of correct usage of adjectives and adverbs, study the miscellaneous rules that follow.

1. Journalists should note that the trend is toward more frequent use of what are called *flat adverbs*. These are words that have an *ly* adverb form but are used in their adjective form to modify verbs. The following are considered correct usage:

> Drive *slow* (or *slowly*). Work *fast*. Tell it *quick* (or *quickly*).

2. Be sure to use a predicate adjective—not an adverb—after such copulative (linking) verbs as *appear, become, feel, look, seem*. The adverb *badly* is correct after the verb *feel* only if it modifies the verb rather than the subject, as in this sentence: The youth feels *badly* the need for getting a college education. Incorrect: The youth feels *badly* about being rejected. (Review of the three kinds of verbs, especially the linking verb, will be helpful here. See pages 49-50 and 52-53.) Study some other examples:

The mayor feels *bad* (not *badly*) about the investigation.
The patient looked *bad* yesterday.
"I didn't hit it that *badly*," said Haas after he had scored his first victory as a touring golf pro.

3. Remember that *well* may be either an adjective or an adverb, according to its use.

The patient feels *well* (not *good*). (Predicate adjective)
His doctor says he is *well*. (Predicate adjective)
He sits *well* in the saddle. (Adverb)
He eats *well* (not *good*). (Adverb)

Webster now accepts *good* as an adverb, but the press associations and most editors forbid the use of *good* for *well*. Apparently, sportscasters are getting by most frequently with such usage: Bostock is really hitting *good*.

4. Remember that *sure* is an adjective, *surely* is an adverb; that *real* is an adjective, *really* is an adverb; and that *very* is an adverb. Don't misuse *sure* for *surely* or *real* for *really*.

Crosby is *sure* of his facts. (Predicate adjective modifying *Crosby*)
He *surely* (not *sure*) should arrive soon. (Adverb modifying verb *should arrive*)
This is a *real* opal. (Adjective modifying *opal*)
I am *really* sorry about that. (Adverb modifying predicate adjective *sorry*)
He spoke *very* clearly over the telephone. (Adverb modifying adverb *clearly*)

5. As a rule, the use of *very* before an adjective is unnecessary. Note these sentences:

The chorus girl is *very pretty*.
The tramp was very offensive in appearance.

Why not omit *very* and say the chorus girl is *beautiful* or *lovely*? And why not say the tramp was *repulsive*?

The pears were *very* rotten.
The marathon runner was *very* exhausted.

If the pears were rotten, the adverb *very* adds nothing to the meaning. Neither can *very* add anything to the word *exhausted*, which means *completely tired*.

Other adverbs are sometimes used unnecessarily. Avoid such expressions as: perfectly beautiful, simply horrible, absolutely correct. The adverbs add nothing to the adjectives.

6. Remember that only adverbs may modify adjectives.

It was *extremely* (not *real*) warm in the courtroom.

Extremely is an adverb modifying the predicate adjective *warm*.

Dunning was considered an *ordinarily* reliable reporter.

The adverb *ordinarily* modifies the adjective *reliable*. If the adjective *ordinary* is used, it should be followed by a comma: *an ordinary, reliable reporter*. But note the difference in meaning. The first sentence refers to Dunning's being reliable under ordinary circumstances. The use of *ordinary* in the second sentence would describe the reporter as being an ordinary type.

7. Avoid the use of *mighty, awful, awfully* (for *very*) in your writing, if not in your speaking. Do not say: The lieutenant was mighty (or awfully) tired. Say he was very (or *extremely*) *tired*. Or if he was *exhausted,* say so!

8. Do not use the adjective *some* or the phrases *sort of* and *kind of* for the adverbs *somewhat* and *rather*.

> Wayne was reported *somewhat* better today.
> Wayne said he felt *rather* (not *sort of* or *kind of*) tired when he entered the hospital.

9. Use *almost,* not *most,* when the meaning is *nearly*.

> Walker executed *almost* all his gridiron feats in the Cotton Bowl.

Almost in this sentence means *nearly. Most* in the sentence below has the meaning of "the majority."

> Walker executed *most* of his gridiron feats in the Cotton Bowl.

10. Avoid the use of *above* as an adjective. Instead of saying "Refer to the above section," have your sentence read "Refer to the *foregoing* section," or less formally, *"See above."*

11. Do not confuse the preposition *to* with the adverb *too. Too* means "to an excessive degree" or "also."

> The soldier was *too* tired to move. He was wet to the skin, *too*.

The adjective *two* will not give you difficulty.

12. Some writers have trouble in deciding what adverb to use with a past participle that is used adjectivally. This is not surprising, because there is no hard-and-fast rule to follow. Perhaps the best guide is this: (1) If the passive participle is used merely as a descriptive adjective, like *distinguished* or *tired,* use a single adverb like *very, too* or *so* as a modifier; (2) if the passive participle is a strong verbal form, that is, if it appears to be a part of the predicate and is used to express deep feeling or emotion or strong force, use *very much, too greatly* and so on. Note the following examples:

His first book, *Roots,* has made Haley a *very* distinguished author.
The marathon runner was *too* tired to go on.
The boy was *very much* depressed over his failure.
She was *too badly* frightened to remember the pistol.
He was *so much* (not *so*) overwrought that he decided to take his life.

13. Nouns modified by the adjectives *each, either, neither* and *every* are singular and take singular verbs.

Neither Amanda nor her brother was injured.
Every woman and child in Quang Ngai *was* saved.

14. Use *from,* not *than,* after the adjective *different* in most instances. There are some strong arguments for *different than*. The most logical argument is for using *than* when it introduces a condensed clause: "It has possessed me in a different way *than* (it) ever (did) before," Cardinal Newman declared. As Bernstein points out, insistence on the use of *from* in the cardinal's quotation would result in some such monstrosity as this: "It has possessed me in a different way *from* the way in which it ever before did." Bernstein rightly recommends the use of *than* to avoid awkwardness, cumbersomeness and elaborate wastefulness with words. But, the writer who confines himself to the use of *different from* will always be grammatically correct.

The colonel's answers were *different from* those of the major.
His copywriting style is quite *different from* Bernbach's (style).
Flying conditions are no *different from* yesterday's (flying conditions). But:
Flying conditions are no *different than* they were yesterday.
The Dallas Cowboys today are a far *different* team *than* (preferred to *from what they were*) when they started competing in the NFL 20 years ago.

15. Journalism teachers agree that a common mistake of their students is the omission of the hyphen in compound adjectives which precede the nouns they modify. The hyphen is used correctly in the following:

an all-star lineup	a seven-foot pole
the three-year-old girl	an old-fashioned ring
a do-or-die expression	a well-developed figure
a pearl-handled revolver	a two-car garage

The hyphen also is used when the adjectives are appositives.

The cowboy, *raw-boned* and *weather-beaten*, hunched over the fire.

When the compound adjective follows the verb as a predicate adjective, however, the hyphen may be omitted, although some authorities sanction its use in some cases. It is always used in a compound predicate noun.

> The little girl is only three years old.
> She is a little three-year-old. (Predicate noun)
> Her project proposal is well developed (or well-developed).

The hyphen is not used between an adverb ending in *ly* modifying a participle that in turn modifies a following noun. Journalists should note that this is one of the most common errors found today in newspapers and in some magazines. Study these examples:

> INCORRECT: The *nationally-broadcast* meeting with reporters came just two days before the third and final debate.
> I have just returned from a columnists' workshop, and I can't wait to dazzle all of you with my *newly-acquired* literary skills.
> CORRECT: The *recently completed* bridge will be opened to traffic Friday.
> The *smartly dressed* women looked out of place in the tavern.

16. *Size* is not an adjective and must not be used to form adjectives. The correct form is *small-sized*.

> They owned a *large-sized* ranch in California.
> The hungry boy gulped down a *platter-sized* steak.

17. The numerals *twenty-one* through *ninety-nine* are always written with a hyphen, of course, and so also are the corresponding adjectives.

> Only *twenty-four* persons were rescued.

18. *Alright* for *all right* is now listed in Webster's and in the *Oxford English Dictionary*. However, *all right* is the established spelling. The AP Stylebook advises: Never use *alright*. Hyphenate *all right* only if used colloquially as a compound modifier: He is an *all-right* guy.

19. *Due to*, in the sense of *because of*, is listed now in Webster's. But strict grammarians still insist that *due to* be used only to modify a noun or a pronoun: Cox's slump was *due to* insufficient batting practice. (*Due* modifies the noun *slump*.) Grammarians and other authorities condemn *due to* used adverbially as a prepositional phrase: Cox's average slumped *due to* insufficient batting practice. (*Due to*, as a preposition, introduces a phrase that modifies the verb *slumped*.)

Most journalists will agree that *due to* could have been discarded long ago in favor of *because of*: Cox's average slumped *because of* insufficient batting practice. And certainly you would use *because of* instead of *due to* in this sentence: *Because of* serious illness in his family, the senator could not attend the hearing.

20. Journalists should never be guilty of using a double negative. Two negatives make an affirmative; therefore, such expressions as "can't hardly" and "couldn't never" defeat their purpose. Use such words as *barely, hardly* and *scarcely* without another negative.

> Tarkenton *can hardly* (not *can't hardly*) raise his throwing arm above his shoulder.
> The fleeing convict *could scarcely* climb the river bank.
> With only a high school education, he *could never* succeed in that job.

21. Another rule to remember in using the adverbs *barely, hardly* and *scarcely* is to use *when*, not *than*, in completing the statement.

> *Hardly* had he reached the gangplank *when* he saw her.
> The driver had *scarcely* reached the city limits *when* the police overtook him.

But *no sooner* must be followed by a *than* clause: *No sooner* had the witness been sworn in *than* the prosecutor began firing questions.

22. The adverb *anywhere* never adds an *s*. Webster lists the adverbs *backward* and *somewhere* as preferred, with *backwards* and *somewheres* as standard variant. When used as an adjective instead of as an adverb, *backward* is correct: a *backward* glance. Webster now lists *towards* as a variant, but the stylebooks forbid its use.

23. Use *anywhere* and *somewhere* instead of *anyplace* and *someplace*.

> You can place the desk *anywhere* (not *anyplace*) in the room.

24. Many writers fail to place *only* near the word or element it modifies. This is one of the most common errors made by sports writers and sportscasters today. Example: Belanger has *only* been thrown out three times. (The *only* should precede *three times*.)

Most editors will insist that you use *only* where it belongs in the sentence—immediately before the element it modifies. Note how the meaning in the following sentences is changed merely by moving *only*.

> Bill Hunter believes that *only* Bert Campaneris can surpass Lou Brock's record for stolen bases.
> *Only* Bill Hunter believes that Bert Campaneris can surpass. . . .
> Bill Hunter thinks that Bert Campaneris can *only* equal (cannot break) Lou Brock's record. . . .
> Bill Hunter *only* supposes (he doesn't know) that Bert Campaneris can equal Lou Brock's record. . . .
> Campaneris needs *only* seven steals to reach 600 by mid-season.

Note this other example of placing *only* in its normally proper position.

> The trustees plan to spend *only* $500,000 on the building. (Not: The trustees *only plan* to spend)

Placement of *only* in other than a normal position may be defended when *only* is used as a sentence adverb to modify an entire statement rather than a word or phrase. In the following sentence *only* correctly precedes the verb because it modifies the entire statement:

The producer *only* felt that he was doing the right thing to reject the script.

Placing *only* just before the verb in the following sentence may be better than placing it in what would be considered the normal order, before *when*:

The purpose of the investigation only became clear when the district attorney asked the vending machine company to open its books.

The same rule holds for *ever* and *almost*.

Jackson does not hope *ever* to break the records of Ruth and Maris. (Not: does not *ever* hope)
Bonds has *almost* the easiest swing I have ever seen in baseball.

25. The dangling participle, a common error of writers, is a serious violation of sentence coherence. Therefore it is treated fully in Chapter 14, Sentence Coherence. (See pages 187—89.)

Just remember here that the participial phrase is used as an adjective and must modify a noun or a pronoun that follows it. Make certain that it modifies the right word. Journalists, of all people, should not be caught writing a sentence like this:

INCORRECT: Running at full speed, the ball was caught near the wall in right field. (Surely the *ball* was not doing the running!)
CORRECT: Running at full speed, McBride caught the ball near the wall in right field.

Gerund phrases also can dangle, another violation of sentence coherence. How to avoid making this error is discussed on pages 187–90.

26. The *split infinitive* was discussed on pages 72–73. Here we give more attention to placement of the *adverb* in relation to the infinitive phrase.

Remember that separating the parts of the infinitive with an adverb is sometimes permissible if emphasis is gained, if smoother writing results, and if the meaning is clear and correct. But do not split infinitives needlessly.

The professor advised her students *to search diligently* for the facts.

Nothing would be gained by writing *to diligently search*.
The split infinitives in the following sentences do add emphasis.

Informed that she had won the contest, Mrs. Mayhew called her husband *to happily tell* him of her good fortune.
Jorgensen was unable *to completely master* Greek.

The position of the adverb gives sentences different meanings, as shown in these examples:

> He told Smith *immediately* to come to the point. *Or*, He *immediately told. . . .*
> He told Smith to *immediately* come to the point.
> He told Smith to come to the point *immediately*.
> The corporal failed to *completely* comprehend the order.
> The corporal failed *completely* to comprehend the order.

27. Certainly no journalist should make a mistake like this: The pond, froze solid overnight, was crowded with skaters by noon. Use the past participle form of the verb as an adjective modifier.

> The pond, *frozen* overnight, was crowded with skaters by noon.
> The challenger, badly *beaten*, went down for the full count.

28. You should never use the plural *freshmen* as an adjective. The singular *freshman* is the adjective form.

> The personable star of the North Carolina Tar Heels was elected president of the *freshman* class.
> The *freshman* congressman is being pressed to vote for the treaties.

But "The *freshmen* outnumber the sophomores" is correct.

29. The misuse of *principle* for *principal* is a common error. *Principle* is always a noun, not an adjective. It means a fundamental law or doctrine or truth or a guiding rule or code of conduct: the *principle* of racial equality; a person of *principle*. *Principal* may be an adjective or a noun. As an adjective it has the meaning of *chief* or *main*: the *principal* parts of verbs; a *principal* bank officer. As a noun, *principal* may refer to a chief or leading person, or it may refer to a sum placed at interest: *principal* of the school; he receives 6½ percent interest on the *principal*.

QUIZ ANSWERS

1. Change *freshmen* to *freshman*. 2. When police entered the room, a hysterical, thinly clad woman rushed out a rear door. 3. Change to: Palmer allowed only three hits as he pitched. . . . 4. Insert *else* after *anybody*; eliminate *very*; and make last of sentence read: is one of the toughest chores that. . . to perform, if not the most difficult. 5. He's an excellent prospect, and his passing is the most effective of that of all the backs, but surely he can hardly hope ever to equal (the record of) the incomparable Sammy Baugh. 6. He began to run toward her, and he had scarcely covered half the distance between them when she recognized him. 7. Correct. 8. Change *most* to *almost*. 9. "All right, I agree that every member of the starting freshman quintet is a good shot-maker," said Coach Prewitt, "but I think Phillips and Berg will prove to be the best sharp-

shooters.'' 10. This kind of old-fashioned mountings is somewhat different from the type your mother's ring is set in. The medium-sized mounting is as attractive as the larger-sized (mounting). It may be even more attractive. 11. Although Webster's now accepts *good* as an adverb, the press associations and most newspaper editors still insist on the use of *well* as the adverb: He said he was hitting the ball as well as he has ever. . . . 12. *Bad* should be used as the predicate adjective. 13. Parton received *an* M.S. degree Monday and told. . .''That is the kind of (omit *a*) car I want. . . . 14. Bernbach's copywriting techniques are the most effective of all those used by advertising men. . . . 15. The larger of the two bream weighed barely (or barely weighed) half a pound.

11

Using Prepositions and Conjunctions Correctly

If verbs and nouns may be thought of as composing the skeleton of the sentence, and if adjectives and adverbs are visualized as forming the flesh on the skeleton, then conjunctions and prepositions may be compared to the ligaments, those bands of tissue that tie the parts together. Just as the ligaments are vital parts of the body, conjunctions and prepositions are essential components of the sentence.

Prepositions and conjunctions are connecting or linking words. These two parts of speech are much alike in function, and many errors are made by confusing them. They are treated together in this chapter.

Turn back to Chapter 3 and review carefully the sections on prepositions and conjunctions. Make sure that you know how these two parts of speech are used in sentences and that you can identify the kinds of conjunctions.

To test yourself on the correct usage of prepositions and conjunctions, take the following quiz.

QUIZ

1. It looks like the new system is going to result in better employer-employe(e) relations at Atlantic-Richfield.
2. He told police his wife was forced in a truck and later raped.
3. The Commissioner will try and show where maintenance costs could be reduced without impairing service.

4. Neither County Judge Lew Sterrett or County Auditor Moore Lynn would comment on reports that the tax rate had been agreed on. *upon*
5. The inheritance of around $130,000 will be divided between (or *among*) him, Dolores and Hazel. *but added she*
6. She said the man identified himself as an insurance salesman, nevertheless she was suspicious of him.
7. Matte had no sooner taken the hand-off from Morrall before Barnes spilled him for a four-yard loss.
8. Collins cut to far to the left, so the pass overshot him.
9. The actors had come to have little regard and appreciation of his ability to direct the cast.
10. An accomplice was waiting in a 1967 Pontiac in front of the bank with its motor running.
11. He demanded to know if the payment could be made by April 1.
12. He said he would dismiss the jury providing the attorney general can present evidence that certain jurors are biased.
13. He left no money or property to the youngest son.
14. He kept boring in relentlessly so La Cruz was kept off balance throughout the fight.
15. The director whispered to the producer, "Between you and I, I think Alan is ready for a leading role. Why, he acts just like Clark Gable!"
16. Frazier's footwork is equal, if not better, than the champion's.
17. District Attorney Wade stoutly declared that he would see that Jack Ruby got the death sentence.
18. "I'll have to differ with you on that. I think his change of pace is different than Gibson's."
19. "Winston tastes good—like a cigarette should!"
20. Commissioner Pickett stated that he proposed two possible solutions besides the one suggested by the county auditor.

How did you do on this quiz? Turn to the end of the chapter to find out.

PREPOSITIONS

Let us first consider the *preposition,* the word that shows the relation between a noun or pronoun and some other word.

1. It is not only correct, but desirable, to end a sentence with a preposition if such a construction sounds natural rather than stilted. And placing the preposition at the end of the sentence often gives the sentence a certain emphasis, as: He took the manuscript home and read it *through.* (Not: . . . read through it.) Note these other examples:

Norman Mailer is the writer the critic referred *to.*
Congressman Teague asked, "What is there for us to talk *about?*"
Dole is the only man they can depend *upon.*

Certainly such sentences sound more natural and also have stronger endings than to write: Mailer is the writer to whom the critic referred, *or*, Congressman Teague asked, "What is there about which we can talk?" *or*, Dole is the only man upon whom they can depend. Let's analyze two more examples:

> Use of drugs by high school students is the biggest problem the school board must deal with. (Not: . . . with which the school board must deal.)
> Jackson said his success in politics was something he had always dreamed of. (Not: . . . was something of which he had always dreamed.)

Consider occasionally placing the prepositional phrase at the beginning of the sentence to call attention to the phrase as containing the more important thought in the sentence.

> To the victors belong the spoils.

2. Avoid ending a sentence with a so-called suspended phrase.

> INCORRECT: Right now the council is concerned with the water-shortage problem and is anxious about its solution.

The phrase *about its solution* is suspended. The sentence should be reworded thus:

> CORRECT: Right now the council is concerned with the water-shortage problem and is anxious to find the solution.
> *Or:* Right now the council is seriously concerned with finding the solution to the water-shortage problem.

3. Remember that the *object* of the preposition is always in the objective case. Watch this construction carefully if the preposition has a compound object and especially when the object is a pronoun.

> This matter must be settled *between you and him* (not *he*).
> Just *between you and me* (not *you and I*), I prefer skating to skiing.

4. Be careful not to confuse prepositions with conjunctions. The most common error of this kind is using the preposition *like* as a conjunction: It looks *like* it might rain. Although Webster's now lists the use of *like* as a conjunction in the sense of *as* or *as if* as standard usage, journalists are asked to follow the old rule of using *like* only as a preposition.

> It looks *like* rain. But: It looks *as if* it might rain.
> Bump Wills looks *like* his father. But: Bump steals bases about as well *as* his father used to do.
> The fruit did not look *like* a peach but tasted *like* a peach.

It is correct to use *like* as a conjunction if it is followed by a word that may be regarded as a simile.

Caruthers is only a sophomore, but he plays like a professional (plays).

Caruthers is not a professional baseball player, but he resembles one in ability. *Professional* has the force of a simile. And since *professional* is a noun, the prepositional phrase *like a professional* is correct. If you use the conjunction and say *as a professional*, you are saying that Caruthers actually does play as a professional in a baseball league, an impossibility.

Remember that not only nouns and pronouns may be objects of prepositions—as *professional* is in the foregoing example—but also true gerunds may be objects: Jogging stimulates the heart and the muscles like *swimming*.

Like as a conjunction has become popular in advertising ("Winston tastes good—like a cigarette should") and also in colloquial usage, especially on the air. Example: "Tell it like it is, baby." *Like* also is used often in newspaper headlines. In time it may supplant *as* as a conjunction in journalistic writing, but for now you should use *like*, on the whole, as a preposition.

5. Do not confuse the preposition *but* with the conjunction *but*. When *but* is used as a preposition, it means *except* and usually takes an object. Watch pronouns, particularly compound pronouns, that follow the prepositional *but*. Such pronouns must be in the objective case if they come at the end of the sentence.

> The instructor dismissed everyone *but (except)* Chuck and *me*.
> The instructor dismissed every one *but him* and *me*.

However, if the pronoun comes somewhere in the sentence other than at the end, it may be said to be grammatically attracted to the noun to which it is linked by the *but* and may be put in the same case as that noun, as Bernstein points out.

> No one (nominative) but *I* (nominative) had the answer.
> To no one (objective) but me (objective) did he reveal his secret.

Some authorities, however, still insist on use of the objective *me* in such a construction as the first one: No one but *me* had the answer. They will not concede that it was correct for the poet to have the boy "stand on the burning deck, whence all but *he* had fled."

6. The conjunction *and* should not be used to follow the infinitive *to try*. *To try* is followed by another infinitive phrase as its object.

> It was up to Fidrych *to try to keep* Detroit's hopes alive.

Do not say "try and keep," at least in formal writing. Use of *try and* colloquially, especially when it adds force to the meaning of the sentence, has gained some acceptance, as in this sentence: "Little one, you must *try and* be brave." Also, *try and* is used colloquially on TV and in radio, especially by sportscasters.

But unless they are quoting someone, journalists working for newspapers and most magazines will always use *try to*.

Journalists also should guard against using the colloquial *sure and* for *sure to*: The captain ordered his men to be *sure to* (not *sure and*) report at 7 a.m.

Avoid, too, such an error as "Be careful and don't. . . ." Say: "Be careful not to. . . ."

7. Guard against using "in back of" for the preposition *behind*. *In front of* is correct, but there is no such phrase as "in back of."

He testified that he had slept on the ground *behind* the garage that night.

8. The preposition *in* implies position; *into* implies motion or change of place. Do not use *in* for *into*.

He lives *in* the last house on this street. He went *into* the house.
They forced the woman *into* (not *in*) a car and assaulted her.

9. *Between* refers to position or action of two persons or objects. *Among* usually is used when there are three or more mentioned.

It sat *between* the window and the door.
The boys divided the money *among* the four of them.

However, *between* may be used when three or more persons are thought of severally or individually, or when three or more objects are being considered in pairs.

A contract was drawn up *between* Leslie Shelton, Bill Orr and Charles Mayhew.
It is hoped that an agreement *between* the four governments will be reached at Paris.

10. Do not confuse *beside* and *besides*. *Beside* means "at the side of." *Besides* means "in addition to."

The car paused *beside* the gas pump.
Paul Savage owns two (other) houses *besides* this one.

11. Do not confuse the preposition *to* and the adverb *too*. Remember that *too* means "also" or "to an excessive degree."

The family went *to* the beach today.
They met the Fields and the Browns, *too*.
It was *too* bad that it rained.

12. The more formal *upon* is rapidly being replaced by *on*. *Upon* is still

used to indicate upward motion or to connote *on top of*, as in:

> The cowboy leaped *upon* his horse.
> The students piled the books one *upon* another.

Otherwise, use *on* in most instances, as in the examples that follow.

> *On* returning from Camp David, the president immediately summoned separate
> groups of lawmakers to the White House to discuss. . . .
> The incumbent said he would campaign *on* three important issues. . . .

Although *on* is steadily shoving *upon* aside, it should not be permitted to run wild in replacing other prepositions such as *in, by, about, against, toward, of, from, at* and *for*. In the following sentences the parenthesized words are much better than *on*.

> Discussing the question *on* (*about* or *concerning*) whether he agreed with the
> Crime Commission on the extent of drug addiction in the high schools, the
> superintendent declared that. . . .
> The Crime Commission registered a vigorous protest *on* (*against*) the laxity of
> school administrators in reporting drug addiction cases.
> The Crime Commission sharply criticized the city council *on* (*for*) its attitude *on*
> (*toward*) drug peddlers.
> The Crime Commission chairman declared he would seek the public's support *on*
> (*of* or *for*) the proposal.
> The chairman exploded with anger on (*at*) the city council's disapproval of the
> report.

Remember that *on* is unnecessary with days of the week: They left (on) Friday.

13. In writing for the printed media, use *about* when you mean approximately and *around* when you refer to motion. However, in broadcast journalism the informal use of *around* for *about* is common:

> The high should be *around* (*about*) 82 degrees.

Bernstein points out that *around* is likewise casual usage in the sense of *from place to place* or *here* and *there*. However, in this sense, *around* has about established itself as correct usage in the printed media: The candidate is barnstorming *around* the state.

Note correct usage of *about* and *around* in the sentences that follow.

> The Braniff International plane arrived at *about* 10:45 a.m.
> *About* (Not *Around*) 5,800 persons attended the Brown rally.
> As the wizened grandmother wound the wool *around* the ball, the ball dropped to
> the floor and rolled *around* and *around*.

Don't use *about* redundantly with ranging figures, as in: She described the robber as weighing (*about*) 165 to 185 pounds.

14. Journalists should not use *over* for *more than*. Webster's accepts such usage (It costs over $5). But the AP Stylebook warns that *over* is not interchangeable with *more than*. *Over* is used as a preposition to refer to spatial relationships, while *more than* is used with figures.

> The Goodyear blimp flew *over* the fairgrounds.
> Payton plunged *over* the goal line.
> *More than* 20,000 delegates jammed the auditorium.

15. The preposition *on* implies position; *onto* implies motion or change of place.

> The passengers walked *on* the deck.
> The sailor jumped from the wharf *onto* the deck.

Note the difference between *onto* and *on to* in the sentence that follows. *Onto* is a preposition. In the phrase *on to, on* is an adverb and *to* a preposition.

> He jumped *onto* the deck and then went *on to* the bow.

16. Discriminate between the meaning of *differ with* and *differ from*. Use *differ from* to indicate dissimilarity and *differ with* to indicate disagreement.

> Mayor Gibson *differed from* Councilman Reilly in temperament, but he did not *differ with* him in local politics.

Usage of *different than* was discussed earlier. Its use is considered correct now if it introduces a clause: The situation is no *different than* it was last week.

17. The preposition may sometimes be omitted from a prepositional phrase, and the infinitive is sometimes written without the *to*. Make sure that the meaning of the sentence is clear if you leave out words. The words in parentheses in the following sentences may be omitted without obscuring the meaning.

> The twins are (of) about the same height and weight.
> The baby resembles his father; he even laughs (in) the same way.
> He will be eligible to play varsity football (for) three years.
> He regards it (as) his own personal problem.
> Calves are selling for (from) 52 to 55 cents a pound.
> The name (of) Smith is listed 116 times in the directory.
> The car ran (to) within six inches of the precipice.
> He helped his wife (to) do the dishes every night.
> Do you dare (to) say he did it?

The use of unnecessary words is called *wordiness* or *redundance*. It is treated in detail on pages 228–30.

18. There are some cases where omission of the preposition would be an error. The italicized words in the following sentences should *not* be omitted.

> He will pass the ball either to Lockett or *to* Jackson.
>
> The members of the Bonehead Club and *of* the Variety Club worked together on the plan.
>
> He has great respect *for* and confidence *in* the city manager.
>
> These men have little grasp of the importance of the problem or *of* its possible solution.
>
> The mayor never wearied *of* telling the story of that fight.
>
> He wanted to cooperate *in* every way he could.

19. Instead of a gerund with the possessive, a prepositional phrase is sometimes preferable. However, either is correct.

> He discouraged *my singing* the aria.
>
> He discouraged *me from singing* the aria.

20. Many journalists fail to use the correct preposition after a verb to convey the right meaning. Note the italicized phrases in these sentences:

> The members of the two clubs *agree in* principle.
>
> The two clubs *agreed on* a common objective.
>
> The Variety Club *agreed with* the Rotarians.
>
> One club *agreed to* the other's plan.
>
> The members of our club have *agreed among* themselves to work with you.

There are hundreds of such combinations of verbs and prepositions. Use the dictionary to know which preposition expresses the exact meaning you want to convey. Many reference books have lists of these combinations, also.

21. Prepositional phrases are used as adjectives and as adverbs. They should always be placed as near as possible to the words they modify.

Compare the faulty sentences with the improved sentences that follow.

> FAULTY: He recovered from a four-month illness at the end of July.
>
> The couple will be at home after a brief trip in Springfield.
>
> The Auxiliary will place flowers on the graves of members who have died on Memorial Day in Rosemount Cemetery.
>
> CORRECT: At the end of July he recovered from a four-month illness.
>
> After a brief trip, the couple will be at home in Springfield.
>
> On Memorial Day the Auxiliary will place flowers in Rosemount Cemetery on the graves of members who have died.
>
> *Or:*. . . place flowers on the graves of deceased members buried in Rosemount Cemetery.

You will have no difficulty in spotting the misplaced phrases in the following "bulls."

> WANTED—Second-hand typewriter by young lady student with wide carriage. (Advertisement)
> Sergeant Acquitted of Drunk Driving in Criminal Court (Headline)
> A former highway patrolman drew a sentence of two years for operating a moonshine still in federal court at Knoxville.
> The hostess chose a cerise dinner dress with a low, oval neckline for entertaining.

CONJUNCTIONS

Always keep in mind the fact that conjunctions are words that join or link two parts of the sentence.

Coordinating Conjunctions

Coordinating conjunctions (and, or, nor, but, yet, for) join words, phrases or clauses of equal rank.

The conjunction *and* denotes addition or enumeration. *But* and *yet* denote contrast. *Or* and *nor* denote choice. You should readily recognize that the wrong conjunction is used in the following sentence: Schlesinger is the best substitute on the basketball squad, *and* his insertion into the starting line-up will definitely weaken the Ponies' attack. Obviously, *but* is the correct conjunction. Even better would be this sentence: Although Schlesinger is the best substitute on the squad, his insertion into the starting line-up will definitely weaken the Ponies' attack.

To obtain parallelism in a sentence, the writer must see that words, phrases or clauses joined by a coordinate conjunction are of equal rank. It may not always be necessary to arrange sentences in an absolutely parallel structure, but such an arrangement usually results in a clearer and more forceful sentence. Strive, then, to use the same structure on both sides of a coordinating conjunction. Study the examples that follow.

> INCORRECT: Reilly is well-educated and of moderate wealth.
> CORRECT: Reilly is *well-educated* and *moderately wealthy*.
>   Reilly is a man *of good education* and *of moderate wealth*.

In the first sentence *well-educated* is an adjective and *of moderate wealth* is a phrase. Change the sentence to have either two adjectives or two phrases.

> INCORRECT: Jeffers was suffering physically and in mind.
> CORRECT: Jeffers was suffering physically and mentally.

In the first sentence, *physically* is an adverb, *in mind* a prepositional phrase. Although the phrase is used adverbially to modify the verb, it differs too much in form from the adverb *physically* and makes the sentence less smooth and clear than the correct sentence.

In the following sentence the writer was thinking and writing loosely. He began with an independent clause, followed by a dependent clause beginning with the conjunctive adverb *as;* then he added to the independent clause.

> INCORRECT: Brock stepped back from the plate as the pitcher shook his head negatively and called for another bat.
>
> CORRECT: As the pitcher shook his head negatively, Brock stepped back from the plate and called for another bat.

In the correct sentence it is now clear that *and* joins the compound verb *stepped* and *called*, and that it was Brock, not the pitcher, who called for another bat. Of course, you can make two sentences: The pitcher shook his head negatively. Brock stepped back from the plate and called for another bat.

Correlative Conjunctions

The *correlative conjunctions*, which are used in pairs, must be watched carefully. You must use parallel constructions after correlatives. Errors occur most often in using the correlatives *either . . . or, neither . . . nor* and *not only . . . but also.* To avoid making errors, learn the following four rules:

1. Use *or* with *either, nor* with *neither*; don't mix them.

> INCORRECT: *Neither* Bolton *or* Irwin will be nominated.
> CORRECT: *Either* Bellmon *or* Monroney will be nominated.
> *Neither* Bolton *nor* Irwin will be nominated.

2. *No* is not a correlative; therefore compound nouns modified by *no* should not be joined by *nor.* Use *or.*

> He has *no* money *or* land. (Not: He has no money *nor* land.)
> *No* man *or* woman in this room can say that he will run.

3. Place correlative conjunctions as near as possible to the words they connect.

> He possesses *neither* land *nor* money. (Not: He *neither* possesses land *nor* money.)
> He possesses *not only* land *but also* money. (Not: He *not only* possesses land *but also* money.)

4. When nouns or pronouns connected by *either. . . or* or by *neither. . .*

nor are both singular, the verb must be singular: Coffey declared that *neither* he *nor* Edwards was planning to give up *his* job. (Note that the possessive pronoun, when one is used, must also be singular.)

But where a compound subject has a singular noun and a plural noun joined by *or*, or *nor*, the predicate agrees in number with the nearest noun.

> Either the *trustees* or the *president is* to issue a statement.
> Neither the *mayor* nor the *councilmen were* at the dinner.

5. Be sure to use parallel constructions after correlative conjunctions.

> INCORRECT: Periwinkle either was driving carelessly or asleep at the wheel.
> CORRECT: Periwinkle either was driving carelessly or he was asleep at the wheel.
> INCORRECT: Jack not only has been a good scholar, but also excels as a debater.
> CORRECT: Jack not only has been a good scholar but also has been an excellent debater.
> *Or:* Jack not only is a good scholar but he also excels as a debater.

Conjunctive Adverbs as Conjunctions

Conjunctive adverbs, remember, can be used as coordinating conjunctions to join independent clauses. Conjunctive adverbs were listed and discussed in detail on pages 24–25 and 43.

Subordinating Conjunctions

Subordinating conjunctions were discussed in detail on pages 43–46.

Miscellaneous Uses of Conjunctions

1. Although some editors frown on using a coordinating conjunction to begin a sentence, most now approve the practice when it adds variety or emphasis to your writing, as in the following:

> These men have robbed the city of millions of dollars. *And* I dare say they will not try to refute this charge. *But* if they do dare to come forth. . . .

2. The use of *so* as a coordinating conjunction is a general practice, but it is not really good usage. Other conjunctions will give a more exact meaning in most cases. Use of a subordinating conjunction or a connective adverb is often preferable. If you do use *so,* place a semicolon before it.

> He neglected to study for the examination; *so* he failed.
> BETTER: He failed *because* he neglected to study for the examination.
> *Or:* He neglected to study for the examination; *consequently*, he failed.

Use *so that*, not *so* or *so as*, to introduce a clause of purpose. Do not use a comma before *so that*.

Jenkins kept talking for an hour *so that* the motion would not be put to a vote.

An infinitive is frequently used to express purpose.

Jenkins talked for an hour *to keep* the motion from being put to a vote.

3. The adverbs *where* and *when* are misused for *that* in some sentences.

INCORRECT: I read in today's paper where he died in Korea.
CORRECT: I read in today's paper *that* he died in Korea.

Do not use "is when" and "is where" in defining words.

INCORRECT: A debate is when two teams argue both sides of a question.
CORRECT: A debate is the discussion of a question by two teams.

4. Do not use *because* or *as* to introduce a noun clause.

INCORRECT: The reason why he failed was because he did not study.
CORRECT: He failed *because* he did not study.
The reason why he failed was *that* he did not study.

5. Do not overuse *that* in a sentence.

FAULTY: The professor insisted *that* in learning to spell correctly *that* the students master four important rules.
CORRECT: The professor insisted *that* the students master four important rules in learning to spell correctly.

6. Use *than* instead of *until, before*, etc., after the comparative *no sooner*.

He had no sooner begun his speech *than* (not *until* or *before*) catcalls were heard.

7. The conjunctive adverb *while* is used to denote time. It should not be used in place of *although* and *but*.

While he was being groomed for the part, he grew a beard.
Although he had been groomed for the part, he failed to make good.
Although she found flaws in the suggested program, she admitted it deserved serious consideration.
Rucker prefers immediate action, *but* Alward advises going slow.

8. Be careful to use *whether*, not *if*, when an alternative choice is indicated.

The senator wanted to know *whether* (or not) the bill could be amended to provide larger sums.

9. The past participle *provided* is still considered preferable to the present

participle *providing* when used as a conjunction in the sense of *if*. For example, *provided* should have been used in this sentence:

> The Tennessee Republican has decided to support the treaties, *providing* Torrijos makes a few concessions.

Provided and *providing*, when used as conjunctions, imply condition or stipulation of some kind. They should not be used as a mere synonym for the more general word *if*, according to both Bernstein and Copperud. It would have been correct to use *if* instead of *provided* in the foregoing example: The Tennessee Republican has decided to support the treaties *if* Torrijos makes a few concessions. However, *provided* perhaps is better usage here because a condition or stipulation is implied by the senator.

But don't use *provided* or *providing* wherever *if* will do. Note correct usage in the sentences that follow.

> A truce can be negotiated *provided that* a satisfactory plan for the exhange of prisoners can be agreed upon.
> Summaries of the panel discussions can be made available *provided* (or *provided that*) the delegates pay for them.
> Summaries of the panel discussions can be made available *if* (not *provided that*) the delegates want them.

QUIZ ANSWERS

1. Change *like* to *as if*. 2. He told police his wife was forced *into* a truck and (was) later raped. 3. The commissioner will *try to* show *that* (preferred to *where*) maintenance costs. . . . 4. Change *or* to *nor*. *On* is preferred to *upon* here. 5. The inheritance of *about* $130,000 will be divided *between* (or *among*) him, Dolores. . . . (Colloquial *around* is all right in electronic journalism or in quoting someone in the printed media.) 6. Change comma to a semicolon, which is needed before the conjunctive adverb *nevertheless*. No comma is used after *nevertheless*, but some editors would accept it. 7. Change *before* to *than*. 8. *Collins cut too* far to the left; so the pass overshot him. Better: When (or Because) Collins cut too far to the left, the pass overshot him. 9. Need *for* after *regard*. 10. An accomplice was waiting in front of the bank in a 1967 Pontiac, with its motor running. 11. He demanded to know *whether* (or not) the payment.... 12. Change *providing* to provided and *can* to *could*. 13. Correct. 14. Change *so* to *so that*. 15. *Change I* to *me; like* is correct here. 16. Frazier's footwork is equal to, if not better than, the champion's. 17. Delete the first *that*. Repetition is not technically incorrect, but this fault should be avoided. 18. Change *than* to *from; differ with* is correct. 19. Accepted as colloquial usage, at least in radio-television and advertising fields. 20. *Besides* is correct.

PART 2

Sentence Construction

12

Requirements of a Good Sentence

Much has been said and written about *readability*. Newspapers, press associations, newspaper groups and magazines have retained such experts as Robert Gunning and Rudolf Flesch to study how to improve the writing of their staffs.

The results have been extremely helpful to practicing journalists. First of all, these experts advise writers that they must have something to say: writing without ideas and information is like trying to breathe in a vacuum. Second, they insist that the really capable writer will develop his subject in simple words and short sentences. What they urge, then, is *clear, concise* and *interesting* writing. They remind the would-be journalist that words and sentences are tools that one masters by constantly using them. The formula is: a good subject plus simple words plus short sentences.

All this is certainly sound advice. But perhaps the experts have been making the task seem a bit easier than it actually is. For instance, they underestimate the amount of knowledge needed by the competent writer. Roscoe Ellard, an outstanding professor at the School of Journalism of Columbia University until his death some years ago, had this to say about a chapter in Rudolf Flesch's book *How to Make Sense*:

> In his chapter on grammar in this book, the author worries me. An impression the unformed writer might get is that formal grammar is outdated, like a top-hat. Dr. Flesch quotes violations of grammar by Lord Bryce, Jane Austen, and a lovely opening sentence by E. M. Forster: "Do you like to know who a book's by?"

Good for E. M. Forster. But it reminds me of a brash defense I made once to a Regular Army colonel who rebuked me for laxity in my lieutenant's uniform. I reminded him that Major General Howze was parading one of the same laxities a hundred feet away.

"A major general," Colonel Julian E. Gaujot reminded me as my eyes fixed on the ribbon of his Congressional Medal of Honor—"a major general can do a hell of a lot of things a lieutenant doesn't know how to get away with."

Which is something to remember in counseling amateur stylists. Jane Austen, Rudyard Kipling and E. M. Forster know how to take liberties with formalties effectively. There are times to split infinitives for clarity—and times not to. This danger often lurks: The young writer who reads in a book that grammar is top-hat may turn up with sentences that force both copy desk and readers to conclude: "That reporter slept through high school. He ought to go back to one and stay awake."[1]

In an earlier book, *The Way to Write,* Flesch and his co-author Lass give full recognition to the fact that writing well and using good grammar are essentially equivalent.

The argument over the importance of formal grammar is endless. But one must face the fact that the journalist cannot hope to produce clear, concise and interesting writing until he learns how to put sentences together and *knows what he is doing*. This is a roundabout way of saying that he must know good grammar and apply it.

A BRIEF REVIEW OF THE SENTENCE

Let us try to tie together some of the points brought out in earlier chapters and add some pointers on sentence structure and word usage.

Make sure that you can always tell the difference between a complete sentence and a fragment of a sentence. The fragment should never be punctuated as if it were a whole sentence.

One body was recovered last night, that of William G. Seymour.

You know that it would be incorrect to make the second part (*that of William Seymour*) a separate sentence.

By now you should also be able to avoid the run-on sentence, in which two complete sentences are run together needlessly; in other words, you will not make the comma blunder—the use of a comma instead of a semicolon to separate two independent clauses when the conjunction is omitted.

By way of review, why not turn back to page 25 for a second look at five ways to avoid writing run-on sentences such as this one: Dry climates are good for persons with tuberculosis, doctors often advise tuberculars to go to

[1] Reprinted by permission of *Editor & Publisher* magazine.

New Mexico. Or, this one: A few years from now Concorde flights will probably be rarities, possibly they will not exist.

To avoid making sentence errors, you must be able to distinguish: (1) between independent clauses and dependent clauses; and (2) between coordinating conjunctions and subordinating conjunctions, including conjunctive adverbs.

If you have trouble telling the difference between an independent clause and a dependent clause, you should review all of Chapter 2. And if you have trouble with conjunctions, you should review not only Chapter 2 but also pages 152–56 of Chapter 11.

It also is essential that writers be able to distinguish between the simple subject and the complete subject, and between the simple predicate and the complete predicate. Without such knowledge, writers may commit many errors, particularly errors in agreement. With such knowledge, the writer should be able to write correct sentences. For example, the writer must learn to recognize that the verb should be the singular *was* instead of the plural *were* in this sentence: The Huskies coach, as well as the players, *were* elated over the victory. And in the following sentence the writer must recognize that the simple subject is *jury,* a collective noun that requires a singular predicate and a singular possessive pronoun: The *jury* of seven men and five women *is* ready with *its* verdict.

Complete understanding of the four types of sentences—simple, complex, compound, and compound-complex—will enable you to give your readers the variety of sentence structure that the readability experts stress. True, you can obtain variety through other methods, but varying the sentence forms is important to good writing.

Note how the use of a variety of sentence forms makes the following excerpt from a World War II story by Hal Boyle highly readable. [S] at the end of a sentence denotes a simple sentence; [Cd] denotes a compound sentence; and [Cx] denotes a complex sentence.

> AT SEA WITH A U.S. TASK FORCE EN ROUTE TO NORTH AFRICA, Nov. 3. (AP) —
> Water rings the gray-clouded horizon, and winds trouble the sea. [Cd]
> Scores of tiny dots slug slowly through the never ending waves, like determined ants painfully inching across a furrowed field. [S]
> The little dots are ships, and each is carrying thousands of American men to battlefields far from home. [Cd]
> Life on a troopship is like wearing a tight shoe. [S] You don't mind it for a few minutes. [S] But on a transport, it may endure a week, two weeks, perhaps longer. [S]
> The packed quarters are the chief cause of grousing among the troops, who wouldn't be American if they didn't complain about the lack of elbow room. [Cx]

Water is available for showers, washing and laundry less than three hours out of
the 24. [S] Officers bunk four to a room. [S] The men are quartered in holds
which become hot and fetid within a few hours. [Cx]

Part of the voyage the officers sleep with the troops in the crowded holds to show
[that] they can take it, too. [Cx]

Said one private when his officer showed up in the hold at bedtime: "Why are
you sleeping here, sir?" [Cx]

"Oh, just for morale," replied the officer. [S]

"Sir," said the private worriedly, "What is wrong with the officers' morale?"
[Cx] . . . [2]

You should be ready now to take a closer look at some of the principles of
sentence structure. You should have already mastered some of the rules.
Those that have been treated in previous chapters are repeated for emphasis;
others are added to make sure that you have a fairly complete review of the
fundamentals of grammar and composition. You are urged to devote major
attention to those principles which you have not yet mastered. Be honest with
yourself. You know whether or not you are thoroughly familiar with any
principle or rule and whether or not you need drill on it.

UNITY, EMPHASIS AND COHERENCE

In your study of grammar and composition, have you ever heard of "the
trinity"? Many older editors were drilled thoroughly in it, but that was before
the advent of "progressive education." These editors will tell you that, no
matter what it is called, a thorough understanding of "the trinity" of grammar
and composition is of primary importance to the journalist. Younger editors
will agree when it is explained that "the trinity" is a term once used to refer to
unity, emphasis and *coherence* in the sentence.

To produce effective sentences and paragraphs the writer must apply the
three primary principles of *unity, emphasis* and *coherence. Coherence* is
usually treated in today's grammar textbooks as a subdivision under the
broader heading "clearness" or "clarity." Clearness is fundamental in all
good writing, and it matters little if grammarians classify coherence as a
subdivision of clearness as long as the journalist recognizes the need of
coherence—as well as of unity and emphasis—in his writing.

If you add *variety* to *unity, emphasis* and *coherence,* you have the four
essentials of effective sentences and paragraphs.

---

[2] Reprinted by permission from AP Newsfeatures.

13
Sentence Unity

As far as grammar and composition are concerned, unity means simply oneness of thought. A sentence is supposed to express a single complete thought. In other words, the sentence must be unified.

To test yourself on sentence unity, take the following quiz. Correct errors that violate sentence unity. Watch particularly for such errors as: the fragmentary (incomplete) sentence; the run-on sentence—the comma fault; the rambling sentence that contains too many ideas, or the other extreme—the choppy sentence; and the sentence in which the writer tries to join unrelated ideas that belong in separate sentences. Also look for omission of a word, phrase or clause needed for sentence unity and clarity; omission of transitional devices needed for unity and clarity; lack of unified thought in the sentence; failure to subordinate minor ideas by using subordinate clauses or prepositional, participial and infinitive phrases; and use of the wrong conjunction.

You may take the quiz by copy editing each sentence or by completely rewriting it.

QUIZ

1. One auto was recovered. That of William Truehart.
2. Seven men were lost and one saved in the crash.
3. He maintained the girl is a prostitute.
4. He asks us to read, to meditate and write.
5. The most famous temple is Vishwanatha, so be sure to visit it.

6. Dorsey W. Waring, who was a retired army officer, age 81, who was a first lieutenant in the Kentucky National Guard and a captain of the 50th Artillery Brigade in World War I, and who, incidentally, was awarded an honorary LL.B. degree last year by the University of Kentucky, died here Friday night.
7. The city manager may be compared to the manager of a big department store. He has the power to appoint employees. He has the power to fire employees. He supervises the work of the employees in the various departments.
8. He is neither interested nor concerned about the problem.
9. A majority of Pacific-10 Conference players have the ability to graduate to the professional ranks, and most of them come from California. (Reconstruct sentence.)
10. The firemen were laying the first hose line when the roof caved in.
11. The man was booked for investigation of burglary, rape and indecent exposure; he is 24 years old.
12. The main point made by the first speaker and the man who followed him on the panel coincided.
13. We watched them from a sightseeing boat, but we could hardly believe what we saw.
14. He had the services of the nation's top lawyers, but he failed to win the suit.
15. Representative Michel says (that) the report points up the need for more in-house auditing. "You will have programs running wild."

COMPLETENESS OF THOUGHT

Because a sentence should express a single complete thought, *completeness of thought* must be stressed as an important part of sentence unity. The main points of sentence completeness may be summarized as follows: (1) Do not punctuate a phrase or a subordinate clause as if it were a complete sentence; (2) do not omit a word, phrase or clause necessary to the sense of the sentence.

Correct Punctuation

Do not put a period at the end of a phrase or a subordinate clause that stands alone.

A *phrase* is a group of related words without a subject or a predicate. It modifies some other word in the sentence. Obviously it cannot be written as a complete sentence.

A *subordinate clause*, even though it has its own subject and predicate, depends on some other clause for its meaning. It must be connected to the independent clause if the sentence is to comply with the principle of completeness.

In the examples that follow, the italicized portions might have been incorrectly punctuated as separate sentences. In fact, they were so punctuated in a metropolitan newspaper.

> One body was recovered last night, *that of T/Sgt. William G. Seymour.*
> The challenger never won a round on the United Press International score sheet, *although he fought on even terms in the first session.*

These sentences are correct, but the writer of the following sentence became so involved in his construction that he forgot to complete the sentence:

> Twittle was a raw recruit who, hailing from the mountains of Tennessee, with only a fourth-grade education, but with a "shooting eye" that was to bring him fame as a sharp-shooter in World War I.

Essential Elements in a Sentence

Do not omit any word, phrase or clause that is needed for sentence clarity and unity.

You have been warned not to omit articles that are necessary to the meaning. Study these examples of the omission of other words, phrases and clauses and the resultant clouding of the meaning of the sentence.

1. A main verb is sometimes omitted in error.

> INCORRECT: Patti launched her career by singing the type of songs that many other girl singers have and still are singing.
> CORRECT: Patti launched her career by singing the type of songs that many other girl singers have *sung* and still are singing.

Just to make sure that this point is clear, consider one more example.

> CORRECT: Forrester *has* never *done* any campaigning and never *will do* any. (Not: and never *will.*)

Both verbs should be given in full, as shown.

2. Do not omit a necessary auxiliary verb.

> INCORRECT: Four dazed airmen were recovered from the rough water after they bailed out.
> CORRECT: Four dazed airmen were recovered from the rough water after they *had* bailed out (of their aircraft).

The auxiliary verb *had* is necessary to show the correct tense, the past perfect.

INCORRECT: Seven crewmen were lost and one saved in the crash.

CORRECT Seven crewmen were lost and one *was* saved in the crash.

INCORRECT: The wrecked car was rolled off the highway, a wrecker called and other drivers told to proceed cautiously.

CORRECT: The wrecked car *was* rolled off the highway, a wrecker *was* called and other drivers *were* told to proceed cautiously.

NOTE: An auxiliary verb may be omitted if it is in the same form as the other auxiliary verbs in the same sentence. The auxiliary is said to be understood. For example, it is correct to write:

Six crewmen *were* lost and three saved in the crash.

Were is understood before *saved*.

3. Do not omit a necessary relative pronoun.

INCORRECT: Collier manages a professional football club that played well on both offense and defense and drew well throughout the season.

CORRECT: Collier manages a professional football club that played well on both offense and defense and that drew well throughout the season.

The second relative pronoun *that* is needed to make the meaning clear.

INCORRECT: The reply followed a reminder on a South Vietnamese station the Viet Cong had not yet mentioned the proposed truce.

The reporter who wrote the sentence failed to note that the omission of the relative pronoun left the meaning of the sentence cloudy.

CORRECT: The reply followed a reminder on a South Vietnamese station *that* the Viet Cong had not yet mentioned the proposed truce.

NOTE: The relative pronoun, particularly *that,* may sometimes be ommitted without clouding the meaning of the sentence. The writer should make sure that the omission does not make the sentence difficult to comprehend. The pronouns given in parentheses in the following sentences could be omitted.

The senator said (that) he thought (that) the legislature "wanted the regents to run a pretty conservative university."

The President ticked off a dozen actions of Congress and said (that) they seem bewildering at first glance.

Compare the sentences above with the following sentence:

Obviously, the wild things are now living jammed up so close to human beings *that* they are beginning to learn human tricks.

If the writer had omitted *that*, readers might think that *they* refers to *human beings* instead of to *wild things*.

A good rule to follow in using *that* or omitting it is this: If its omission would cause the reader to assume that the subject of the dependent clause is the object of the preceding verb, the pronoun should be used. Consider this sentence from a newspaper story: He maintained the woman is a prostitute.

At first glance *woman* might be taken to be the object of *maintained*. And think of the embarassment if the sentence had been set as "He maintained the woman *as* a prostitute," and the error had got by. It would certainly be safer to write: He maintained *that* the woman is a prostitute.

On the other hand, be careful not to use *that* twice in a sentence for one subordinate clause.

> INCORRECT: The coach said that if Kirkpatrick had been available for service, that the team could have won the game.

The second *that* is wrong and should be omitted.

However, the relative pronoun needs to be repeated in a series of clauses like those in the following sentence.

> The City Plan Commission Wednesday advised the City Council *that* Dallas should stay strictly within its 260-square-mile drainage area in annexing new territory, (*that* it should) adopt a flexible annexation policy, and (*that* it should) head off undesirable residential developments.

Some editors would advise you to write the sentence this way: ". . . advised the City Council to stay. . . , to adopt. . . and to head off. . . ."

4. Do not omit a necessary preposition.

In the sentences below, the prepositions that are set in italic type are necessary to the sentence. They should not be omitted.

> He never worried *about*, nor tried to help with, her problems.
> He admits that he is more apprehensive for his own safety than *for* that of (*for* the safety of) his family.
> The strange writings were found on the box, which had been broken open, and *on* the wrappings that had been torn away.

Make sure you do not omit prepositions that are needed to make the sentence clear. Many prepositions are little words. Don't judge their importance by their size!

5. Do not omit the *to* of any of the infinitives in a series.

> He wants us to write letters, *to* present our arguments and *to* convince the council of the necessity for this action.
> The student must learn to read extensively, *to* analyze what he reads and *to* summarize the main points presented.

6. Do not omit the conjunction before the final item in a series. Using a comma in place of *and* is not sufficient.

Read extensively, analyze what you read *and* summarize the main points.

7. Do not omit the participle in a phrase, especially when the main verb contains a different idea from that of the participle.

> In addition to *having* a nose for news, the good reporter must also possess integrity.

But note that the participle may be omitted when the phrase follows the independent clause with the same verb:

> That reporter has integrity, as well as a nose for news.

8. Do not omit words, phrases or clauses that are needed to make the meaning clear and to unify the sentence.

Because the demonstrative pronoun *that* is omitted, the incorrect sentence below has a *main point* and a *man* coinciding, an impossible feat.

> INCORRECT: The main point made by the first speaker and the man who followed him on the panel coincided.
>
> CORRECT: The main point made by the first speaker and *that of* (*that made by*) the man who followed him coincided.

The words italicized in the following sentences are needed:

> Gold was sharply higher. In Zurich it closed at $186.625 *an ounce*, up from Friday's $184.125.
>
> Twenty armed soldiers and seventeen People's Police escaped to West Berlin from *the duty of* enforcing a government ban on free United States food for East Germans.
>
> Two of the five critically injured rioters were found *to be* dead on arrival.
>
> The kind old woman gave us a sightseeing tour to talk about *when we got* back home.

Try omitting the italicized phrases and clauses to see whether you think the reader would get a clear meaning of the sentences without these.

9. Do not omit transition words or phrases that help make the connection between the parts of a sentence clear to the reader.

This is a common fault of newspaper reporters, many of whom have been warned by some editors and by some journalism instructors to be extremely sparing in the use of transitional words and phrases. However, today the use of transitional devices has become common practice in both newspapers and magazines. In fact, expert use of transitional words and phrases within the sentence is considered one of the distinguishing marks of the good writer. Journalists, then, should use transitional words and phrases whenever needed to make the sentence clearer to the reader. The use of such words and phrases within a sentence contributes greatly to clarity and to unity.

In the sentence that follows, omission of the transition word *however* would make the meaning obscure.

> Colby is protected in his job under the Civil Service Act. *However*, he is (He is, *however*,) subjected to tremendous pressures.

Note the effective use of a transitional phrase in this sentence:

> Muse expected to be reelected chairman of the board with little opposition. *On the contrary*, he was ousted.

You should note in the foregoing examples that the transitional expressions are placed at or near the beginning of a sentence to indicate the relationship of the sentence to the preceding one. Thus, the transitional device not only contributes to clarity within the sentence, but it also helps the reader to make a smooth transition from sentence to sentence—and often from paragraph to paragraph. Failure to use such transitional devices often results in the writer's leaving too great a gap between sentences or even between paragraphs. This makes it difficult for the reader to "follow" the writer.

Being parenthetical, such expressions are, therefore, set off by commas, as *therefore* is in this sentence. If the transitional word or phrase comes in the middle of the sentence—as *therefore* does in the preceding sentence—it must be set off. If the expression introduces the sentence or the clause, it may or may not be set off by a comma. *However* is always set off, but other transitional words and phrases should be set off only if the comma is needed for clarity. No comma is needed here: *Therefore* such words and phrases need not be set off. But the comma is essential here: *Otherwise*, (or *On the other hand*,) the tax increase cannot be avoided.

You must not overuse transitional expressions, but you need to learn to use them carefully whenever their use contributes to unity and clarity, particularly by providing a bridge over which the reader may cross easily from one sentence or from one paragraph to another.

Some of the conjunctive adverbs listed on page 43—such as *otherwise, therefore, consequently, hence, else* and *still*—may be used effectively as transitional words that connect either clauses or sentences. Even the coordinate conjunctions *but* and *and* may serve as transitional words to introduce the second of two sentences.

The journalist should find use at times for many of the following transitional words and phrases, which may be used most often to establish the connection between the sentence in which the transitional expression occurs and a preceding sentence: *meanwhile, heretofore, therefore, otherwise, temporarily, incidentally, consequently, naturally, lately, hence, also, at last, by that time, as soon as, as long as, actually, of course, at least, in contrast (with), in addition (to), for that reason, for example, for instance, as a result, after all, in the meantime, at the same time, after awhile, in conclusion, to conclude, to sum up, in summary, in short, in brief, on the whole, on the contrary, on the other hand, although true, it is true.* Study a few more examples of the use of transitional expressions:

> "We're trying to use persuasive means rather than an order of some sort," said Rehkemper. . . . *Meanwhile,* a group which instigated a petition in support of the priest has organized and plans to support Father Vogel in his appeal.

> *By that time,* a large number of embassy employees had arrived, including two officials who tried to find out what was happening.

> The President denied overpromising in the campaign. *However,* a key presidential aide admitted that "some of the promises in the campaign were made without the knowledge available today in the White House."

> The senator says the report points up the need for more in-house auditing. "Otherwise, you will have programs running wild."
> *Or:* The senator argued, "The report points up the need for more in-house auditing; *otherwise,* you will have programs running wild."

> *Heretofore,* federal welfare programs have been based on need, such as aid to dependent children, the aged and disabled.

> The attack had no apparent goal other than to create carnage and gain headlines. It succeeded in both purposes.
> *But* the latest massacre also succeeded in underlining the Israeli argument that the PLO is not a serious group, seeking peace and compromise, but a gang of killers. *To cap it all,* PLO headquarters in Lebanon quickly took credit for the rampage, calling it "a heroic operation."

(For punctuation of parenthetical transitional expressions, see pages 246–47.)

10. Do not use two sentences if the use of one sentence is clearer.

Two sentences often can be combined by making one sentence a subordinate clause introduced by a subordinating conjunction; for example, *if, unless, although, even if, in order that, so that, because, or since.* Let's look at some examples of this.

> Streaming north through Panmunjom were North Korean Communist prisoners. They were transported in closed ambulances. They did not appear to be sick or wounded.

Why were the prisoners being transported in ambulances? Were they sick or wounded? Use of a subordinate clause to introduce the second sentence would answer the questions at once, and the addition of a phrase at the end of the construction would further clarify the meaning. Read the following sentences and compare them with those in the previous illustration.

> Streaming north through Panmunjom were North Korean Communist prisoners. Although they did not appear to be sick or wounded, they were being transported in closed ambulances, apparently to prevent incidents.

Often the omission of a necessary sentence makes it difficult to keep pace with the writer, as in this excerpt:

> The ROK's moved cautiously as they began the ascent of Old Baldy. At the summit they found only a remnant of the North Korean division that had defended the mountain for 21 days.

The writer asked his readers to make quite a jump from the foot of Old Baldy to the top of the mountain! At least one transition sentence is needed between these two sentences, something like: "It took them two hours to work their way to the summit." Or the second sentence might be started with the subordinate clause: "When they reached the summit, . . ."

Sometimes you may find that you need to use transitional devices throughout a series of paragraphs, or at least between several paragraphs within a story. Do not hesitate to do this if these expressions make it easier for the readers to follow the meaning of the paragraphs and of the complete story. In the following Associated Press story excerpt note how the italicized transitional devices and other interesting paragraph beginnings help hold the story together and make it easy to read.

> Panmunjom, Aug. 11 (AP)—A bitter band of die-hard Americans came back from their Red prison camps today—vowing vengeance on weaker comrades who turned to communism under pressure.
>
> *They* spat out "progressive" as a dirty word, and wore with honor the badge of "reactionary" fastened on them by Red Chinese who clubbed and tortured them but did not break their spirits.
>
> *One of these tough Americans* had to be held back by force when he spotted a "progressive" at the Freedom Village reception center.
>
> "I'll get him when I get home," he said.
>
> *One hundred Americans* came back from the North, along with 24 British, 25 Turks . . .
>
> *Meanwhile,* 328 Americans repatriated earlier sailed from Inchon aboard the troopship Gen. Nelson M. Walker, . . .
>
> *At the same time* a plane bearing 17 seriously ill Americans, litter patients, landed at Honolulu for a night of rest,. . .

OTHER PHASES OF UNITY

Besides completeness, there are other phases of unity that are important. You know by now that unity means oneness of thought and that a correct sentence expresses a complete thought, but this does not mean that a sentence can contain only one statement. Although a sentence should express only one main idea or fact, you know that most often that main idea or fact is modified by other statements expressed in other clauses. Thus we have complex, compound and compound-complex sentences. What the journalist needs to remember is this: If the sentence is composed of two or more parts—two or more statements—the parts must be closely related. In other words, make sure that the parts of a sentence fit together to make up one unified larger thought or idea that is clear to the reader.

If this kind of unity is to be obtained, consideration must be given the main principles that are discussed below.

1. Keep each sentence to one unified thought. The statements or ideas of the sentence must be related. Study these examples:

> POOR: The blaze spread rapidly through the sprawling plant, which is of modern, functional design.
> BETTER: The blaze spread rapidly through the sprawling plant. The brick structure is of modern, functional design.
> INCORRECT: War damage totals more than $1,000,000,000, with one building in every six having been destroyed, and industry and agriculture are almost dormant.
> CORRECT: War damage totals more than $1,000,000,000, with one building in every six destroyed. Industry and agriculture are almost dormant.

The thoughts in each case are not closely related. They should be put into separate sentences, as shown.

Certainly the two statements in the following example do not go well together as independent clauses. Subordinate the second clause.

> INCORRECT: A majority of Pacific-10 Conference players have the ability to graduate to the professional ranks, and most of them come from California.
> CORRECT: A majority of Pacific-10 Conference players, most of whom come from California, have the ability to graduate to the professional ranks.

If you make the change of putting the idea in one independent clause into a subordinate clause, make sure that the idea does have some relation to the idea in the main clause. This subordination of one idea to another is an important phase of coherence.

2. Avoid going to the other extreme and chopping your sentence into small units.

Although the reporter is urged by readability experts to use as many simple sentences as possible, he should avoid the choppy writing that sometimes results from this practice.

If the ideas expressed in two or more short sentences are evidently related, they may be put into one unified sentence. This usually means subordinating one or more ideas.

> CHOPPY: The city manager may be compared to the manager of a big department store. He has the power to appoint employees. He has the power to fire employees. He supervises the work of the employees in the various departments.
>
> BETTER: The city manager may be compared to the manager of a big department store. He supervises the work of the employees and has the right to hire and to fire personnel.

There are times, of course, when the stringing together of short sentences is permissible. The sports writer may employ the style to express fast action. Writers use it sometimes for emphasis. If you use it, make sure that it serves a legitimate purpose.

Here is a good example of a sports writer's reporting:

> Ulmer backtracked several paces. He feinted to the left. He hesitated another few seconds. Then he rifled a 20-yard pass, straight over the middle, into the arms of Haynes for the winning score.

3. Prospective journalists do not need to be reminded that the childish habit of stringing clauses together with the conjunction *and* will not be condoned in any publication office. However, some of you may need to be reminded that you must keep superfluous details out of your sentences. Avoid the rambling sentence that contains too many details.

In the following sentence, some of the details—possibly including birthplace, birth date, parents and education—belong in separate sentences. Some of the details might be omitted, unless this is an obituary.

> Rathbone Deberry, born in New Orleans Dec. 1, 1894, the son of James and Stella Deberry, received a B.E. degree from Tulane in 1916, and has served as assistant city engineer in New Orleans, as assistant location engineer for the Illinois Central Railroad, and has engaged in architectural practice since 1926.

4. You may be failing to use enough subordinate clauses or prepositional, participial and infinitive phrases.

If you study the writings of professional journalists, you will find that they have learned to subordinate minor ideas in their sentences, using dependent clauses and, in many instances, phrases to express the less important ideas. When you have mastered this technique, you will be well on your way to becoming a first-rate writer.

Here are examples of poor sentences and ways to improve them.

> POOR: We harvest raw sap and the water content is reduced from two-thirds to a third by a centrifuge similar to a cream separator, and then the concentrate is treated with ammonia to prevent souring and shipped.

BETTER: We harvest raw sap, whose water content is reduced from two-thirds to a third by a centrifuge similar to a cream separator. After the concentrate is treated with ammonia to prevent souring, it is ready to be shipped.

POOR: Treating the concentrate with ammonia to prevent souring is the next step in the process, and it is the most important one.

BETTER: Treating the concentrate with ammonia to prevent souring, the next step in the process, is the most important one.

The important idea is stressed in the better sentences, as it should be.

POOR: The third season of the television show, "Bewitched," has been completed, and the producer is planning to send Elizabeth Montgomery and Agnes Moorehead, the first socially acceptable witches, on a personal appearance tour.

BETTER: With the third successful season of the television show, "Bewitched," (having been) completed, the producer is planning to send Elizabeth Montgomery and Agnes Moorehead, the first socially acceptable witches, on a personal appearance tour.

The main idea—that the two TV stars will make a personal appearance tour—is given the emphasis it deserves by changing the first independent clause to a phrase.

Take care to subordinate the minor ideas, not the principal statement. Notice this sentence:

POOR: The firemen were laying the first hose line when the roof caved in.

BETTER: The roof caved in while the firemen were laying the first hose line.

The important idea is the roof collapse.

Putting a *when* clause at the end of a sentence may result in faulty subordination, as shown in the first sentence about the firemen. Sometimes the subordinate clause needs to come first in a sentence, for emphasis, as in the following example:

POOR: The vote on letting the bridge contract was taken when Commissioner Pickett arrived.

BETTER: After Commissioner Pickett arrived, the vote on letting the bridge contract was taken.

The following are other examples in which the main ideas were incorrectly subordinated by being placed in dependent clauses or phrases:

POOR: The blackmailer hesitated several minutes before he opened the post office box, which gave the officers sufficient time to spot him and to make the arrest.

BETTER: The officers gained sufficient time to spot and to arrest the blackmailer when he hesitated several minutes before he opened the post office box.

POOR: He looked like a tramp, although he is a multimillionaire.

BETTER: Although he looked like a tramp, he is a multimillionaire.

POOR: The governor glanced across the lobby to see two senators taking pokes at each other.

BETTER: When the governor glanced across the lobby, he saw two senators taking pokes at each other.

POOR: Wainwright lapsed into a coma, dying 24 hours later.

BETTER: Wainwright died Wednesday after lapsing into a coma 24 hours earlier.

5. Earlier you were warned to be habitually on the alert against commiting the comma fault, or comma splice.

You should recognize that the comma fault is a violation of the principle of unity. The following examples should be sufficient to demonstrate how to correct this fault.

INCORRECT: The water content in the raw sap is reduced from two-thirds to a third, then the concentrate is treated with ammonia.

The second clause should be preceded by a semicolon because *then* is not a coordinate conjunction.

CORRECT: The water content . . . to a third; then the concentrate . . . .

The writer would have obtained even more unity by expressing the minor idea in a subordinate clause:

BETTER: After the water content in the raw sap is reduced from two-thirds to a third, the concentrate is treated with ammonia.

A common error of the worst type is illustrated by this sentence:

INCORRECT: Richardson hit the middle of the line three times, he failed to make a first down.

The error can be corrected in several ways: *(a)* by use of a coordinating conjunction; *(b)* by use of a subordinate clause; *(c)* by conversion of one clause into a phrase; *(d)* by making two sentences.

a. Richardson hit the middle of the line three times, *but* he failed to make a first down.

b. Although Richardson hit the middle of the line three times, he failed to make a first down.

c. After hitting the middle of the line three times, Richardson failed to make a first down.

d. Richardson hit the middle of the line three times. He failed to make a first down.

The following sentence violates the principle of unity even more seriously because the two clauses are not so closely related as those in the foregoing example.

INCORRECT: Gene and Lynn Phillips are brothers, they will both be in the starting lineup for the Ponies this fall.

The error is corrected below in three ways: (*a*) by making two sentences; (*b*) by use of a subordinate clause; (*c*) by use of a prepositional phrase and an appositive.

a. Gene and Lynn Phillips are brothers. The will both be in the starting lineup for the Ponies this fall.
b. Gene and Lynn Phillips, who are brothers, will both be in the starting lineup for the Ponies this fall.
c. In the starting Pony basketball lineup this fall will be two brothers, Gene and Lynn Phillips.

Which type of construction you use will depend upon where you wish to place the emphasis.

Avoid the comma fault. If the two statements are not closely related, use separate sentences. Otherwise, you will not achieve unity in your sentence.

The comma fault is often committed when *so* is used to introduce the second clause. This results in a weak construction in most cases.

WEAK: Johnson is needed, so he will go.

Even with a semicolon before *so,* the sentence would still be weak. Better unity could be obtained in the following ways:

CORRECT: Johnson is needed. He will go.
Johnson is needed, and he will go.
Because he is needed, Johnson will go.
Being badly needed, Johnson will go.

Many editors prefer the conversion of one statement into a subordinate clause or into a phrase.

6. Exercise care in the choice of the conjunction.

Use the conjunction which expresses exactly the meaning you intend to convey. There is a wide variety to choose from, and there is no excuse for violating the principle of unity.

INCORRECT: Bernard Buckheit entered politics and became governor, and his twin brother became a peanut vendor.

The conjunction *and,* which implies addition, is wrong; the correct conjunction to use is *but,* which expresses contrast.

INCORRECT: Bobo is not observing training rules, and his batting average is dropping sharply.
CORRECT: *Because* Bobo is not observing training rules, his batting average is dropping sharply.

INCORRECT: The victim was given two blood transfusions, but he died.
CORRECT: *Although* the victim was given two blood transfusions, he died.

7. Do not violate the principle of unity by using the incorrect sentence form.

As a rule, the compound-complex sentence finds little place in journalistic writing. Conversion of these sentences into complex sentences is often the best way to achieve better unity.

POOR: Bruce Portillo was especially good at backing up the line, and later the coach found that he was even more effective at fullback on the offensive.
BETTER: Later the coach found that Bruce Portillo, who was especially good at backing up the line, was even more effective at fullback on the offense.

The second sentence has greater unity and places the emphasis where it belongs—on the fact that the coach found Portillo more effective at fullback.

Of course, two ideas which are truly coordinate should be written as a compound sentence. Don't try to force a coordinate idea into a subordinate clause.

POOR: Bowers and McCloud brought in a third detective, with whose help they solved the murder of the councilman.

The second idea is as important as the first, if not more important. It belongs in an independent clause.

BETTER: Bowers and McCloud brought in a third detective, and with his help they solved the murder of the councilman.
Or: After Bowers and McCloud brought in a third detective, they solved the murder of the councilman.

QUIZ ANSWERS

1. One auto was recovered, that of William Truehart. 2. Insert *was* before *saved.* 3. Insert *that* before *the.* 4. Insert *to* before *write.* 5. Change comma to semicolon or make two sentences. 6. Break up into more sentences; be sure to have the honorary degree fact in a sentence by itself. 7. Combine into two sentences, preferably. For example: The city manager may be compared to the manager of a big department store. He supervises the work of employees in the various departments and has the right to hire and to fire personnel. 8. He is neither interested *in* nor concerned about. . . . 9. A majority of Pacific-10 Conference players, most of whom come from California, have the ability. . . . 10. The roof caved in while the firemen were laying the first hose line. 11. The man, 24, (or *The 24-year-old man*) was booked for rape, burglary and indecent exposure (in order of importance). An investigation of the charges is continuing.

12. The main point made by the first speaker and *that of* (or *that made by*) the man who followed him coincided. 13. Change *but* to *and*; or, even better, convert first sentence into a subordinate clause: As we watched. . . . 14. *But* is correct conjunction; however, this would be better: Although he had. . . top lawyers, he failed to win the suit. 15. Needs transitional word between sentences: Representative Michel says. . . points up the need for more in-house auditing. *"Otherwise,* you will have programs running wild."

14

Sentence Coherence

A study of sentence coherence logically follows the study of sentence unity. A sentence—or a paragraph—may be unified without being coherent. To obtain sentence coherence, the writer must be sure to arrange ideas in logical order and to see that all parts of the sentence fit together (cohere) logically and consistently to express a main idea. The connections between different parts of the sentence must be natural and logical if the sentence is to be unmistakably clear to the reader.

It is essential to make sure that the sentence is *complete*, that no words are omitted which are needed to make the meaning clear. Such words include necessary verbs, articles, pronouns and prepositions.

Two other main ways to attain sentence coherence are the correct placement of modifiers and the use of parallel construction.

Before proceeding with your study of coherence, test your knowledge of the essentials of sentence coherence by taking the quiz that follows. Rewrite or copy edit the sentences to correct errors that violate sentence coherence or clarity. Watch for such errors as: missing words needed in the sentence, misplaced modifiers or dependent clauses, needlessly split phrases, wrong correlative conjunctions, incorrect reference of pronouns, and dangling words and phrases. Also, correct all violations of parallelism and consistency—unnecessary shifting of voice, subject, person, number and tense.

178

QUIZ

1. He has only hit two home runs so far.
2. While playing quarterback for the Jets last year, his passing average was 28.2 yards.
3. He tripped and fell forward into the mud when he hit the last hurdle. (Revise)
4. Charles Johnson of Abilene caught 11 black bass on a black Hula Popper lure, the biggest one weighing five pounds.
5. He neither owns land nor cattle.
6. He is honest, a hard worker and has confidence in his ability to make good.
7. Bring the mixture to a boil, and then it should be stirred briskly.
8. Her sister told her that she had won the prize. (Revise)
9. Each salesman will be allowed a commission also.
10. To provide the city with more water and finding more parking space downtown are the two big problems facing the city council.
11. Coach Shula began to listen to his assistants, and the team's morale was improved.
12. There is no panacea either for farm market problems or dwindling profits ahead, Dr. Timm told the vocational agriculture teachers.
13. Being a rabid anti-Semitic leader, the Congressional subcommittee probably will not invite him to appear.
14. He offered to advise the county commissioners on home rule, but they refused it.
15. He gunned the motor while it veered sharply to the left.

PLACING MODIFIERS CORRECTLY

Modifiers should be placed as near as possible to the words they modify or in such a way that the meaning of the sentence is clear to the reader. Guard against misplacing word, phrase or clause modifiers.

Adverbs

You know that such adverbs as *only, nearly, hardly, scarcely, even, almost, also* and *not* can change the meaning of the sentence if they are placed near different words in the sentence. The word *only*, which can be used as an adjective or an adverb, must be watched particularly.

Note the difference in meaning of the following sentences because of the change in position of the word *only*:

The champion won *only* two fights last year.
Only the champion won as few as two fights last year.
The champion, *only*, won as few as two fights last year.

Almost and *ever* should always be placed carefully. Study the different meanings of the following sentences.

> INCORRECT: Jenkins *almost has* a perfect batting stance.
> CORRECT: Jenkins has an *almost perfect* batting stance.
> INCORRECT: The manager said he didn't *ever think* the recruit could learn to play first base.
> CORRECT: The manager said that he did not think the recruit *ever could* learn to play first base.

Many adverbs can be used at different places in the sentence: (1) to gain variety; and (2) to give the exact emphasis desired. Be sure that the adverb is not used ambiguously, however. Study the following sentences to see the difference in meanings.

> He was *even* polite to his mother-in-law.
> He was polite *even* to his mother-in-law.
> *Even he* (of all persons) was polite to his mother-in-law.
> *Surely* the Tigers will win this one.
> The Tigers will win this one, *surely*.
> The Tigers *will surely win* this one.

Beware of using a "squinting adverb," one that may modify either of two words, one preceding and one following the adverb. Such adverbs usually modify an infinitive. Note these sentences.

> To miss batting practice *often* results in suspension from the team.

Does *often* modify the infinitive *to miss* or the verb *results?* To avoid confusion, it would be permissible to split the infinitive in this case and say: *to often miss*.

Another case would be an adverb placed between a verb and an infinitive, like this:

> The players were told *constantly* to concentrate on the fundamentals.

Does *constantly* modify *were told* or *to concentrate?* The probable intention is to have it modify the infinitive, and this may be made clear by saying: *to constantly concentrate*.

Phrases and Clauses

1. The *prepositional phrase*, used either adjectivally or adverbially, must be watched closely.

> POOR: They found him beneath the overturned car with a broken left leg.
> BETTER: Beneath the overturned car they found him, *with a broken left leg*.
> BEST: They found him beneath the overturned car. He had a broken left leg.

Of course you would know that the first sentence did not mean that the car had a broken leg, but the phrase should be near the word *him,* which it modifies. However, this may make a rather stilted sounding sentence. The best solution is to make two sentences.

Consider this lead that the United Press International editor called to the attention of telegraph editors: His rejected mistress confessed today that she stabbed the man *with the bushy mustache* who died of his wound on a midtown street yesterday, police said.

Here's another example of this type of error. It is not as glaring as the foregoing errors, but it is obvious that the prepositional phrase *to Jaworski,* used adverbially, should follow *turn over* more closely.

> FAULTY: The committee hopes to complete and to turn over by Friday if possible its report to Jaworski.
>
> BETTER: The committee hopes to complete and to turn over its report to Jaworski by Friday if possible.

2. *Participial phrases* used at the end of sentences are often dangling phrases; they have no word to modify. The error may be corrected by placing the phrase at the beginning of the sentence or by rewording the sentence entirely.

> INCORRECT: Funeral services will be held at Keever Chapel at 10 a.m. Thursday, the Rev. W. J. McCawley, pastor of the First Christian Church, officiating.

The phrase *the Rev. . . officiating* is a dangling participle phrase. Such phrases may be used to introduce sentences occasionally. The following sentence has a correct participial construction at the beginning of the sentence. This construction is called the nominative absolute (see page 213).

> His shirttail flying in the breeze, the boy raced down the street.

In the incorrect sentence above, the correction could be made in several ways:

> CORRECT: Funeral services will be held at Keever Chapel at 10 a.m. Thursday *with* the Rev. W. J. McCawley, pastor of the First Christian Church, officiating.
>
> *Or:* Funeral services . . . Thursday. The Rev. W. J. McCawley . . . will officiate.
>
> *Or:* Funeral services will be conducted (read) by the Rev. W. J. McCawley, pastor of the First Christian Church, at Keever Chapel at 10 a.m. Thursday.

3. *Elliptical expressions* that dangle are sometimes found in sentences. Such expressions usually begin with *when* or *while.*

> INCORRECT: While making an entrance from the wings, the actress' feet became entangled in her long dress and she sprawled on her face.

CORRECT: While *she was* making an entrance from the wings, the actress' feet became entangled. . . .

Or: While making an entrance from the wings, the actress got her feet entangled. . . .

An elliptical expression is really an incomplete clause, that is, a clause from which one or more important parts have been omitted. The error can be corrected by supplying the missing parts. If that is not done, care must be taken to see that the phrase modifies the correct word, such as *actress*, not *feet*, in the last example given.

Here are other examples of the dangling elliptical expression:

INCORRECT: When idling, the noise of the motor becomes louder.

CORRECT: When *the motor is* idling, the noise becomes louder.

INCORRECT: The old man's 1955 pick-up always seems to stall when making an important delivery.

CORRECT: The old man's 1955 pick-up always seems to stall when *he is* making an important delivery.

Some editors would pass the following sentence:

Candidates failing to report regularly for practice cannot make the team, the coach declared.

However, the meaning would be clearer if a relative clause were used:

Candidates *who fail to report for practice* cannot make the team, the coach declared.

Surely most editors would require you to revise this sentence:

Candidates failing to report for practice by the deadline which will be observed by all schools in the conference will be ruled ineligible for varsity competition.

The meaning of the sentence is vague. It might be revised thus:

All candidates who fail to report by the deadline set by conference officials will be ruled ineligible for varsity competition.

Do not confuse dangling elliptical expressions with the transitional devices often employed by good writers to connect sentences or paragraphs. A sentence like the following is correct. The transitional phrase *speaking of taxes* is used independently, not being attached to any particular noun or pronoun.

Speaking of taxes, what does the committee chairman think of the new income tax proposal?

4. Most editors would call the introductory *when* clause in the sentence

below a dangling clause because it does not modify the main verb *can look* in the independent clause.

> When the Mississippi Rebels opened the season in such high spirits, their supporters can look back now and see that they were certain to have a successful season.

The sentence would be better this way:

> Supporters of the Rebels can look back now and see that when the players entered the season in such high spirits, they were certain to have a successful season.

5. Guard against misplacing a dependent clause. Both relative clauses and adverbial clauses are often placed incorrectly in sentences.

> INCORRECT: Sidden apparently had put the gun into the car *while it was loaded*.
> CORRECT: Sidden had apparently put the gun, *while it was loaded,* into the car.
> BEST: Sidden apparently had failed to unload the gun before placing it in the car.
> INCORRECT: He tripped and fell forward into the mud *when he hit the last hurdle*.
> CORRECT: *When he hit the last hurdle,* he tripped and fell forward into the mud.

You can avoid this type of error if you arrange the parts of the sentence in chronological order—in the logical time sequence in which they occurred. In the last example, what was the sequence in the hurdler's accident? He first hit the hurdle; then he tripped; then he fell forward into the mud. Note this further illustration:

> INCORRECT: His car hurtled over the 25-foot embankment when Johnson reached the slick pavement and lost control.
> CORRECT: When Johnson's car reached the slick pavement, he lost control, and the automobile hurtled over the 25-foot embankment.

It is always safest to place a relative clause next to its antecedent.

> POOR: All girls and boys are eligible for prizes who send in the box tops.
> CORRECT: All girls and boys *who send in the box tops* are eligible for prizes.
> POOR: The soldier pulled a bar of chocolate from his pocket, which he fed to the gaunt waif. (He did not feed his *pocket* to the waif!)
> CORRECT: The soldier pulled from his pocket a bar of chocolate, which he fed to the gaunt waif. *Or:* From his pocket the soldier pulled a bar of chocolate which he fed to the gaunt waif.

6. Do not place a phrase or a clause where the reader cannot tell whether it belongs with what precedes it or with what follows it. As we observed earlier, such a construction results in what is called a "squinting" modifier—a modifier that look both ways.

> POOR: The manager when he was fouled repeatedly protested to the referee.

There are two misplaced modifiers in this sentence. The clause *when he was fouled* seems to refer to the manager, and the adverb *repeatedly* squints—it may modify either *fouled* or *protested*. The sentence should be written this way:

CORRECT: When his fighter was fouled repeatedly, the manager protested to the referee.

Note two more examples:

POOR: Tell him, if he is in his office, I will see him this afternoon.
CORRECT: If he is in his office now, tell him I will see him this afternoon.
Or: Tell him I will see him this afternoon if he is to be in his office then.
FAULTY: Because prices are difficult to control when they begin to rise, the government should act soon to check this. (Does the time clause, "when they begin to rise," modify the introductory dependent clause or the independent clause that comes last in the sentence?)
BETTER: Because prices are difficult to control, the government should act to check inflation as soon as prices begin to rise.

7. Avoiding the misplacing of a modifier is simply a matter of refraining from the needless separation of these sentence parts: (*a*) subject and verb; (*b*) verb and object; (*c*) a compound verb; (*d*) a verb phrase; (*e*) an infinitive phrase. Here is an example of separation of the subject and verb (*a*):

INCORRECT: The new committee, in its first meeting after being appointed by the mayor, could reach agreement only on the matter of recommending a study of taxicab service to and from the airport.
CORRECT: In its first meeting after being appointed by the mayor, the committee could reach agreement only on the matter of. . . .

In this example the verb and object were needlessly separated (*b*):

POOR: His car careened to the right and hit hard and almost demolished the abutment.
BETTER: His car careened to the right and *hit* the *abutment* hard. The abutment *was* almost *demolished*.

The parts of a compound verb (*c*) were separated in this example:

POOR: His car careened to the right and, traveling at almost a 45-degree angle, smashed into the abutment.
BETTER: His car careened to the right. Traveling at almost a 45-degree angle, it smashed into the abutment.

The parts of the compound predicate, *careened* and *smashed*, are too widely separated in the first sentence.

It is correct to separate a verb phrase with adverbs if this makes the meaning clear. It is also considered correct to place the adverb after the first auxiliary verb thus:

> The mayor had *definitely* decided that the tax rate must be raised by five cents.

It is also permissible to split the infinitive with an adverb if the construction is clear and reads smoothly.

> He was able to *slowly* cross the ledge.

But needlessly separating the parts of a verb phrase (*d*) or of the infinitive (*e*) is an error illustrated in the following examples.

> INCORRECT: He declared that he would, despite strong opposition, continue his project.
> CORRECT: He declared that he would continue the project despite strong opposition.
> INCORRECT: He is far too slow afoot to within three days' time switch from guard to halfback.
> CORRECT: He is far too slow afoot *to switch immediately* from guard to halfback.

Conjunctions

The *correlative conjunctions* should be placed correctly in the sentence. *Either. . . or, neither. . . nor, both. . . and* and *not only. . . but also* should be placed so that each conjunction immediately precedes the word it connects with another word.

> INCORRECT: *He neither* possesses land *nor* money.
> CORRECT: He possesses *neither* land *nor* money.
> INCORRECT: The Gibsons raise *not only* geese *but also* a herd of goats.
> CORRECT: The Gibsons *not only* raise geese *but also* keep a herd of goats.
> *Or:* The Gibsons raise not only geese, but goats.

Pronouns

Correct *reference of pronouns* is an essential of coherence. If necessary, review Chapter 6. Remember that it must always be clear what word is the antecedent of the pronoun.

Avoid having a double reference.

> POOR: Johnson told Hall that his car had been stolen.

Whose car had been stolen, Johnson's or Hall's?

CORRECT: Johnson told Hall, "*My* car has been stolen."
Or: Johnson told Hall, "*Your* car has been stolen."

Make sure that the pronoun has a definite antecedent to which it refers. For example, there is no antecedent for *it* in this sentence:

INCORRECT: He offered to advise the councilmen, but they refused it.
CORRECT: He offered his *advice* to the councilmen, but they refused *it*.
Or: He offered to *advise* the councilmen, but they refused *to hear him*.

Avoid the use of the pronoun *which* to refer to the entire clause used as the antecedent.

INCORRECT: Aaron Spelling was given the leading part, which some of the other actors did not like.

The reader might think that *which* refers to *part* or even to *Spelling*, when actually the intention was to have it refer to the entire independent clause. The sentence will be clear if changed like this:

CORRECT: Spelling's being given the leading part displeased some of the other actors.
Or: Some of the actors were displeased at Spelling's being given the leading part.[1]

In most cases, the pronoun should refer to a specific word, and that word should be an important word in the sentence. The pronoun should not refer to a parenthetical expression or to a word in the possessive case.

POOR: Baseball is a difficult game to master, one that requires a good *physique* and more *skill* than most other games, and *they* must be developed while you are young.
BETTER: Baseball is a difficult game to master, one that requires a good physique and more skill than most other games. You should develop a sound body and baseball skill while you are young.

POOR: The face leered at her in the semidarkness. It looked like a *murderer's* face, *which* made her swoon.
BETTER: . . . .It looked like the face of a murderer. At the sight, she swooned (or *fainted*).

Make sure that the pronoun has the correct antecedent, and place the pronoun as near that antecedent as possible.

INCORRECT: He introduced the car-inspection bill early in the session, which was promptly acted upon.

[1] Yes, the Aaron Spelling referred to here is today's top TV producer and writer. Spelling is a journalism graduate of Southern Methodist University, where he had many roles in Arden Club productions.

CORRECT: Early in the session he introduced the car-inspection bill, which was promptly acted upon.

POOR: The youngest daughter in the Scarborough family, who was both beautiful and talented, was Vicki.

BETTER: In the Scarborough family the youngest daughter was Vicki, who was both beautiful and talented.

POOR: Jocko was memely a puppet in her hands that was controlled by expertly manipulated wires.

BETTER: In her hands Jocko was memely a puppet that was controlled by expertly manipulated wires.

The pronoun *it* may be used as an expletive to introduce a sentence, but this construction should be employed sparingly and carefully.

Note these sentences:

CORRECT: It is snowing hard.

FAULTY: It says in today's paper that Premier Abdullah Yafi may be replaced by a pro-Egyptian former premier, Rashid Karami.

The same rule applies to the impersonal pronouns *they* and *you*.

FAULTY: They take a siesta every day in Mexico.

BETTER: *Mexicans* take a siesta every day.

FAULTY: All play and no study makes you dull.

BETTER: All play and no study makes *one* a dullard (*or* makes a person dull).

USING VERBALS CORRECTLY

Journalists must be alert to avoid using dangling modifiers, especially dangling participles. Failure to do so may result in misleading and even ludicrous sentences, such as this one given earlier: Running at full speed, the ball was caught near the wall in right field. Analyze the sentence:

Running at full speed is a participial phrase that appears to be used adjectivally to modify *ball*. A modifier dangles when it clearly does not modify the word to which it is attached. The sentence should read: Running at full speed, *McBride* (or *he*) caught the ball near the wall in right field. The participial phrase, used adjectivally, now clearly modifies the noun *McBride* or the pronoun *he*.

Note that the dangling participial phrase cannot be corrected by changing the order or position of the phrase. It is necessary to add words or to change the structure to clarify what the phrase modifies.

Dangling modifiers, which most often come at the beginning of the sentence, usually are verbals—participial phrases, gerund phrases and infinitive phrases. Phrases that dangle at the end of the sentence, however, are common. (These, along with dangling elliptical expressions, were treated on pages 181–82.)

Because all verbals either describe an action or make an assertion, it is most important to construct the sentence so that the reader clearly sees who is doing the acting or who or what is being acted upon. Let's take a closer look now at dangling verbals.

Participles

Remember that the participial phrase is used adjectivally, that it must have a word (substantive) to modify and that it must modify the right word to make sense.

If the participle introduces the sentence, the word modified by the participial phrase is almost always the subject of the sentence. Study the examples that follow.

> INCORRECT: Having only a month to live, they gave him his Christmas presents early.
> CORRECT: *Having only a month to live,* little *Tommy* was given his Christmas presents early.
> INCORRECT: Being a dissenter, the committee probably will not invite him.
> CORRECT: *Being a dissenter, Ferguson* probably will not be invited by the committee.
> *Or:* As (Because) Ferguson is a dissenter, the committee probably will not invite him.

In the following incorrect sentence, in which the participial phrase comes at the end, there is no specific word in the independent clause for the participial phrase to refer to. This is a violation of coherence. The sentence should be recast as shown in the correct version.

> INCORRECT: Highway 80 is much too narrow to accommodate present-day traffic, causing unnecessary traffic casualties.
> CORRECT: Unnecessary traffic casualties are occurring on Highway 80 because it is much too narrow to accommodate present-day traffic.

The past participle may be used incorrectly, also. The reference is vague in the following sentence. Note the revision of it.

> FAULTY: Unnecessary traffic casualties are occurring on Highway 80, caused by the narrowness of the road.
> CORRECT: Unnecessary traffic casualties, caused by the narrowness of the road, are occurring on Highway 80.

The dangling past participle phrase may introduce the sentence, thus:

FAULTY: Caught in the late-afternoon traffic on Main, it was impossible for Maxwell to get his wife to the hospital before the baby arrived.

CORRECT: *Caught* in the late-afternoon traffic on Main, *Maxwell* found it impossible to get his wife to the hospital before the baby arrived.

Placing *thus* or *thereby* before a participle does not keep it from dangling if there is no specific word for it to modify.

FAULTY: Abandonment of the two-platoon system required coaches to use men who could play on both the offense and the defense, thus largely eliminating the football specialist.

CORRECT: Because abandonment of the two-platoon system required coaches to use men who could play on both the offense and the defense, the football specialist was largely eliminated.

The misplaced participial phrase often violates correct use of tense.

FAULTY: The injured man was rushed to the hospital, entering the emergency operating room at 8:30 p.m.

CORRECT: The injured man *was rushed* to the hospital for emergency treatment and *was wheeled* into the operating room at 8:30 p.m.

Or: The injured man, *rushed* to the hospital for emergency treatment, *was wheeled* into the operating room at 8:30 p.m.

In the faulty sentence the participle *entering* not only is too far removed from the word it modifies (*man*) but the idea expressed in the participial phrase needs to be in the same tense as the predicate *was rushed*.

Another example of faulty tense is the following:

FAULTY: Olivares died in a rest home Tuesday at the age of 113, being born March 9, 1840, in Rosario, Argentina.

The sentence can be corrected by changing *being born* to *having been born*.

Gerunds

A *gerund* is a verb form ending in *ing* that is used as a noun. It may be the object of a preposition, the object of a verb or the subject of a sentence. It can have the same kind of modifiers that a noun can have—adjectives and pronouns—but unlike a noun it can take an object. The phrase in which the gerund is used is called a gerund phrase and, like the participial phrase, it must not dangle.

INCORRECT: After considering the problem from all angles, a vote was taken.

CORRECT: *After considering* the problem from all angles, *the committee* voted.

The gerund phrase cannot modify *vote*. The noun *committee* must be used.

INCORRECT: In jumping from the plane, the parachutist's head banged against the door.

CORRECT: *In jumping* from the plane, *the parachutist* banged his head against the door.

Sometimes the use of a dependent clause instead of a dangling gerund phrase is advisable. Why not change the sentence concerning the parachutist to read: When the parachutist jumped from the plane, he banged his head against the door.

Errors in the use of the gerund usually result from failure to use the active voice rather than the passive voice, that is, failure to have the subject doing the acting rather than being acted upon.

INCORRECT: The feature article should be outlined before attempting to write it.

CORRECT: *Before attempting to write* a feature article, *the writer* should outline it.

The dangling gerund phrase occurring at the end of the sentence is corrected by placing it at the beginning of the sentence and having the correct noun in the main clause for it to modify. Note, too, use of the active voice.

Infinitives

An introductory *infinitive phrase* must properly refer to the subject of the sentence. Make sure you have a true subject in the active voice for the infinitive phrase to modify. Otherwise, you have a dangling infinitive phrase. Study these sentences.

INCORRECT: To become a champion swimmer, the shoulder muscles should be developed while you are young.

CORRECT: *To become* a champion swimmer, *one* should develop the shoulder muscles while young.

INCORRECT: To prevent soil erosion, terraces should be built and crops should be rotated.

CORRECT: *To prevent* soil erosion, *the farmer* should build terraces and rotate crops.

Note that the subjects in the correct sentences are doing the acting; in other words, the verb in the main clause is in the active voice.

PARALLEL STRUCTURE

Parallel structure is an important element of coherence. It is simply the principle of placing ideas that are parallel (alike) in thought or meaning into grammatical forms or constructions that are alike. (Parallelism was treated briefly on pages 78 and 153–54.)

Parallelism is not called for or even possible in much journalistic writing, but knowledge of the principle will keep journalists from writing sentences that are not uniform and not clear in meaning.

The most common violations of parallel structure occur when there is an unnecessary interchange of: (*a*) an infinitive with a gerund; (*b*) a noun with a gerund or with an infinitive; (*c*) a noun with a dependent clause; (*d*) an adjective with an independent clause; (*e*) an adjective with a verb; and (*f*) an infinitive or a gerund with an independent clause.

The error in the following example occurred because of incorrect use of an infinitive with a gerund (*a*)

> INCORRECT: To provide the city with more water and finding a solution to the downtown parking problem are the two big matters to be discussed tonight.
> CORRECT: *Providing* the city with more water and *finding* a solution to the downtown parking problem are the two big matters to be discussed tonight.
> *Or: To provide* . . water and *to find.* . . .

Juxtaposing a noun with a gerund and with an infinitive (*b*) gave rise to the errors in these examples:

> INCORRECT: The council must consider two matters: the shortage of water and finding a solution to the downtown parking problem.
> CORRECT: The council must consider two problems: *providing* a sufficient supply of water and *solving* the downtown parking problem.
> INCORRECT: The answers to the water-shortage problem may be to tap Red River and stricter enforcement of lawn-watering regulations.
> CORRECT: The answers to the water-shortage problem may be *to tap* Red River and *to enforce* more strictly the lawn-watering regulations.

Interchanging a noun with a dependent clause (*c*) is illustrated in this example:

> INCORRECT: Mayor Tisdale announced his candidacy for a second term and that he would conduct a campaign based on his present platform.
> CORRECT: Mayor Tisdale announced *that he would run* for a second term and *that he would conduct* a campaign based on his present platform.

An independent clause is used inappropriately as an adjective (*d*) in this example:

> INCORRECT: The bank robber was dark-eyed, sharp-nosed and he had an olive complexion.
> CORRECT: The bank robber was *dark-eyed, sharp-nosed* and *olive-complexioned*.
> *Or:* The bank robber had *dark eyes*, a *sharp nose*, and an *olive complexion*.

The error in the following example occurred because of incorrect juxtaposition of adjectives and a verb phrase *(e)*.

INCORRECT: Cindy was graceful, well-dressed and had charming manners.
CORRECT: Cindy was graceful, well-dressed and *well-mannered*.
Or: Cindy had grace, she dressed well, and she had charming manners.

An infinitive and a gerund are interchanged with independent clauses *(f)* to create errors in the following sentences:

INCORRECT: The city council is considering two possible solutions: to tap Red River, or it can drill a large number of artesian wells.
CORRECT: The city council is considering two possible solutions: *tapping* Red River or *drilling* a large number of artesian wells.
INCORRECT: The committee of businessmen offered two alternative proposals: raising the parking-meter charge to ten cents, or more of the downtown streets could be converted into one-way thoroughfares.
CORRECT: The committee of businessmen offered two alternative proposals: *raising* the parking-meter charge to ten cents or *converting* more of the downtown streets into one-way thoroughfares.

By now you have observed that there are three important principles to follow to obtain parallelism. (1) See that coordinating conjunctions join constructions which are alike. (2) See that correlative conjunctions join constructions that are alike. (3) See that the parts of a series are alike in construction.

1. Do the coordinating conjunctions *and, but* and *or* join constructions that are alike in these sentences?

To provide the city with more water and *to find* more parking space downtown are the two big problems.
Raising the parking-meter charge or *widening* the streets may be the solution.
Not wider streets but *more one-way thoroughfares* may be the answer.

2. Do the correlative conjunctions *either . . . or, neither . . . nor* and *not only . . . but also* join constructions that are alike in the sentences below?

The driver was either *asleep* or *drunk*.
Neither the *car* nor the *driver* was harmed.
He was wise not only *in slowing down* but also *in sounding* his horn.

3. Are the parts in the series in each sentence alike in construction?

The mayor is *honest, cooperative* and *tenacious*.
A policeman has no legal right *to make* you talk or *to force* you to answer questions you do not choose to answer or *to prevent* your lawyer from talking with you or *to keep* you in jail on mere suspicion.
The mayor has fought hard *for* better *streets, for* adequate *parks, for* lower utility *rates* and *for reelection*.

CONSISTENCY OF STRUCTURE

Consistency in sentence structure is an important element of coherence. Do not change the point of view within a sentence without a good reason for the shift, or your sentences will lack unity, coherence and forcefulness.

1. Do not shift from one *voice* to another.

> POOR: Under the proposed plan the engineering student would study three years at Baylor, and then he would be admitted to Texas Tech for two years and a summer session.
>
> BETTER: Under the proposed plan the engineering student *would study* three years at Baylor and then *would attend* Texas Tech for two years and a summer session.
>
> POOR: The head coach began to accept the advice of his assistants, and the morale of the team was improved sharply.
>
> BETTER: The head coach *began* to accept the advice of his assistants, and the morale of the team *improved* sharply.
>
> POOR: Trout had been employed by the bank since 1969, and he became chairman of the board of directors in 1976.
>
> BETTER: Trout *had been connected* with the bank since 1969 and *had been* chairman of the board of directors since 1976.
>
> Or: Trout *joined* the staff of the bank in 1969 and *became* chairman of the board of directors in 1976.

Always keep in mind this rule: Use the *active voice* rather than the passive voice as far as possible. Of all the parts of speech, the one that will make your copy sparkle brightest is the active verb. Use of the active verb gives a sentence concreteness, forcefulness, life, vividness, originality and variety. Only the concrete noun comes close to matching the action verb as an indispensable tool for the journalist.

In cultivating the use of the active verb, however, do not forget that the passive voice is sometimes useful in your writing. A fairly safe rule to follow is this: If the person or thing receiving the action is more important than the person who is acting, use the passive voice rather than the active voice. A review of pages 65–66 will refresh your memory on this point.

2. The *subject* of the verb should not be shifted unnecessarily.

> POOR: Conrad established the business in 1966, and most of the firm's commercial loans were handled by him until 1974.
>
> BETTER: *Conrad established* the business in 1966, and *he handled* most of the firm's commercial loans until 1974.
>
> POOR: In the last four minutes Earl Campbell went in at fullback, and the game *was won*.
>
> BETTER: In the last four minutes Earl Campbell went in at fullback and *won* the game with an 11-yard plunge.

POOR: Baugh played professional football longer than any other man, and practically all the league's records in forward passing were set by him.

BETTER: *Baugh played* professional football longer than any other man and *set* practically all the league's records in forward passing.

Or: Baugh, who played. . . , *set* practically all the league's records. . . .

3. The *person* of the pronoun should not be shifted unnecessarily.

POOR: You should keep your eyes on the players in the middle of the line, for one cannot learn to appreciate the fine points of football by watching only the backfield.

The error can be corrected by changing *one* to *you*, to make both pronouns second person. A better change would be to alter the construction of the sentence, thus:

BETTER: To learn to appreciate the fine points of football, *you* should keep *your* eyes on the players in the middle of the line instead of watching only the backfield, the coach told his players.

4. Unnecessary shifting of *number* must be avoided.

INCORRECT: The big Ohio Redskins fullback grinned and replied, "Each player was informed at the beginning of spring practice that we must learn to block first of all."

Each player is third person singular, and *we* is first person plural. The error will be corrected if *we* is changed to the third person singular *he*.

5. Do not shift the *mood* without good reason for the change.

INCORRECT: Grasp the ball firmly with all five fingers; then you flick your wrist slightly as you throw.

Grasp is in the imperative mood. *Flick* is in the indicative mood. Make both verbs imperative.

CORRECT: *Grasp* the ball firmly with all five fingers and *flick* your wrist slightly as you throw.

6. The *tense* of the verb should not be shifted within the sentence.

INCORRECT: Sales threads his way down the east sideline and fell over the goal line for the winning touchdown.

CORRECT: Sales *threaded* his way down the east sideline and *fell* over the goal line for the winning touchdown.

Remember that the past tense is used in most news stories which are largely reports of events which have already taken place. Consistent use of the past tense in the story makes for clearer writing. Also, if each sentence and each paragraph is kept in the past tense, the copy editor has more leeway in cutting the story or in changing the order of the paragraphs. This is often necessary to fit the story into the space available for it.

For example, it would be better writing to say, "Moore *did* not *play* against Notre Dame because he *was* crippled" than to say "is crippled," even though Moore may still be crippled when the story is written. Here is another illustration:

> CORRECT: A middle-aged woman was arrested Tuesday and is being questioned about the robbery.
>
> BETTER: A middle-aged woman *was arrested* Tuesday and *was held* for questioning about the robbery.

The first sentence is grammatically correct, but most editors would prefer the consistent use of the past tense. Also, this insures accuracy of facts, as the woman may have been released before the story is printed.

QUIZ ANSWERS

1. He has hit only two home runs so far. 2. While playing quarterback for Oakland last year, he compiled a passing average of only 28.2 yards. 3. When he hit the last hurdle, he tripped and fell. . . . 4. Use a second sentence: The biggest one weighed five pounds. 5. Transpose *neither* and *owns*. 6. He is honest, hard-working (or industrious) and confident of his ability to make good. 7. Bring the mixture to a boil; then stir it briskly. 8. Her sister told her, "You (or *I*) won the prize." 9. Each salesman also will be allowed a commission. 10. To provide the city with more water and to find more parking space. . . . 11. Change *was improved* to *improved*. Better: When Coach Shula began . . . assistants, the team's morale improved. 12. There is no panacea ahead for either farm market problems or dwindling profits, Dr. Timm told. . . . 13. Correct dangling participle: Since he is a rabid anti-Semitic leader, the Congressional . . . . 14. He offered to advise the county commissioners on home rule, but they refused to hear him (or *they refused his advice*). 15. He gunned the motor while the car (or the boat) veered sharply . . . .

15
Sentence Emphasis

Emphasis, the third member of "the trinity," is a rhetorical principle that journalists must recognize as important in the practice of their profession. *Emphasis* is the principle of stressing a certain word or words within a sentence or a paragraph. Because emphasis is obtained by position and arrangement of ideas in the sentence, journalists are especially concerned with seeing that the most important idea is featured in the sentence, particularly in a news story lead. Emphasis is obtained by arranging the words in a sentence so that they give prominence to the central idea, with the minor details subordinated.

However, the journalist must bear in mind that his public reads silently—and often under hurried and distracting conditions. The newspaper reader may not even bother to complete the reading of every sentence. Thus, the beginning of the journalistic sentence is the best place for emphasizing a point. For the same reason a news story must register its important facts at the beginning and let the finer details fall into place later.

With radio and television copy the case is different. Here the copy is spoken aloud and must therefore be in a style that is more informal, more conversational than that of the newspaper. Also, because the audience is less hurried and distracted, the copy may build up to its important points more gradually—this is particularly the case with dramatic writing.

One cue may certainly be taken from the radio and television media: the readability experts urge newspaper men and women to write "like you talk."

If this advice is taken, as a rule clearer writing results. But Gunning and Flesch recommend that you do not go all the way in writing as you talk. They recognize that their rules are not always applicable, and they suggest a compromise between formal written English and informal spoken English for newspaper writers.

Before you begin your study of sentence emphasis, take the short quiz to test your knowledge of this important rhetorical principle.

Rewrite the sentences to obtain emphasis of major ideas.

QUIZ

1. It is impossible to enforce the ordinance.
2. Before he died he had lost his property, his family and his friends.
3. The general lapsed into a coma, dying 24 hours later.
4. The sheriff carried a John Doe warrant which he served on the suspected robber.
5. The roof caved in and six firemen were seriously injured.
6. After he was shot six times following a midnight argument at another tavern in the 2100 block of Northwest Highway, a tavern owner died at 5:05 a.m. Thursday.
7. The boy was running across the street near his home at 8:45 p.m. Wednesday when he was struck and killed.
8. The driver of the runaway car is going to have to show up with greenbacks clutched in hand, if he wants his car back, because Mrs. Price chained the vehicle to a tree.

LOOSE VERSUS PERIODIC SENTENCES

The basic sentence in most news writing is the declarative sentence with its parts arranged in normal order: subject—predicate—object. Grammarians term this type of sentence the *loose sentence*.

The *periodic sentence* is one that builds to a climax, with the important matter coming at the end. This type of sentence is best adapted to fiction writing. It is used in news writing largely for variety.

The loose sentence, in which the facts are recorded simply and straightforwardly, is the reporter's workhorse.

LOOSE SENTENCE: Miss Selma Adele Ullman wrote two checks for $2,100 the day she was murdered in her fashionable Highland Park home at 3605 Mockingbird Lane. (This was the lead for the follow-up story. The murder, rather than the check writing, was featured in the first story, of course.)

PERIODIC SENTENCE: The day she was murdered in her fashionable Highland Park home at 3605 Mockingbird Lane, Miss Selma Adele Ullman wrote two checks for $2,100.

In the loose sentence, normal sentence order is followed: subject (*Miss Selma Adele Ullman*)—predicate (*wrote*)—object (*two checks*). Placed last are the minor details, which many readers will not bother to read in a follow-up story such as the one this lead was taken from. The periodic sentence would be all right in fiction, but the newspaper copydesk would probably blue-pencil it. Newspaper editors insist that you "put first things first" in most of the sentences you write.

Do you think a copy editor would pass the following sentence as the lead for a follow-up news story?

> Police Chief W. H. Naylor said Tuesday that Miss Selma Adele Ullman wrote two checks for $2,100 the day she was murdered in her fashionable Highland Park home at 3605 Mockingbird Lane.

The sentence would be turned down because the beginning is devoted to the minor detail that the police chief was the source of the information. The important news was *what* the police chief divulged.

In his zeal to put first things first, the journalist must not forget that the end of the sentence is also a good spot in which to place interesting or important information. If the sentence is not too long, the reader will read it through and will get this piece of information.

> Elimination of sex or robbery motives from the killing, he said, virtually removed male suspects.

The sentence ends with an idea that is as important as the idea which begins the sentence. This emphasis is achieved by placing the source of information—a minor detail—between the important ideas. Note how much weaker the sentence would be if *he said* were placed at the end of the sentence.

> WEAK: The questioning of the woman got negative results, as did the lie-detector test.

Why not shift the concluding phrase to the middle of the sentence, giving the sentence a stronger ending?

> BETTER: The questioning of the woman, as well as the lie-detector test, got negative results.

In the following sentence, likewise, the idea placed at the end should be tucked into the middle of the sentence.

> WEAK: The mayor will request the city council to raise parking meter rates in his first attempt to solve the downtown traffic problem.
> BETTER: The mayor, in his first attempt to solve the downtown traffic problem, will request the city council to raise parking meter rates.

The journalist should use the periodic sentence occasionally in news stories, and he should find much use for it in feature stories and editorials. In the following example observe that the periodic sentence, with the emphasis at the end, is more effective than a loose construction would be.

Walter Williams, as head of the committee in its fight, was able to state facts and to sell his idea to the mayor.

The next sentence was taken from an editorial. Note how the sentence builds to a climax.

So long as Texas agriculture is bankrupt in the sense that it can not stand alone without government control and subsidy, the supreme contribution of the A & M System will be to show Texas farmers and ranchers how to make a living from the yield of their own acres, *under their own efforts and with their own capital*.

The writer of the feature story from which the following sentence was taken used one of the most common devices for writing a periodic sentence—the introductory subordinate clause.

Although he was far beyond the regular age limit for membership in 20-30 International, Shimen's avid interest in the group's activities *led to his nomination as its first "honorary member and ambassador of good will."*

The periodic sentence given next comes from a feature article.

Though he has planned the make-up (makeup) of his newspaper every week for 36 years, the editor of The Watkins Glen Express has never seen his front page, *for since the age of eleven he has been totally blind.*

This periodic sentence builds to a forceful climax.

The following sentence illustrates how the reporter sometimes can give a news story lead emphasis at the end of the sentence.

A man who looked down on the earth from a height of some 16 miles today told how his tremendous momentum in a Douglas Skyrocket enabled him *to climb almost another one and one-half miles without fuel.*

The beginning of a news story lead must be interesting and important, but do not overlook any opportunities to make the end emphatic as well.

SUBORDINATION OF MINOR IDEAS

You have observed by now that emphasis is achieved by placing the main idea at the beginning or at the end of the sentence and by subordinating the minor ideas.

The subordination of minor ideas is achieved by placing the ideas in subordinate clauses or phrases. If you wish to be a first-rate writer, you must learn to use subordinate clauses and phrases correctly.

You have been warned to be careful that you subordinate the *minor* ideas, not the principal statement of the sentence. You have been given special warnings not to place the main idea in a clause beginning with *when* or *which*, or in an infinitive phrase or in a participial phrase. If you feel that you need to review subordinate clauses, turn back to Chapters 2, 3 and 11, and study the sections that deal with subordinate conjunctions. Then study these additional illustrations of good use of subordination of minor ideas.

The important idea may be at the beginning or at the end of the sentence. The minor idea is put into a subordinate clause or into a phrase.

> Control Data went ahead to file its suit against IBM because it became convinced that the Justice Department would not act. (The more important idea comes first, with the other idea placed in the subordinate clause.)
>
> Although he was considered one of the top university administrators in the nation, he simply could not deal with the rioting students. (The more important idea comes last, with the other idea subordinated in an introductory clause.)

Often it is better to use the shorter phrase rather than a subordinate clause to begin a sentence. Note these examples:

> After being in a coma for 24 hours, Wainwright died. (*Not:* Wainwright had been in a comma for 24 hours when he died. Don't subordinate his death.)
>
> Wainwright died after being in a coma for 24 hours. (*Not:* Wainwright lapsed into a coma, dying 24 hours later.)

Do not overlook the element of reader interest in determining what goes into the principal clause.

> The bank, which recently moved into its new building on Avenue E, plans to hold open house Tuesday.

The element of timeliness makes the idea of holding open house more important than the fact that the bank recently moved into the new building.

Do not hesitate to use the introductory subordinate clause—even in straight news stories—if you are sure that such a construction helps make your sentence more effective. Although the device can be employed in straight news leads on occasion, its more frequent use will be in the body of the story. This type of construction can help you give your writing variety.

(Turn to pages 208–13 for many examples of effective use of introductory subordinate clauses and also of introductory prepositional, participial and gerund phrases used adverbially.)

SEVEN WAYS TO OBTAIN EMPHASIS

Seven other main devices for obtaining emphasis in the sentence are: (1) use of the active voice rather than the passive voice; (2) repetition of words; (3) balancing ideas of equal importance; (4) use of parallel structure; (5) variety in sentence structure, especially in sentence beginnings and endings; (6) arrangement of a series of words, phrases or clauses in the order that builds to a climax; and (7) use of separate sentences for important ideas.

1. Note the use of the active rather than the passive voice to achieve emphasis.

> Foss *carried* the state by an overwhelming majority. (*Not:* Foss was elected by an overwhelming majority throughout the state.)
> Governor D. X. Buchanan *shot* and *killed* a burglar Friday night. (*Not:* An unidentified burglar was shot and killed by Governor D. X. Buchanan.)

Readers are far more interested in reading that their governor killed a man than they are in finding out that an unidentified burglar was shot.

2. What better example of the effectiveness of the repetition of words can be given than this excerpt from Lincoln's Gettysburg Address?

> . . . and that government of the people, by the prople, for the people shall not perish from the earth.

3. Emphasis is obtained by using both coordination and balance to give ideas of equal importance equal prominence in the sentence. Try balancing two clauses which are similar in construction and of about the same length. Join the clauses with a coordinating conjunction.

> "Get it first, *but* first get it right." (A press association slogan)
> The Tarheels could finish first, *or* they could finish last.

The balanced sentence should be used only occasionally, usually to emphasize two ideas that are strongly contrasted.

4. Parallel structure may be used to give equal emphasis to two or more similar ideas that are about equal in importance. However, to make sure that the sentence is both correct and effective, see that the parallel ideas are parallel in form. In other words, if one of the equal ideas is expressed by an infinitive phrase, then the other ideas need to be in infinitive phrases. Note the examples that follow.

> INCORRECT: Providing the city with more water, a possible solution of the airport taxicab dispute and how to combat pornography are three important problems the city council will consider tonight.

CORRECT: How to provide the city with more water, how to solve the airport taxicab dispute and how to combat pornography are three important problems. . . .

(For a review of parallel structure, turn back to pages 190–92.)

It is important, also, to maintain the same point of view throughout a sentence. You cannot make a sentence strong and effective if you confuse the reader with shifts in construction. Avoid unnecessary shifts in tense, number, person, subject, voice and mood. (For a review of consistency of structure, see pages 193–95.)

5. Emphasis through *variety* is a most important way to obtain emphasis—and, of course, to attract the attention of readers and to keep them reading. To be a successful writer, you must learn to vary the beginnings and even the endings of sentences and of paragraphs. And you need to use varied kinds of sentences of varied lengths. You will have thorough instruction in variety of sentence structure in the next chapter.

6. An effective sentence climax can sometimes be obtained merely by arranging events in the order of their importance.

CLIMATIC: He gambled recklessly and lost his friends, his family and finally his life.
WEAKER: Before he died he had lost both his family and his friends.

7. Certainly you will have no trouble seeing that the following sentence should be broken up into two or more sentences in which emphasis can be given to the main ideas.

A colorful array of exhibits—including antiques, paintings and leathercraft—will go on display in the Fine Arts Building, and a foods show will be held in the Women's Building, with judging in all events scheduled for 8 p.m. Saturday.

Note how much better the emphasis on the main ideas is in this revision:

A colorful array of exhibits—including antiques, paintings and leathercraft—will go on display in the Fine Arts Building for the three-day event. A foods show, featuring pies, cakes and cookies, will be held in the Women's Building. Judging of all events will take place at 8 p.m. Saturday.

The news writer should be particularly careful to separate any *direct quotations* he uses from important explanatory material. Study the following example:

You might say the Lone Star Steel Company dug into the pension files to build a top-notch fire department.
But Vice-President L. D. Webster puts it this way:

"We wanted experience—and got it. Back of the five veterans on our eight-man force are 160 years of fire-fighting know-how."

The inexperienced writer might have crowded into one paragraph the information contained in the three paragraphs. Such a crowded paragraph would be difficult to read and would not put the emphasis where it belongs— on the quotation. Look at another example, which shows the *wrong* way to do it:

"My baby is dead; my baby is drowned!" cried the young woman, Mrs. William A. Varnell of Arsenal, Ark., as she ran screaming to the curb, with an unconscious child in her arms, and stopped Mrs. Drake, who was driving along Grand. "Take us to the hospital."

See how an expert reporter separated the direct quotation from the explanatory material in handling this story:

Mrs. Drake was driving along Grand when a young woman with an unconscious child in her arms ran screaming to the curb and stopped her.
"My baby is dead, my baby is drowned!" cried the young woman, Mrs. William A. Varnell of Arsenal, Ark. "Take us to the hospital."

In using fairly long quotations, it is best to place *he said* or its equivalent in the middle of the sentence or paragraph, rather than at the end. (Some editors do not agree that attribution should be placed this far into a quote.)

"A hobo is a transient worker of varied occupations. So many people misconstrue the word," Zollner says. "It's used by the men themselves, but they sometimes resent others' using it, particularly when they are identified with tramps. These men don't want charity, but occasionally they may have to ask for it."

Note the position of *Zollner says*. Remember that you must not keep the reader in the dark too long as to the identity of the person speaking. (Placement of the attribution is treated in more detail on pages 255–56.)

In the report of a speech or in an interview, you should bring the name of the person quoted into your report often, particularly in a lengthy quotation.

QUIZ ANSWERS

1. Enforcement of the ordinance is impossible. Or: To enforce the ordinance is impossible. 2. Before he died he had lost his property, his friends and his family. (Build to a climax.) 3. The general died 24 hours after lapsing into a

coma. Or: The general, after lapsing into a coma, died 24 hours later. 4. The suspected robber was served with a John Doe warrant which the sheriff carried with him. Or: Taking along a John Doe warrant, the sheriff served it. . . . 5. Six firemen were seriously injured when the roof caved in. 6. Begin with the independent clause: A tavern owner died at 5:05 a.m. Thursday after he was shot six times. . . . 7. The boy was struck and killed at 8:45 p.m. Wednesday while running across the street near his home. 8. Begin with: If he wants his car back, the driver of the runaway car . . . clutched in hand, because Mrs. Price chained . . .

16

Variety of Expression

Variety is the spice not only of life but also of good writing. You can keep a reader reading by varying sentence structure and by using other devices to obtain variety in the expression of your ideas.

The subject of variety of sentence structure has been treated throughout this book. Remember that you can avoid monotonous writing in the following ways: (1) By varying the beginnings of sentences and of paragraphs; (2) by using varied kinds of sentences of varied lengths; (3) by using direct quotations; (4) by using fresh figures of speech; (5) by using simple, concrete words and action verbs.

In the first half of this chapter, then, you will be studying many examples of the five methods of obtaining variety in your writing, particularly examples of varying the beginnings of sentences. Many of the examples were taken from news leads and from the bodies of newspaper stories or articles. Included also are examples from magazine articles.

But learning to write with variety is not enough. You must write with correctness—with proper grammatical usage and with exactness, precision, accuracy and propriety. Writing with both variety and correctness will enable you not only to attract readers but also to hold them.

Before you begin your study of the methods of obtaining variety in your writing, test your comprehension of this most important subject by taking the first half of the test that follows. Then, in the second half of the test, which deals with correctness, rewrite the ten constructions to correct all errors in usage that you find.

QUIZ

In the following ten sentences you are to obtain variety in the beginnings of sentences by rewriting so as to use the type of rhetorical device called for:

1. Combine the two sentences and begin with a *present participle phrase:* Directors of the GI Transportation Company Thursday announced they would continue their fight to win a city taxicab franchise. They declared they had the cabs necessary to public operation.

2. Revise to begin with a *gerund:* Juan Mason's business is understanding people.

3. Revise to begin with an *infinitive phrase:* The PTA's chief goal has become bringing the home and the school closer together.

4. Combine the two sentences and begin with an *adverbial clause of concession*—a dependent clause: The number of deaths from Hong Kong influenza may rise sharply this week, City Health Officer Tav Lupton said. However, he feels that the epidemic is now under control.

5. Revise to begin with a *prepositional phrase:* L. M. Crandall Jr. engineered his way into the finals of the Public Links Golf Association championships today with a surprising upset of George Bennett. Crandall had a pinstriped railroad man's cap cocked on his blond head.

6. Combine the two sentences and begin with an *adverbial clause of cause:* Control Data went ahead last week to file suit against IBM. It filed because it had become convinced that the Justice Department would not act.

7. Revise to begin with an *adverbial subordinate clause of condition:* Transsexual tennis player Renee Richards said Sunday that she will start suing players if they continue to retire or default instead of playing her.

8. Combine the two sentences and begin with an *adverbial clause of time:* The astronauts' spaceship dashed ever nearer to home, and the three tired astronauts caught as much sleep as they could. They were resting for the critical reentry through the earth's atmosphere.

9. Revise to begin with a *past participial phrase:* A young man and his wife are in City-County Hospital today in critical condition. They were injured in saving their three-year-old baby from a speeding automobile.

10. Revise to begin with a *noun clause:* Police Chief Naylor said that what they first thought might be human hair under the fingernails of the murder victim turned out to be cat fur.

Rewrite the following sentences so as to eliminate stereotyped words and expressions (clichés); unnecessary slang; wordiness, especially circumlocutions; provincialisms; unacceptable colloquialisms; non-idiomatic expressions, including misused prepositions in phrases; jargon or gobbledygook; and vulgarisms.

11. At this point in time his outlook on life is quite different than his partner's.

12. He continued on for a half an hour until he met up with his brother.

13. They plan on going to the island soon, since the area is now free of disease.
14. All of a sudden the walls caved in, and despite the gallant efforts of the hook-and-ladder heroes, the hungry flames completely destroyed the warehouse.
15. With the agreement finalized, the two firms will now be merged together.
16. They sure would like to get on that TV show and win some loot.
17. "The state faces a serious crisis in the winter months," the rival of the incumbent governor declared prior to the election.
18. He couldn't of gone irregardless of the date set for the show.
19. Hardy dashed the hopes of the opposition when he tucked in the pigskin and scored standing up.
20. The police quickly threw out a dragnet. The drunk hit-and-run driver was caught around one hour later. He had a half-emptied bottle of hooch in his car. He was promptly booked and tossed into the jug.

VARYING THE BEGINNINGS OF SENTENCES

Although the lead for a straight news story most often begins with a noun (the subject), do not overlook the opportunity to begin with any other part of the sentence if it will get the attention of the casual reader. However, you should be sure to begin the lead with an idea or a fact which is an important and interesting element of the story, and no conscientious newspaper editor will permit you to forget that rule.

What has been said about the lead applies equally to other sentences in the story. Strive to give the majority of the sentences interesting beginnings.

The following rhetorical devices—grammatical beginnings—are used by the skillful writer to play up the features in the lead or in any sentence.

1. Beginning with a *noun* (subject).

A *mother* was killed yesterday in Albuquerque in a futile effort to save her five-year-old daughter from death under the wheels of an automobile.

The subject *mother* is modified by the article *a* in this lead. As far as possible, it is best to avoid using *the* or *a* or *an* in leads. If the article is needed, however, use it. Here the article is unnecessary:

Jurors also could have considered a probated sentence, since Ott's record apparently reflected no prior felony convictions.

Here are good examples of sentences beginning with nouns, the first having been the lead of an AP story:

Japanese explorer Naomi Uemura became the first person to reach the North Pole alone by dog sled Monday in a 500-mile, 57-day adventure delayed by a hungry polar bear, blizzards, ice floes and the pregnancy of one of his huskies.

Norman Lear thinks Washington is where the action—as well as the lights and cameras—is today.

2. Beginning with a *prepositional phrase*.

Of the nation's ten largest advertising agencies, Leo Burnett Co. is probably one of the corniest.

In the eight Son of Sam's attacks thus far, resulting in six deaths, the victims all have been young women or their escorts.

For hundreds of thousands, possibly millions of people, Son of Sam has shattered those assumptions.

With one vote to spare, the Senate ratified the Panama Canal treaty Tuesday, paving the way for return of the 40-mile waterway to the Republic of Panama.

After a decade of impressive gains in cleaning up the nation's air and water, the environmental movement is falling on hard times.

Despite two weeks of intensive research and interviews with thousands who attended the Legion convention, health officials remain puzzled about the cause of the disease. . . .

Before an audience that overflowed Municipal Hall Friday night, the rival candidates debated the issue of liquor by the drink.

Among the seizures of enemy stores was a cache of 3,200 rounds of heavy machine-gun ammunition, 82 mortar rounds and 2,700 pounds of rice.

As a judge on Hitler's dreaded wartime People's Court, Hans-Joachim Rehse signed 231 death sentences. (*As* is a preposition in this construction.)

3. Beginning with a *present participial phrase*.

Watching the vapor trails of MIG fighters about 30,000 feet below him, Powers had no doubt that the Soviets were determined to put an end to the U-2 missions.

In the foregoing sentence about Powers' U-2 mission, it would have been an error to write: Watching the vapor. . . feet below him, it was obvious to Powers that the Soviets were determined. . . . The participial phrase could not modify *it*, an expletive. The proper noun *Powers*, immediately following the participial phrase, is the only correct usage here.

Avoid the dangling participle! Be sure that any participial phrase you use properly modifies the noun or pronoun which follows the phrase. Don't write a sentence like this: "Falling down the elevator shaft, Smith's leg was broken." After all, Smith accompanied his leg in the fall.

Here are some other correct examples:

Confounding nearly all the experts, French voters have dealt a body blow to Socialist-Communist hopes to take control of the government.

"Attending Mr. Gibbs' Preparatory School for Boys in London, I learned how to survive by emphasizing the clumsy and comic aspects of my character," Ustinov said.

Passing and pounding in impressive fashion, Arizona State whipped Arizona, 23–7, and became the Western Athletic Conference representative in the Fiesta Bowl. (Note the use of the compound present participle *passing and pounding*.)

Starting with the Brazilian series, Stella used the most precise-looking of all materials, metal, to carry the paint.

Racing toward earth on a near-perfect course, the Apollo 8 astronauts were to splash down in the Pacific Ocean a thousand miles southwest of Hawaii Friday.

Arriving at the Brutons' home, De Mohrenschildt let himself in the rear gate and led Marina and Jeanne Oswald to the swimming pool.

4. Beginning with a *past participial phrase*.

Relieved of his severe neurotic symptoms, Brooks said he began to get some emotional maturity, though he was still hard-pressed financially.

Troubled by growing problems that include declining academic standards, more colleges are placing renewed emphasis on raising the quality of education.

Undaunted by such setbacks, feminist leaders say that they are emerging stronger than ever.

Assumed to represent the highest Soviet technology, the highly sophisticated and supersonic "Backfire" bomber has been reclassified (by the United States) in the proposed treaty.

Injured in saving their baby from an oncoming automobile, a young man and his wife are in critical condition in City-County Hospital today.

Note the use of the compound past participle in the following opening phrase:

Delayed by bad weather and half hidden by mist over the harbor, the 83,673-ton Queen Elizabeth arrived in New York late yesterday with 1,758 passengers.

Here is another example of the use of a compound past participle. We hope that other journalism students will not, like Donald Withers, assume that journalism is an "easy racket" offering easy riches!

Caught and *booked* on robbery charges for an attempted holdup, Donald Withers of New York City told police he was studying journalism "because it's an easy racket and I want some easy dough."

5. Beginning with an *infinitive phrase*.

To match the razzle-dazzle politicking of the premier, Quebec's Liberals had to set off some pre-election fireworks of their own.

Note that the infinitive phrase is used adverbially to modify the predicate *had to set off*. It plays up purpose by answering *Why*?

To write a biography of William Allen White took courage, for he left behind one of the great American autobiographies.

Note that this infinitive phrase is the subject of the verb *took*.

Remember that the infinitive phrase placed at the beginning of the sentence is used either as a *noun* or as an *adverb*. Note the following:

> *To believe in Christ* has always been, as Kierkegaard put it, an inexplicable leap of faith.

> *To emphasize his discontent with the U. S. stand*, (Prime Minister) Ecevit once again threatened to shut down U. S. bases and lower Turkey's contribution to NATO forces. (The infinitive phrase is used adverbially to modify the predicate *threatened*.)

The infinitive phrase that is used as an adverb must be set off with a comma. When the phrase is used as a noun, no comma is needed.

6. Beginning with a *noun clause*.

> *What was thought might be human hair under the fingernails of the murder victim* was cat fur, Police Chief Naylor said.

The entire noun clause *What was thought. . . of the murder victim* is the subject of the verb *was*.

Here are other good examples of the use of noun clauses to begin sentences:

> *That the traditional moral system in the United States still has widespread acceptance* was made clear in the survey.

> *What has caused the most confusion in the minds of consumers* is the split between the medical and nutrition professions over the Senate report.

> *Whether there will be a lessening of the tensions between the two under the premise that all's fair in love and politics or whether they would operate at arm's length* remains to be seen. (The compound noun clauses are the subject of *remains*.)

Avoid overuse of the noun clause to begin news leads. Some editors do not permit its use because it may make the lead run too long. Glance back at the last example. You can readily see that this sentence is too long to have been a news lead. But you will find you can use the noun clause effectively to begin sentences in the body of the news story, the feature article or the editorial.

If the beginning noun clause runs too long, it is better to break up the parts and make two sentences.

> AWKWARD: *That the United Nations could be used "to settle little conflicts that might grow into big ones" like the conflict between India and Pakistan but could not be used effectively to settle conflicts in which major nations were involved* was the senator's conclusion when he appeared before the committee Thursday.

> BETTER: The United Nations could be used "to settle little conflicts that might grow into big ones" like the conflict between India and Pakistan, but could not

be used effectively to settle conflicts in which major nations were involved. That was the conclusion reached by the senator when he appeared before the committee Thursday.

7. Beginning with a *subordinate adverbial clause of cause*.

Because it became convinced that the Justice Department would not act against IBM, Control Data went ahead to file its suit.

Since (Because) he didn't get his new suit back from the cleaners in time and was forced to get married in a "soiled and unkempt" gray ensemble, Thomas J. Mitchell of Shreveport has filed suit for $2,500 against the Shreveport Laundries, Inc., and its agent.

Often a phrase beginning with *Because* may be used rather than a cause clause. It is shorter, of course, and often just as effective as a clause: *Because of its size*, U.S. Steel has far less flexibility than its smaller counterparts. Another example: As a result (of the debate), lawmakers decided to take an alternative approach.

8. Beginning with a *subordinate adverbial clause of concession*.

Although nuclear-fueled power plants still enjoy an economic advantage in all but coal-producing regions, the cost of nuclear energy is far outpacing the general rate of inflation.

Though our satellites do a remarkable job of keeping an eye on the Soviet Union, they cannot look inside underground laboratories or elaborately camouflaged installations. . . .

While (Although) he was considered one of the top university administrators in the nation, he simply could not deal successfully with the rioting students.

Note that *While*, usually used to mean *at the same time as*, is used here in the sense of *Although*. Use it in this sense sparingly, and only as a *while* clause preceding a main clause.

9. Beginning with a *subordinate clause of condition*.

If players continue to retire or to default instead of playing her, transsexual tennis player Renee Richards said Sunday that she will begin to sue.

If they were gravely concerned about the amount the world is spending on ways to make war, most delegates were not showing it as they joked and laughed in the hallways and corridors of the United Nations.

Unless the situation is turned around soon, White House leadership could be damaged beyond repair, political experts agreed.

And note this effective use of a conditional clause in the lead of a newspaper feature story:

If the young chick hatched by a Rhode Island hen in the back yard of Ernest Horn, 4141 Odessa Street, grows to maturity, it will be able to furnish four drumsticks for the dinner table.

10. Beginning with a *subordinate clause of time*.

Before he was the night-stalking "Son of Sam," convicted mass murderer David Berkowitz, according to a detailed diary he kept, roamed city streets, setting some 2,000 fires as the "Phantom of the Bronx."

When the prisoner comes to the rehabilitation program, he has to wean himself from the high-voltage jolts he got out of crime to a steady current of satisfactions from self-respect and responsible living.

While investigators today sought the cause of an Army air tragedy on Hawk Mountain, authorities at Davis Monthan Airfield at Tucson reported that three of 12 persons killed in the crash had been identified definitely.

As their spaceship dashed ever nearer to home, the three tired astronauts caught as much sleep as they could, resting for the critical reentry through the earth's atmosphere.

As far back as written records exist, people are described as dying suddenly while in the throes of fear, rage, grief, humiliation or joy.

Since Robert Lee Pauling was born five days ago, there are now five generations living and present in the baby's family.

Often a time phrase, rather than a time clause, may be used effectively and usually with a saving of space.

Less than a week before that gathering, Don Bolles, an investigative reporter for The Arizona Republic and an IRE member, was killed by a bomb planted in his car in Phoenix.

For the second straight year, the Seattle Mariners will be hosts to the American League's season opener when they entertain the Minnesota Twins April 5.

About once a month, reporters and editors at The New York Times receive a single-sheet homegrown bulletin that praises some of them and damns others. The praised are named; the damned are granted anonymity.

Make sure that you know how to punctuate introductory subordinate clauses and phrases.

A *comma* is needed to set off introductory subordinate cause clauses, concessional clauses, conditional clauses and time clauses.

A *comma* is used after a beginning present participial phrase and after a beginning past participial phrase.

A *comma* is needed with an infinitive phrase used adverbially but not with an infinitive phrase used as the subject.

Unless they run very long or need a comma after them for clarity, introductory prepositional phrases do not need a comma. Such a sentence as this would require one to avoid confusion: "After a few years in Washington, politicians can detect. . . ."

An introductory noun clause that is used as the subject of the verb is not followed by a comma.

There are other types of grammatical beginnings which may be used by the journalist. Most of these devices can be easily overused, especially in the writing of leads, where they should be used only for special effect or for the purpose of giving variety to your writing. But much use can be made of most of these devices in the bodies of stories and articles, primarily to obtain variety in the beginnings of sentences and paragraphs.

11. Beginning with a *gerund*.

> *Running* is the newest treatment for depression.
> *Changing a criminal's thought patterns* is a long and tedious process.

The gerund *Running* is the subject of *is*, and the gerund phrase *Changing a criminal's thought patterns* is the subject of *is*.

Note the use of the compound gerund in the next sentence:

> *Planning and constructing a nuclear plant* takes 10 to 12 years. Some take much longer.

And here's a magazine article lead in which a gerund is used as the subject and another gerund used as the object of the preposition *like* in the first clause:

> *Tracking down the Hobo King* was like *stalking Santa Claus;* it allowed me the rare luxury of believing in a myth as big as Paul Bunyan and Johnny Appleseed.

12. Beginning with a *nominative absolute*.

> *Her right hand still paralyzed from a snakebite,* 13-year-old Fay Nolan fondled the rattlesnake which had bitten her while 6,000 persons watched atop Little Black Top Mountain.

The nominative absolute is a phrase, you will recall, in which a noun precedes the participle, as in *hand . . . paralyzed*. The nominative absolute is used like a participial phrase and modifies the noun or the pronoun that follows it. The journalist will not use the nominative absolute often.

13. Beginning with a *verb*.

> *Look* for both exports and imports to rise appreciably in 1979. A major trading partner will be Japan.
> *Shed* a tear for the Dolphin Dolls, the pretty teen-aged girls who are cheerleaders for the Miami Dolphins football team. (A news story lead)

14. Beginning with an *adjective*.

> Lyle contributes more than a game-saving arm and savvy coolness to his team's success. *Exuberant and free-spirited,* he deflates tension with a variety of practical jokes.
> *Subdued and pleasant,* Stans fitted into the sprawling Department of Commerce as unobtrusively as a wastebasket.

Jubilant over their long-sought World Series victory, the Yankees whooped it up in the locker room.

A huge, shambling, genial man with massive double chin, large red nose and an undisciplined thatch of white hair, he looks like a caricature of the cigar-waving, ham-fisted "old pol." But Thomas P. "Tip" O'Neill Jr., speaker of the House of Representatives, proves that appearance can be deceptive.

15. Beginning with an *adverb*.

Suddenly the hold-up man pulled a pistol and fired three shots at the liquor store manager.

Yet another "Howard Hughes will" has surfaced, and an exasperated judge recessed the "Mormon will" trial in Los Angeles until after the holidays.

Actually, much of the work overseen by the corps is military only in a technical sense.

Finally, the Saudis are deeply concerned about Soviet activities in areas close to their kingdom.

Still later, the confession continued, the aunt watched doctors cut open the body for the autopsy that revealed the presence of arsenic.

Now and then her face twitched and she swallowed, but she held her composure until the verdict was rendered.

Then the wounded general, caked with dust, climbed out of the Jeep without help.

Meanwhile, doubts about some new uses for computers are being raised inside the bureaucracy itself. (The adverb *Meanwhile* is used here as a *transitional* word. For a review of this popular device, see pages 167–69.)

16. Beginning with a *pronoun*.

None of his three quarterbacks has played a minute of a varsity game.

This caused small steering rockets to fire and send the spacecraft into the uncontrolled roll.

Many called him Der Bingle, The Ol'Groaner, but for half a century those who knew him well thought of him as King Bing, entertainer supreme.

That would give the astronauts a chance to fly up to the station late next year and attach a small rocket to it.

Those who oppose selling warplanes to the Arabs want each sale considered individually, on the theory that Congress would find it easier to reject an Arab arms deal not tied to new arms for Israel.

You can't win for losing in this tough league.

17. Beginning with an *expletive*.

Although journalists should be careful not to overuse the expletive, they will find the expletive beginning effective at times.

It was the first time a woman had been executed in Alabama.

There is, however, a common thread that runs through the private non-profit sector: a belief in being of service to one's community and other people, without relying on government and without any expectation of personal profit.

> *It's* not uncommon for returning graduates to make long journeys back to their
> school reunions. But Sally and Richmond Curtis did it the hard way—they
> walked 130 miles.
> It was five years ago Sunday that Patricia Campbell Hearst, screaming and
> half-naked, began an odyssey of terror and mystery that baffled the nation.
> *There's* only one way to do it.

And how could we phrase it any other way than: *It* was the night before
Christmas.

18. Beginning with a *conjunction*.

Grammarians used to condemn the use of the coordinating conjunctions *and*
and *but* to introduce sentences. Then they yielded a bit by saying it might be
permissible to begin with *And* or *But* if the conjunction was set off by a
comma. *But* today it is popular practice to begin sentences with *And* and *But*.
And now you are warned *not* to use the comma after these introductory
conjunctions, unless the comma is needed for clarity.

> *And* Coach Sutton in defeat had some kind words as well for Rose. "I've always
> felt he was one of the most underrated players in the league. . . ."
> *But* the central role of organized labor remains collective bargaining.
> *And*, the more we spend, the more we compound what has come to be known as
> the welfare mess. (Note that the comma is needed here for clarity.)

VARYING THE BEGINNINGS OF PARAGRAPHS

For the journalist, the *beginning* of a paragraph—like the beginning of a
sentence—is the most important part.

Naturally, you cannot get the most important part (idea or fact) of every
paragraph into the first line or two. However, you must strive to do this as far
as possible. You must make the opening of every paragraph interesting if you
expect the reader to go on with your story. Try, then, to begin each paragraph
with an arresting fact or idea—if not with the most important fact or idea—
and then devote the remainder of the paragraph to building the details.

Use *key words* to begin as many paragraphs as possible. Newspaper
readers, remember, read silently and hurriedly. Just as they may fail to finish
many sentences, they may fail to finish even more paragraphs. Avoid
beginning paragraphs, as far as possible, with the articles *the, a* and *an* or
with the expletives *there* and *it* or with the prepositional phrase *according to*.

Use the greatest possible variety of grammatical beginnings for paragraphs,
just as you do for sentences. Variety in paragraph beginnings, in fact, is even
more important than variety in sentence beginnings. You will use the subject
for paragraph beginnings more often than any other kind of grammatical
beginning, just as in beginning sentences; but give the reader as much variety
as you can manage.

Of course, you know that you must keep paragraphs short if you are writing for newspapers. Because you can get only five to six words in a narrow newspaper column, and as lengthy paragraphs will slow up and discourage the hurried newspaper reader, newspaper journalists must write shorter paragraphs than magazine journalists or book writers. They will find themselves writing many one-sentence paragraphs.

Remember that the paragraph is used simply as a mechanical, visual device to break up the subject matter into units and to facilitate reading. Because unity is desired in the paragraph, this may best be obtained by confining the paragraph to one idea or fact, rather than to two or more. Thus, the writer will achieve better unity by keeping paragraphs short.

You were told earlier that *transitional devices* must not be overworked in news writing, but you should not hesitate to use a transitional word, phrase or sentence that is needed to tie a paragraph to a preceding paragraph or paragraphs. Use the transitional device to begin a paragraph whenever you feel that the meaning otherwise would not be clear to your readers.

Only one word may be needed to make the transition clear. In the following example, note how the use of *Meanwhile* helps the reader to move easily from one paragraph to another:

> Airport opponents of the Concorde will meet Friday night to discuss ways they can protest Concorde service to and from Dallas-Fort Worth Airport.
> *Meanwhile,* the Dallas and Fort Worth City Councils said they would consider complaints from residents of the airport area and from others protesting that the supersonic jetliner exceeds the legal noise level on landings and takeoffs.

A prepositional phrase may be used to make the transition clear:

> *In addition,* Mayor Johnson will ask the Council to visit the airfield and look over the situation.

Note how the use of transitional expressions, along with other interesting paragraph beginnings, in a report of William Anthony Toomey's winning of the Olympic decathlon makes it easier for the reader to continue with the story.

> Of all Olympic competition, *the decathlon* most closely reflects the original Greek ideal of all-around athletic excellence.
> *An entire track and field meet in miniature,* its ten events in two days add up to the toughest individual test of speed, stamina, strength and spirit ever devised.
> The man who wins the Olympic decathlon well deserves to be known as the finest athlete in the world.
> *That man* last week was William Anthony Toomey, a 29-year-old schoolteacher from Santa Barbara, Calif., who not only captured the gold medal but set an Olympic record in the process.

Toomey modestly insists that "behind every good decathlon man there's a good doctor," and indeed the demands of the brutal competition are enough to strain the strongest body.

Meanwhile, Kurt Bendlin, West Germany's world record holder, arrived in Mexico City complaining of two sore knees and tendonitis in one elbow. Toomey had a pulled hip muscle for which he was being treated with cortisone.

Even so, in the first test, the 100-meter dash, Toomey hit the tape in 10.4 seconds, best time for the day. . .

Then, a soaring 25-ft. 9¾-in long jump, best of Toomey's career, gave him another 994 points and kept him in the lead.

After that, a poor 45-ft. 1¼ in. shotput and a disappointing 6-ft 4¾ in. high jump dropped him to second behind East Germany's Joachim Kirst.

Next came the grinding 400-meter run, and after ten straight hours of competition, Toomey somehow managed to sprint the distance in 45.6 sec.

It was the fastest time ever recorded in the decathlon and it put him back in the lead as the first day ended.

The second day's competition began with the 110-meter hurdles. . .

Now the gold medal was riding on the last event, the 1500-meter run. If he could beat Toomey by 10 sec. or so, Bendlin could still win.

But Bendlin never came close . . .

Gasping in the thin air, every muscle rubbery with fatigue, Toomey led all but a few strides of the way and drove to victory by 30 yards . . . "That was the worst competition I've ever been in," said Toomey. "I've never had to endure anything so intense. They shouldn't call this the Olympic Games. It's not a game out there."

VARYING THE KINDS OF SENTENCES

The journalist's workhorse is the declarative sentence, but he should use interrogative, imperative and exclamatory sentences occasionally to give his writing variety. Note these examples:

1. Using *interrogative sentences*.

What has happened to Fitzgerald as a result of his testimony? In late 1969, after his name was out of the headlines, the Air Force fired him.

Is it really true that a "defeatist consensus" is preventing the United States from making adequate response to the global challenge of the Soviet Union?

What are little atoms made of? Nothing to be afraid of! Neutrons, protons and little electrons. That's what little atoms are made of.

Do you feel tired? Run down? Have you tried blood? The folks down at Kenya, Africa, have, and it works fine.

Note the effective use of a series of questions in the last example.

2. Using *imperative sentences*.

Just lie in bed, pick up your telephone receiver and hear a Sunday morning sermon by your favorite pastor.

Relax! Kick off your shoes and stretch out on the sofa some Sunday afternoon. Wriggle your toes if you want to, but don't go to sleep.

Note that the second of these imperative sentences may be classed as exclamatory also.

3. Using *exclamatory sentences.*

Earthquakes to order! That's the business of Geophysical Service, Inc., and Saturday it had a new half-million-dollar instrument with which to do the job.

Don't push the call button! The sudden *ping* in the cockpit might startle the jet hijacker and provoke him to fire his pistol.

You might save a life—and it may be yours!

One of the most effective ways to obtain variety in your writing is to use a judicious mixture of simple, complex, compound and compound-complex sentences. The newspaper writer will find himself using the simple sentence most often, followed by the complex, the compound and the compound-complex sentences, in that order. Just be sure to mix them up!

The effective use of a variety of sentence forms—with interesting sentence and paragraph beginnings—is shown in the analysis of a feature story on pages 219–23.

USING DIRECT QUOTATIONS

The use of *direct quotations* is popular in journalistic writing. Study news stories and features written by top-ranking journalists and note how they obtain variety by this device.

In the sentences that follow, observe how the use of a direct quotation at the beginning of a sentence is likely to capture the attention of the reader.

"Bing always believed that the best possible cure for any kind of personal trouble was to keep yourself busy," she (Kathryn Crosby) said. "So that is what the children and I will be doing for a long time to come. I have to work, I have to. I go crazy if I do nothing."

"The child is just as dead as if the crime had been committed by a man," the governor told newsmen in announcing that he had rejected Mrs. Dennison's final plea for mercy. "The law does not contemplate any difference between a man or woman convicted of murder."

Note in each of the two examples that the source of the quotation was placed in the middle of the quotation. Remember that you should not give too much of the quotation before letting the reader know the source of the excerpt.

It is possible to obtain variety by putting the source first occasionally.

After he had passed sentence, the judge paused just a few seconds.
And then he said: "God have mercy upon your soul."

Putting the quotation first in a separate paragraph may be effective, but this device should be used sparingly.

"I'll take him in the third round!"
That was the boast made today by Muhammad Ali concerning his title bout with Leon Spinks.

Let's look at an example of *misplacement* of the source in a story that appeared in a metropolitan newspaper. Sen. James Abourezk, D-S.D., was quoted as saying that "the agreement was not reached by mutual concession since the president, in the middle of the bargaining process, deserted the American consumers and joined the other side."

The following paragraph read: "I and a number of my colleagues who have fought against deregulation for many years are willing to agree on this bill because we feel it is the best we can get and we believe the nation and the world are looking to us for leadership in resolving our national energy policy," said Rep. Harley Staggers, D-W.Va., chairman of the conference committee.

Few readers could have guessed that it was not Abourezk, but **another** representative who was being quoted, since Staggers' name does not **appear** until the very end of the lengthy, confusing quotation.

The use of quotations to obtain variety is the only device not employed in the feature story that we will analyze next.

ANALYZING A FEATURE STORY

Here is an example of a brilliantly written feature story. The writer was Louis Cook Jr. and the piece appeared in *The Des Moines Register*. Cook is now with *The Detroit Free Press*.

We will use the story to review methods of obtaining variety in sentence structure by varying the grammatical beginnings of sentences and paragraphs, by using different kinds of sentences of varied lengths, by using simple, concrete words and by using fresh figures of speech. The author's figures of speech are italicized.

S.U.I. ATOM BUSTER NEARLY READY
By Louis Cook Jr.
(Register Staff Writer)

(1) Iowa City, Ia.—Deep in the earth just east of the physics building on the State University of Iowa campus, scientists are preparing to give an atom the surprise of its life.

(2) The final phase in the construction of the University's new $23,000 device to bust atoms now is under way.

(3) Since the golden age of Greece the atom has been a subject for guessing and theorizing, and it still remains one of the enigmas of modern physics.

(4) Within a few months, researchers at the state university will be able to take an atom apart, see what makes it do the things it does, and, perhaps, put it back together.

(5) The atom buster is *an unromantic-looking job of plumbing, resembling an overgrown water heater* more than anything else.

(6) Made of inch-thick boiler plate, it rests in an underground concrete vault connected to the basement of the physics building by a zigzag tunnel *somewhat like the entrance to a world war dugout*.

(7) It's 50 feet over-all in length, 8½ feet in diameter. *Two grown men could run foot-races in it*. At either end is a round door of 3-inch-thick steel, held in place by 32 1¼-inch bolts.

(8) It takes a substantial piece of apparatus to bust up something that for centuries has been regarded as the smallest possible subdivision of matter.

(9) Thirty thousand volts of direct current, produced by an ordinary transformer and rectifier system, will start things going in the atom buster.

(10) An ordinary 22-inch-wide woven cotton belt, *like those used on a threshing machine*, will run on pulleys from one end of the apparatus to the center.

(11) A positive charge of electricity will be placed on the end of the moving belt by *a business that looks like a rake with the handle removed*. Electrons will be sprayed on the belt *just like water from a lawn-sprinkler*.

(12) The belt will carry the charges to the center of the buster. There another rake proposition, oppositely charged, will hold the electrons back, *as a dam stores up water*.

(13) When the mass of electrons becomes great enough—about five million volts worth—they will then flow onto a piece of metal in a 22-foot-long vacuum tube *similar to a regular radio tube except in size*.

(14) That's where the fun begins. The number of volts in an electrical circuit *is the same thing as the number of pounds of pressure behind the flow from a water faucet*. Volts are merely a measure of electrical pressure.

(15) When an electron is kicked down the 22 feet of empty space in the vacuum tube by five million volts, it's really traveling. Electrically charged plates surrounding the path of the electronic beam will keep it moving along.

(16) The electrons stream into the far end of the atom buster *like a watermelon seed squirted out from the fingers of a small boy*—but at an inconceivable speed.

(17) What will happen when this stream of electrons beats upon a substance placed in its path is anybody's guess, but previous experience with a lower-powered device at the university indicates many possibilities.

(18) For one thing, X rays, neutrons, alpha rays and beta rays *will spray out like sawdust when a saw whirls into a log*.

(19) Observers, peering through a periscope arrangement working through a water-filled six-inch pipe extending into a chamber 40 feet away, won't see much.

(20) But delicate counters will record the number and distribution of the rays emitted.

(21) An atom is made up *like a solar system.* In the center is *something like our sun, of great mass—the nucleus.* Around it revolve the electrons, *as the earth revolves about the sun.*

(22) Electrons will be ripped away from the orbits they have held since the beginning of things. Nuclei will be driven from their complacent positions *as heads of little universes.*

(23) Actually, sodium will be changed into magnesium; platinum to gold—but not lead into gold. . .[1]

First, note that there is great *variety in the grammatical beginnings of paragraphs and sentences.* Grammatical beginnings for paragraphs alone include the following: adverbs (1, 23); prepositional phrases (3, 4, 18); past participle phrase (6); pronouns (7, 14); expletive (8); adjectives (9, 10); subordinate clauses of time (13, 15); noun clause (17); subjects (19, 22); and conjunction (20).

You will note that seven paragraphs in the story do begin with articles (*a, an, the*)—which are not regarded as interest-arousing words. However, remember that the journalist must begin many paragraphs—and sentences—with articles. As long as the journalist strives to begin a *maximum* number of paragraphs and sentences with something other than an article, he will not draw the ire of the editor. In the story, Louis Cook has given the reader plenty of variety in paragraph and sentence beginnings.

Second, check the *variety in sentence lengths.* The lead is the longest sentence—as is often the case in news writing. It runs 31 words. The opening sentence in. the fourteenth paragraph is the shortest—six words, counting the contraction as two words. You will find sufficient variety in sentence length.

Third, note the *variety of sentence forms.* The reporter followed the advice of the readability experts in making maximum use of the *simple* sentence. Of the 33 sentences in that part of the story which is quoted, 22 sentences—two-thirds of the sentences used—are *simple.*

Also, note that the next most commonly used type of sentence is the *complex* sentence—not the compound. Eight complex sentences are used, unless you want to call the sentence composing paragraph 5 a complex rather

---

[1] Reprinted by permission of *The Des Moines Register and Tribune*, Des Moines, Iowa. (Italics and paragraph numbers are the editor's.)

than a simple sentence by reading into it some words that are not there. Only two *compound* sentences appear and, as you might expect, but one *compound-complex* sentence.

You are urged to check the sentence forms used, which may be easily done by following this numbering system. Where a paragraph contains but one sentence, the sentence is given the number of that paragraph: where two or more sentences make up a paragraph, each sentence is given the paragraph number plus an *a, b* or *c* designation.

Simple sentences: 1, 2, 4, 5, 6, 7a, 7b, 7c; 9, 10, 11b, 12a, 14a, 14b, 14c, 15b, 16, 19, 20, 21a, 21b, and 22b. Complex sentences: 8, 11a, 12b, 13, 15a, 18, 21c and 22a. Compound sentences: 3 and 23. Compound-complex: 17.

When you first look at the sentence making up paragraph 16, you may be inclined to classify it as something other than a simple sentence. As you analyze it, however, you will note that the lengthy expression modifying atom-buster is composed of a prepositional phrase (like a watermelon seed), followed by a participle (squirted), followed by a prepositional phrase (from the fingers), which in turn is modified by another prepositional phrase (of a small boy); and you will find that the conjunction *but* is followed not by a clause buy by a prepositional phrase. This sentence, then, is a good illustration of the use of phrases rather than independent and dependent clauses. Such usage usually makes for tighter writing, and remember that any editor will bless the reporter who saves newspaper space.

The use of phrases rather than clauses usually will save space, but not always. In the sentence being analyzed, for example, the use of the dependent clause "that a small boy squirts out from his fingers" would run no longer than the three phrases "squirted out from the fingers of a small boy." However, Cook apparently felt that the participial construction "squirted out" sounded more natural as a modifier of *watermelon seed* than a relative clause introduced by the pronoun "that."

Of course the use of a series of phrases can be overdone. Writers certainly should avoid the practice of stringing together so many phrases that the writing becomes choppy and sing-songy. One of the best ways to save space and to provide flowing narrative is to eliminate some prepositional phrases by using the object of the preposition as a direct modifier. For example, the phrases "from the fingers of a small boy" could have been shortened to "from a small boy's fingers."

Saving space by the use of phrases instead of clauses is well illustrated in many of the other simple sentences in the story. For example, you should note in paragraph 2 that an infinitive (to bust) is used rather than a dependent clause, such as *that will be used to bust atoms*. In paragraph 4 the writer uses a triple predicate, rather than three independent clauses, to save space. In the sixth paragraph, the introductory past participle phrase not only gives the sentence an interesting beginning but takes less space than a subordinate clause like: (The atom buster) *which is made of inch-thick boiler plate.* Note the use of a past participle phrase at the end of paragraph 7, rather than the use of a space-wasting subordinate clause like: *which is held in place.* A prepositional phrase used appositively in the middle of 10 is very effective and saves space. In 12 note the use of the phrase *oppositely charged* in place of a subordinate clause. Finally, notice how space is saved in paragraph 23 by dropping the verb from the last two clauses: *platinum to gold–but not lead into gold.*

Fourth, observe that the reporter does not begin *every* sentence in the story with the most important or most interesting idea. Some of the sentences are periodic, rather than loose, in their construction; that is, *they build to a climax.* The lead itself in paragraph 1 is an excellent illustration of the periodic sentence. "Deep in the earth just east of the physics building on the State University of Iowa campus, scientists are preparing to give an atom the surprise of its life."

The sentence that makes up the third paragraph of the story is another good example of the periodic sentence, and one of the best examples in the story is sentence 4. "Within a few months, researchers at the state university will be able to take an atom apart, see what makes it do the things it does and, perhaps, put it back together."

USING FIGURES OF SPEECH

In Cook's story on the University of Iowa's atom buster you surely observed that much of the superior quality of this piece of writing resulted from the reporter's deft use of figures of speech.

Remember that the four elements of writing style are words, sentences, paragraphs and figures of speech.

In case you have forgotten, the main figures of speech are simile, metaphor and personification.

SIMILE: The boy was as nervous as a cat on a windy day.

A *simile* is an expressed comparison. In the sentence above, the word *as* expresses the fact that the boy's nervousness is being compared to a cat's. Here's another one: As subtle as a sailor with a six-hour pass.

METAPHOR: Before his first solo flight, he had butterflies in his stomach.

A *metaphor* is an implied comparison. Reading the example, you will find that a disturbed, uneasy feeling is being compared to butterflies in the stomach. The comparison is implied, that is, not plainly stated, because the word *as* or *like* is not used to signal the comparison. Here's a second example: To the ski novice a molehill is a mountain.

PERSONIFICATION: The dishes in the sink cast dirty looks in my direction.

Personification consists in speaking of an abstract quality or an object as if it were a human being. Here's another one: Streaks of light probed from room to room and dived under chairs and tables like thieves.

Original and appropriate figures of speech will contribute clearness, concreteness, vividness and conciseness to your writing. Well-chosen figures of speech help the reader to grasp ideas quickly because they present a new idea by comparing it with something with which the reader is familiar.

In writing about the atom-buster, Cook was aware that he was dealing with a highly complicated apparatus which hardly anyone could have seen and about which readers knew little or nothing. He knew that he could not use the technical terms of the scientests. Therefore, he employed figures of speech profusely, likening the parts of the atom-buster and its functions to things familiar to most readers.

Note how he did this with such figures of speech as the following: "resembling an overgrown hot water heater"; "like those used on a threshing machine"; "a business that looks like a rake with the handle removed"; "similar to a radio tube except in size"; "like a watermelon seed squirted out from the fingers of a small boy"; "made up like a solar system"; "as the earth revolves about the sun."

You can't become a first-class writer like Mr. Cook, who today is with *The Detroit Free Press*, until you learn to use expertly the fourth element of writing style, the *figure of speech*. However, writers must avoid using figures of speech that are trite, incongrous or mixed:

> He was sly as a fox. (Trite)
> The strains of music fell upon the ear like a soothing poultice. (Incongrous)
> The manager's torrent of abuse was the last straw for the players. (Mixed)

In our analysis we have considered the handling of sentences in great detail. We have not devoted much attention to the development of paragraphs, but it will be well for the student to note how cleverly Cook manages these larger elements. There is sufficient variety in paragraph length, for instance; yet no paragraph is too long. In fact, sixteen of the twenty-three paragraphs are composed of single sentences.

The last thing to note about Cook's excellent story is its vocabulary. The most casual reading of the piece will convince the student that the words used by this reporter are sharp and vigorous. The subject of words is so important that it is worth close attention.

USING SIMPLE, CONCRETE WORDS

Many excellent English textbooks that stress diction are available. You will do well to read some of them and to refer frequently to an unabridged dictionary, a thesaurus and a book of synonyms. The journalist must never stop developing his vocabulary; every year brings new words into our language.

Using Simple Words

The readability experts stress the use of *simple words*. You must follow their advice in most straight news writing, but you must not write *down* to the reader. The educational level of the average reader is rising, and his *reading* vocabulary is larger than his *speaking* vocabulary. But don't use words that are beyond the comprehension of the average reader, because he seldom will bother to keep a dictionary beside him as he reads his newspaper. If you must use a word that is big or technical, explain it to the reader; in other words, do a bit of interpretative reporting.

On the whole, then, you must use a simple vocabulary for clearness. Can you find in the atom-buster story a single word that the average newspaper reader would not comprehend? I doubt it. And this story deals with a highly technical subject.

Using Specific, Concrete Words and Action Verbs

In addition to using words that are clear to the reader, you should strive to use *specific, concrete words*—not general, abstract words. For example, don't use the verb *said* if the man actually *exclaimed, shouted, bellowed, thundered, ranted*—or perhaps *whispered*. Be sure, of course, that the person *did* shout or bellow or thunder or whisper before you use a synonym for said. Newspaper editors and press associations call the forms of the verb *to say* the most serviceable words in the journalist's language. You will use *says* or *said* far more often than you will use synonyms for this verb, but don't fail to employ the specific and more concrete term where it is appropriate.

Instead of using the general term *walked,* you should use, if appropriate, such specific, concrete verbs as: *strode, hurried, raced, dashed, strutted, strolled, limped, shuffled* and so on.

Observe that the verbs suggested here are not only specific and concrete, but also are *action verbs*. Why not have the speaker *hurry* (not *walk hurriedly*) to the podium, and have him *thunder* his message—if he actually thundered? You won't need adverbs like *hurriedly* if you use forceful, active verbs.

In the atom-buster story, note that Cook made effective use of verbs and verbals that are not only *concrete* and *specific*, but which also show action. Check these, in the indicated paragraphs: (8) *to bust up;* (11) will be *sprayed;* (12) *stores;* (15) is *kicked;* (16) *squirted;* (17) *beats;* (18) will *spray;* (19) *peering;* (21) *revolve(s)*: (22) will be *ripped* away, will be *driven.*

Take advantage of *audio-active* verbs whenever possible, advises Lucile Vaughan Payne in *The Lively Art of Writing.* Instead of writing in the passive voice "Thunder was heard in the mountains," make it "Thunder *growled* in the mountains." Now you have the subject acting. It's doing the thing that thunder does, points out Payne. It could also *grumble* or *rumble* or even *snarl,* depending upon the kind of thunder-sound it is. Nobody cares about thunder that "was heard." Give the reader thunder he can hear, that may even make him jump. Sound is a sign of life and movements. Transmit it with audio-active verbs at every opportunity, urges Payne.

But journalists, of course, must be selective in their use of action and audio-active verbs. Their use in straight news reporting may be somewhat limited. Sports reporters and columnists probably have the greatest freedom in using them, because they are covering *action.* Reporters covering crime also will make good use of action verbs. And, certainly, the action verb may be used most effectively in writing feature stories and feature articles.

The nouns you use should also be concrete and specific. You will most often call a house a house, to be sure, but there may be times when you could appropriately use such words as *shack, shanty, lean-to, cabin, bungalow, duplex, apartment house, mansion* and so on.

The readability experts also advise the use of a maximum number of human-interest words. *Human-interest words* are words that appeal to the emotions. Grammarians would say that such words are those that are used for their *connotation,* which is defined as the suggestive emotional content or significance which a word has in addition to its explicit literal meaning. Words like *mother, sweetheart, home* and *Old Glory* are simple examples of words that have rich connotations for different readers.

USING CORRECT WORDS

Journalists, whether working for newspapers or magazines or for the electronic media, must be careful in their choice of words, especially in regard to correctness, clearness, variety and effectiveness. Use of diction that is correct and clear is most important. To make sure their writing is both clear and correct, journalists writing for newspapers need to write primarily for average, middle-class readers who are educated but not intellectual. That level of writing will be adequate, at least, for highly educated readers, many of whom take *The New York Times* or *The Wall Street Journal* as a supplement to their local newspapers. Also, editorials and columns, together with interpretative or investigative reporting, certainly will appeal to this group of readers as well as to middle-class readers.

Because readers of magazines vary from the select, highly educated group to those who have less than an average education, writers must be careful to choose words that fit the audience of the particular magazine they are writing for—learned words for the highly educated, common words that are clear for the average reader, and short, simple words for the reader with a less-than-average education.

Journalists in television and radio may choose words much as do newspaper journalists. However, because broadcasters work with spoken language, they are permitted more freedom, particularly in the use of colloquialisms—expressions that may be correctly used in informal conversation or informal writing but which are not appropriate in formal literary writing for magazines and newspapers.

Always keep in mind the class and the educational level of the readers or viewers or listeners you are trying to reach—and use words that they can understand without necessarily having to go to the dictionary. But don't allow your writing to be patronizing toward any group.

Not only must your writing be clear, but it must be correct, exact and effective.

As a living language, English is constantly changing. For example, much of what used to be identified in dictionaries as slang is now accepted.

Journalists know, of course, that there are several standards of diction. Generally recognized today are three levels of usage: formal English, informal English and the Vulgate (substandard). Formal English is usually written and is used in scholarly works, business letters, and so on. Informal English, both written and spoken, is used by literate persons carrying on their daily activities. This is the diction that most journalists will use. The Vulgate—the substandard—is used mostly by uneducated persons and illiterates.

Journalists must recognize that there are kinds of expressions that must not be used, that there are some which usually must be avoided and that there are other types of usage that are acceptable when appropriate to the situation, to the medium and for the audience.

Journalists, therefore, should refer when necessary to a current dictionary or to an up-to-date stylebook to determine the level of usage for a word or an expression.

An entire new section on the usage of words, to be found as a Glossary of Usage on pages 289–299, should be most helpful. The glossary is a list of about 145 words and phrases that are often misused. The list is alphabetically arranged for easy reference. It is not complete, but it should serve as a valuable checklist of the most common faulty expressions.

Also, students may refer to Chapter 18 for a greatly expanded list of Troublesome Homonyms and Other Words Easily Confused. Dozens of words added to that list would have fitted into the Glossary of Usage, but we did not want the glossary to run too long. Students should make much use of that list, as well as of the glossary.

Before you can make full use of these, however, you need to study first the following sections on Using Correct Words. These deal with: expressions that should be avoided altogether; words and phrases that generally should be avoided; and words and phrases that may be used whenever appropriate.

Always Avoid Wordiness, Vulgarisms and Improprieties

1. *Wordiness* is a common fault of many writers. Do not use more words than are necessary to express the intended meaning. Editors, who demand concise writing, complain that many cub reporters are wordy.

There are many forms of wordiness, and they go under such names as tautology, circumlocution, verbosity, verbiage, redundancy, prolixity and euphemism. This book cannot attempt to explain these terms and discuss them. If you wish to know more about them, consult any good book on rhetoric or look in the various reference books on language. Just remember that the journalist must avoid wordiness. He must not be longwinded. He must write in a style that is not only accurate and clear but also terse. Learn to "boil down" your writing.

John Dean made "at this (that) point in time" the most popular example of wordiness when in the Watergate hearings he testified: "I had no idea the CIA was involved at that point in time." And later he stated, "I was at Camp David at that point in time." Today this wordy expression is heard on TV and radio in all areas of reporting, and it is found in newspapers and magazines. Certainly the expression could be cut to *at that time*—or why not simply make it *then?*

A partial list of wordy expressions is all that can be given here. The words that can be omitted are in italics. The word that could be used for a phrase or a longer word is given in parentheses.

rest *up*	half a hundred (fifty)
passed away (died)	25 acres *of land*
refer *back*	made his home (resided)
check *up on*	made his escape (escaped)
jumped off *of*	effected his entrance (entered)

end *up*
lift *up*
inside *of*
all *of*
fold *up*
paid *out*
high noon
noon luncheon
summer *months*
true facts
continue *on*
feel *of*
later *on*
over *with*
large *in size*
many *in number*
eye witness
quite unique
pair of (or *two*) twins
visible *to the eye*
final outcome
regular meeting of
ugly *in appearance*
consensus *of opinion*
in spite of (despite)
old veteran
off *of*
close *down*
his *own* home
will be leaving
 (will leave)
Jewish rabbi
head *up*
wide variety
join *together*
terminate (end)
personal friend

downy couch (bed)
kind of (rather) rattled
all of a sudden (suddenly)
devoured by flames (burned)
totally destroyed
present incumbent; the *incumbent* senator
as a *general* rule
invited guest
55 *guests* attended
10 a.m. *in the morning*
met *in regular session*
made a statement (stated)
was in possession of (had)
was in receipt of (received)
the issue *in question*
acted as chairman (presided)
was the speaker (spoke)
quite a few (several or many)
a number of (several)
both the two sons
widow *woman*
widow *of the late*
general public
There are many *who* recommend
at that point in time (at that time or then)
controversial issue
future planning
Both Smith and Jones were sentenced
Both the two sons. . .
prior to (before or preceding)
serious crisis
at a later date (later)
important essentials
met *up with*
in my opinion, I firmly believe. . .
check *up on*
purple *in color*

You see that wordiness often results from the use of unnecessary prepositions and adverbs, unnecessary adjectives, unnecessary prepositional phrases, and faulty repetition. Watch your writing for these errors.

The bad practice of adding unnecessary particles to verbs is considered in the discussion of *idioms* on page 237.

2. *Vulgarisms,* also called *barbarisms* and *illiteracies,* are words and phrases that are not accepted even in colloquial (conversational) language. The only time journalists might use such an expression would be in quoting someone literally. Even then it will be best to eliminate the expression unless it is needed to present an accurate picture of the person quoted.

Here are some examples of vulgarisms:

irregardless   *couldn't of* done   hisself   *can't hardly* do it.
ain't got none   *liked* for *lacked*   hadn't ought to
don't want no (or *nothing*)   anywheres (anywhere)   drownded

3. *Improprieties* are good English words used in the wrong way grammatically. For example, in the sentence *They sure served some good eats last night, eats,* a verb, is incorrectly used as a noun. Most grammarians—and most editors—also would condemn the use of the adjective *sure,* an adjective used here as an adverb. However, *Webster's Third International Dictionary* now accepts the use of *sure* as an adverb.

Most editors probably will disagree also with Webster's approval of such uses as these: the noun *holiday* used as a verb, but *to vacation* is now considered correct; converting *concert* into a verb, *concertize;* the use of *to suicide* as a verb; the use of *to orate;* etc. (The conversion of nouns and adjectives into verbs—*politicize, minimize, positionize, finalize, internalize,* etc.—is discussed in the next section under the heading of jargon and gobbledygook.)

Webster's, however, cannot accept the use of improprieties that are caused by the misuse of words similar in form, such as: sound *affects* for *effects; suspect* for *expect; infer* for *imply* or vice versa; *liable* for *likely; uninterested* for *disinterested; compliment* for *complement; avenge* for *revenge* and so forth.

Generally Avoid Stereotypes, Slang, Jargon, Gobbledygook and Provincialisms

In choosing words or phrases that are correct, appropriate and effective, journalists usually should avoid using stereotypes (clichés), slang, jargon, gobbledygook and provincialisms. But journalists should recognize that although they generally will avoid using these types of expressions, they may occasionally use one or more of the types when appropriate. Always keeping your readers in mind, choose words that will effectively communicate your meaning to them.

1. *Stereotypes* are words or phrases that have been worn out through

overuse. They are often referred to as trite or hackneyed words or expressions, bromides or clichés.

In the atom-buster story, the only expression that might be called a stereotype is *golden age* in the third paragraph. The writer of that feature story has learned what *you* must learn—that the use of stereotypes in newspaper, magazine and radio-TV writing is a fault to be avoided.

Because the use of bromides constantly crops up in news writing, journalists should be particularly alert in recognizing trite words and phrases and in eliminating them from their working vocabulary for the most part.

Most editors recognize that use of stereotypes cannot be avoided altogether and that, in fact, a cliché may be used effectively at times. However, editors will expect you to realize what you are doing when you use a stereotype, and you certainly should make it clear to the readers that you know what you are doing. Bernstein recommends use of the cliché "only with discrimination and sophistication." For example: "The delegates to the conference seem unable to see the disarmament forest for the weapons trees." The writer has made it clear to his readers that he knows what he is doing in using a stereotype.

The sports writer and the police reporter must exercise extra caution in this regard, because stereotypes abound in their departments. The sports writer must learn to avoid such words and expressions as these:

pill	rifled the ball
apple	sent to the showers
horsehide	battled furiously
pellet	charity toss
pigskin	a brilliant 70
hoghide	chalked up a victory
tangle with	in the shadow of their own goal posts

Sports writers and sportscasters certainly must add to this list *on the year* (or *season* or *game*): He has hit 19 homeruns *on* (for) *the year*, or He has hit three homeruns *on the game*. Although this expression was introduced only a few years ago, it is already recognized as the cliché most commonly used by sports writers and sportscasters today.

The police reporter must beware of such expressions as these:

grilled	hail of bullets
angry mob	fusillade of bullets
brutal murder	a shot rang out
reign of terror	miraculous escape
lodged in jail	caught red-handed
pitched battle	shrouded in mystery
pool of blood	struck with a blunt instrument

Writers in other fields of reporting must avoid the use of expressions which have been overworked. A few examples of expressions to be avoided are given below. There are hundreds of others.

acid test	mourned their loss
admiring friends	in the nick of time
at long last	nipped in the bud
avenging justice	pale as death
blanket of snow	paramount issue
bolt from the blue	point with pride
bonds of matrimony	proud father (parent)
bone of contention	proud possessor
breakneck speed	reigns supreme
breathless silence	riot of color
colorful display	ripe old age
dashed the hopes of	rode roughshod over
deadly earnest	round of applause
devouring (hungry) flames	saw the light of day
enjoyable occasion	second to none
fair sex	select few
Father Time	soul of honor
feathered songster	supreme sacrifice
goes without saying	tender mercies
grim reaper	time immemorial
host of friends	too numerous to mention
in our midst	took (him) to task
iron out (their troubles)	untiring efforts
large and enthusiastic audience	view with alarm
lingering illness	weaker sex
long-felt want	worse for wear
met head-on	wreathed in smiles

2. Generally, the use of *slang* in journalistic writing should be avoided. *Slang* is defined as words or phrases that have been invented or have been altered from their standard meanings. Slang, then, is highly informal language that is outside conventional or standard usage. Slang words and phrases have popular currency, but most of them are short-lived. Here are a few examples, some old, some new:

the cat's whiskers   Says you!   Do you dig me?   Natch!   Cool it!
Swell! Neat! and Far out! (for Fine!)   You know, you know, you know. . . .

You will note that we said the journalist must avoid the *unnecessary* use of slang. Newspaper editors try to keep their papers comparatively free of slang, but most editors permit their writers to follow a middle-of-the-road policy. They recognize that many words and expressions which originated as slang have been accepted as good usage by the compilers of dictionaries, and that more such words and expressions will become good English in the future. In fact, we must recognize that slang has played an important role in enriching the English language. Most editors would approve the use of the following expressions, all of which are accepted by Webster's now:

dogface	hooker	disc jockey
jail bait	pizzazz	overkill
groupie	hornswoggle	clip joint
debunk	cops	rip off, rip-off
yes man	bamboozle	mob (of gangsters)
gob (sailor)	highbrow	fortune-telling racket
rubberneck	stooge	big house (penitentiary)
roughneck	blurb	razzle-dazzle
cold feet		gobbledygook

Many editors, however, would disapprove use of much slang that has been approved only recently in the more permissive dictionaries. For example, these words are no longer identified as slang in *Webster's New Collegiate Dictionary:* shrink; head shrinker; snow (cocaine); freak out and freak-out; with-it (adj.); lousy (with money); and lounge lizard.

The AP Stylebook advises: In general, avoid slang. And most editors will agree with that policy. However, a majority likely would approve use of slang that has enough quality to add *pizzazz* to your writing—and if it fits in appropriately. Slang will not be appropriate in most straight news stories, but you may find you can use it effectively in some feature stories and columns. For example, Bob Greene had this recently in his syndicated column: For most people the word gigolo conjures up an image of a slimy creature slinking around diamond-dripping matrons at society parties, a *lounge lizard*, a snake who is generally to be avoided.

Make sure that any slang you use is not only appropriate but that its use also gives the reader a more specific, clearer idea of the subject.

3. Use of slang may no longer be a main question for editors and writers. A much bigger problem today is the increasing overuse of *jargon* and *gobbledygook*. *Jargon* is confused, unintelligible language, and *gobbledygook* is wordy and generally unintelligible jargon, most of which originates in Washington. Big business and the social scientists, as well as government officials, also are offenders.

After former President John F. Kennedy used the word *finalize* in a press conference and was criticized by some for using slang, Dr. Phillip B. Grove, the editor-in-chief of the Merriam Webster dictionaries, came to his defense by stating that *finalize* had been in use "by a wide variety of erudite publications and personages" since World War I.

In *The American Language*, H. L. Mencken noted a vast coinage of similar verbs in recent years from adjectives, common nouns and proper names: slenderize, tenderize, permanentize, pressurize, hospitalize, routinize, moisturize, winterize, Texanize and Sovietize.

Criticism of using such a word as *finalize*, declared Dr. Grove, would be "a typical reaction by those who shudder over the use of particular words they don't like and who refuse to recognize the obligation of a dictionary to report the language as it is spoken and written by educated people."

Remarked one newspaper editorial writer, after reading Dr. Grove's statement: "Such criticism, Dr. Grove means, should be *funeralized*."

Recently the author heard this usage in a TV sermon: "You must *positionize* yourself in the right relationship with God." Really, to what ridiculous lengths can we go in creating "new verbs" by adding *ize* to adjectives and nouns?

Today, however, *finalize, maximize, minimize* and even *accessorize* (used in advertising) are approved by Webster's. Also accepted are such words as *interviewee, standee* and *escapee*, but so far *offendee* and *protectee* haven't made it. Just possibly they never will. But *prioritize*, which has become a popular word in the average bureaucrat's vocabulary, is likely to be accepted in the next edition of the dictionary.

Although *finalize* and some similar "new verbs" are accepted in the new *Webster's International Dictionary*, you will find that most newspaper editors, at least, will frown upon such usage. And, you will find authorities such as Copperud stating: "*Finalize*, like *implement* as a verb, is hopelessly associated with gobbledygook, and its user may bring scorn upon himself." And even Rudolf Flesch, a liberal in English usage, calls *finalize* jargon. Flesch advises: Don't use *finalize* when *complete, finish, end* will do.

Consider this bit of gobbledygook from a top man in national government: "Once the inflation genie has been let out of the bottle, it is a very tricky policy problem to find the particular calibration and timing that would be appropriate to stem the acceleration in risk premiums created by falling incomes without prematurely aborting the decline in the inflation-generated risk premiums. This is clearly not an easy policy path to traverse, but it is the path which we must follow."

Before using jargon or gobbledygook, then, you certainly should consult the stylebook or your editor. The AP Stylebook says: In general, avoid jargon. When it is appropriate in a special context, include an explanation of any words likely to be unfamiliar to most readers.

4. *Provincialisms* are words or expressions that are used and understood in a limited section of the country. For instance, you will hear such a sentence as this in some parts of our country: "She *carried* her husband to work in the station wagon." Another part of the country would say *took* instead of

carried, and still others would use *drove.* Would you know what was meant if you heard someone say, "He's *fixing* to go," or "I *reckon* that's right"? Use such expressions as these only if they give color to a story or are used by the person you are quoting.

If a newspaper circulates in only a limited section of the country, the journalist may be warranted in using expressions that are native to the section. If you expect to write for publications that cover the nation, however, you must limit your use of expressions that will not be understood outside the region of their origin.

Check the dictionary to identify *provincialisms,* also called *localisms.* Webster's identifies such expressions as *regional* or *dialectical.* For example, *goober* is listed as used only in the South and the Midland. (As a synonym for *peanut,* it could be that *goober* may soon be used nationally!) *Reckon,* used as a verb in place of *suppose,* is labeled *chiefly dialectical,* for example.

Use Colloquialisms and Idioms When Appropriate

1. *Colloquialisms* are informal words and phrases used largely in conversation and to some degree in very informal writing. They have been regarded as unacceptable in formal writing, and many of them are not suitable in newspaper writing. With the emphasis on readability, however, and on writing as you would talk, many colloquialisms are finding their way into newspaper articles and stories. Certainly the reporter need not hesitate to use such acceptable contractions as *isn't, don't, doesn't, I'll* and such common words as *phone* and *auto.*

In revising this edition of *Grammar for Journalists,* the author found that *all* the examples he listed ten years ago as "colloquialisms to be avoided by journalists" are now approved by Webster's. Some of the examples were:

I *guess* (believe) it's true.
Jones *located* (settled) here in 1895.
Smith *runs* (manages) a barber shop or a factory.
I *sure* (surely) would like to go.
It's a *deal.* (Webster's lists *dirty deal.*)
They were all *mighty* (very) tired.
This is a very *healthy* (healthful) climate.
We drove along *real* slow (very slow or slowly).
They sold 90,000 *pair* (pairs) of hose.
He *suspicioned* (suspected) that Fagan was a thief.
completed for *complexioned*
last for *latest* (edition)
towards for *toward*
enthuse (They were enthused. . .)

It is difficult today to use a dictionary to identify colloquialisms. Only *Webster's New World Dictionary* and *The American College Dictionary* continue to use the label *colloquial.* *Funk and Wagnalls Standard College Dictionary* uses the label *informal.* And *Webster's New Collegiate Dictionary* and the Third International no longer use either the *colloquial* or *informal* label. *Webster's New World Dictionary* identifies many words as colloquial with the label *Colloq.* The label itself, the dictionary says, "does not indicate substandard or illiterate usage."

The Associated Press and United Press International, which chose *Webster's New World Dictionary,* Second College Edition, as the guide in compiling the 1977 stylebooks, agree that the test for the use of colloquialisms is appropriateness. "Many colloquial words and phrases characteristic of informal writing and conversation are acceptable in some contexts and not in others," it is pointed out. Examples given include *bum, giveaway* and *phone.* It also is noted that *ain't* is a substandard contraction that should not be used in news stories unless needed to illustrate substandard speech in writing. Most newspaper editors would agree with the press associations on usage of colloquialisms. However, many editors would never approve the use of such expressions as these: *last* for *latest* (edition); *towards* for *toward; suspicioned* for *suspected;* or *enthused* used as a verb with the meaning of "to make enthusiastic" or "to show enthusiasm."

Journalists, then, will find they may use colloquialisms effectively in newspaper writing that is conversational in style, particularly in feature stories. And, of course, they are often appropriate in direct quotations. Television and radio journalists, naturally, have much more freedom to use colloquialisms than do newspaper writers. Examples: The high is expected to be *around* (about) 90 degrees. As far as thunderstorms (are concerned), they should be rather severe. Palmer will try *and* (try to) win his sixth straight game.

What was said about the use of slang applies also to the use of colloquialisms: Use colloquialisms where they are appropriate and where their use will keep your writing from sounding artificial or pompous.

2. *Idioms* are words or expressions that are peculiar to a particular language, and they often have some grammatical irregularity. Perhaps the majority of idioms in the English language which may be regarded as correct are idioms in which a verb is modified by one or more prepositions used adverbially. Using the preposition as an adverb to modify the verb radically

alters the meaning of the verb. Some examples of correct idioms are given below.

to make good	Let's don't	comply with (not *to*)
to catch a cold	fall in	have a try at
to put up with	hold up	identical with (not *to*)
to be up against	drop in	up to his neck in trouble

The *use of prepositions* is one of the most delicate and tricky problems in English. Here are some incorrectly used phrases and the correct idiomatic forms:

INCORRECT	CORRECT
comply to	comply *with*
die with	die *of*
free of disease	free *from* disease
pleased with an idea	pleased *at* or *by* an idea
pleased by a toy	pleased *with* a toy
speak *or* talk to him	speak or talk *with* him
identical to	identical *with*
different than	different *from*
plan on going	plan *to go*
sort of a person	sort *of* person

You will note that most of the examples include one or more prepositions used adverbially. All good writers make great use of idioms. Journalists should use idioms frequently but must see that they are correct.

Hundreds of words may be followed by any one of several prepositions, according to the meaning to be conveyed. Dictionaries help to supply the correct preposition in an idiomatic expression. *Webster's New World Dictionary* is especially useful. Also, a most helpful book is Funk & Wagnalls' *Standard Handbook of Prepositions, Conjunctions, Relative Pronouns and Adverbs*. And there is an excellent list of correct use of prepositions in idioms in Skillin and Gay's *Words Into Type*.

Writers certainly must recognize that there is a trend toward adding unnecessary particles to verbs, and you will find that most editors condemn such usage. Examples: *face up to* for *face; paid off* for *paid; meet up with* for *meet; lose out* for *lose; heat up* for *heat; continue on* for *continue; merged together* for *merged; postponed until later* for *postponed; or reduced down* for *reduced*.

QUIZ ANSWERS

1. Declaring they had the cabs necessary to public operation, directors of the GI Transportation Company announced Thursday that they would continue their fight to win a city taxicab franchise. 2. Understanding people is Juan Mason's business. 3. To bring the home and the school closer together has become the PTA's chief goal. 4. Although the number of deaths from Hong Kong influenza may rise sharply this week, City Health Officer Tav Lupton feels that the epidemic is now under control. 5. With a pinstriped railroad man's cap cocked on his blond head, L.M. Crandall Jr. engineered. . . . 6. Because it was convinced that the Justice Department would not act, Control Data went ahead last week to file suit against IBM. 7. If they continue to retire or default instead of playing her, transsexual tennis player Renee Richards said Sunday that she will start suing players. 8. As their spaceship dashed ever nearer to home, the three tired astronauts caught as much sleep as they could, resting for the critical reentry through the earth's atmosphere. 9. Injured in saving their three-year-old baby from a speeding automobile, a young man and his wife are in City-County Hospital today in critical condition. 10. What was thought to be human hair under the fingernails of the murder victim was cat fur, Police Chief Naylor said. (The noun clause is subject of the second *was*.) 11. At this point his outlook on life is quite different from his partner's (*or,* from that of his partner). 12. He continued (on) for half an hour (*or* for a half hour) until he met his brother. 13. They plan to go to the island soon, since (because) the area is now free from disease. 14. Suddenly the walls caved in, and despite the efforts of firemen, the flames destroyed the warehouse. 15. With the agreement signed, the two firms will now be merged. 16. They surely would like to get on that TV show and win some money. 17. "The state likely faces a crisis in the winter," the rival of the governor declared before the election. 18. He couldn't have gone regardless of what date was set for the show. 19. Avoid using stereotypes (trite words and expressions) like *dashed the hopes, pigskin* and *scored standing up*. However, these terms, especially the last one, may be used occasionally. 20. The police quickly began a search of the area and caught the drunk (drunken) hit-and-run driver about an hour later. He had a half-emptied bottle of whiskey in his car. He (*or,* the man) was promptly booked and jailed (*or,* placed in jail).

PART 3

Punctuation and Spelling

17
Punctuation to Make the Meaning Clear

If you have been convinced that clarity in writing must be a primary objective of the journalist, you recognize the fact that correct, effective punctuation is essential to clear writing. An understanding of sentence structure should enable you to grasp, with a minimum of effort, all the rules of punctuation which you need to know. For, in your study of sentence structure, you could not fail to observe that correct punctuation is closely related to correct sentences.

You cannot punctuate a sentence correctly unless you know the proper relationship of the parts of the sentence. Once you have learned how to put a sentence together and understand why you put it together that way, you will see that punctuation serves the primary purpose of helping to make clear to the reader the thought relationships that make up the sentence. And don't forget that no amount of punctuation will enable you to make a good sentence out of one that you have not constructed properly.

Punctuation marks, then, are not to be used like ornaments on a Christmas tree, to dress up the sentence. To a certain degree they are used for emphasis, but punctuation is functional rather than ornamental. Its purpose is to make reading easier and to bring out the meaning intended by the writer.

The Associated Press, with which Rudolf Flesch worked for several years in a program to improve readability of copy, offers in its 1977 *Associated Press Stylebook* this suggestion: Think of punctuation as a courtesy to your readers, designed to help them understand a story. Inevitably, a mandate of this scope involves gray areas. For this reason, the punctuation entries in this book refer to guidelines rather than rules. Guidelines should not be treated casually, however.

In an earlier publication, AP gave this excellent definition of punctuation and its purpose: "Punctuation is the visual inflection. The marks should clarify meaning and, like shouting, should be employed sparingly. Skillful phrasing avoids ambiguity, insures interpretation and lessens need for punctuation."

In other words, the only reason for using punctuation marks is to convey the exact thought and the desired tone to the reader. Punctuate for clarity and for emphasis, and in all instances use as few punctuation marks as possible. The author of *The Dallas News Style Book* makes this trenchant comment: "Avoid necessity of involved punctuation by avoiding long and intricate sentences." Flesch, Gunning and other readability experts say "Amen" to that.

But remember that, fundamentally, punctuation is determined by the grammatical construction. Learn the rules, and make your punctuation consistent.

PERIODS
When to Use the Period

1. Use a period at the end of a declarative sentence or an imperative sentence that is not exclamatory.

> The thief was caught an hour later only a block from the store.
> Put the books on that desk in the corner if you will.

2. Use a period after most abbreviations.

Mr.	Sen.	LL.D.	etc.	*ibid.*	Mass.	a.m.	U.S.
Mrs.	C.P.A.	Ph.D.	i.e.	Feb.	Sgt.	p.m.	B.C.
Dr.	B.A.	c.o.d.	e.g.	Oct.	E. Elm St. 12 ft.		A.D.
the Rev.	M.A.	f.o.b.	o.k.	Dec.	Ga.	vol.	No. 1

Use the abbreviations Jr. *or* Sr. after a person's name.

Months are abbreviated only when used with an exact date: Feb. 5, Dec. 21. Months with short names, such as April, May and July, are never abbreviated, even when used with a date.

Abbreviate the names of all but eight states when they follow names of cities: He was found in Fullerton, Calif. Do not abbreviate these eight: Alaska, Hawaii, Idaho, Iowa, Maine, Ohio, Texas and Utah.

3. Use a period as a decimal point.

$15.75	101.5 degrees
25.5 percent	a .325 batting average

4. Use three periods to indicate omission of words.

> "We are not . . . going to delay or put a freeze on these negotiations because of Africa or because of domestic considerations," Powell said.

Webster defines ellipsis as:
"Omission of one or more words that. . . to make the expression grammatically correct."

Use four periods at the end of a sentence from which words were omitted: Before Eric Sevareid signs off Wednesday, there will be one last gulp . . . and just before that little light goes off, one last word . . . "Walter". . . .

When Not to Use the Period

1. Do not use a period after *percent*: They received a 12 percent increase. Note that *percent*, not *per cent*, is now correct usage.

2. Do not use a period after nicknames like *Tom, Dick* and *Sam*.

3. Do not use a period after initials or abbreviations that name well-known organizations, persons or things.

FBI	AAF	GOP	YMCA	Station WFAA		Texas Tech
LSD	JFK	LBJ	UFOs	ERA	NATO	CIA

4. Do not use a period after abbreviations of common words that are used in colloquial language, such as: *ad, bus, gas, phone, photo, exam, gym*.

COMMAS
When to Use the Comma

1. A comma is used to separate two independent clauses joined by the coordinating conjunction *and, or, nor, but, yet* or *for*. Note these sentences:

> "Coaching for coaching's sake is fine, but there are other things like teaching boys to compete in society, and I don't know if I could have done some things I've done anywhere else but Grambling," said Robinson.
> Moynihan has had certain advantages over his fellow freshmen, for he was already an international figure by the time he reached the Senate.
> Grasshoppers descended upon the fields in huge waves, and the corn soon was stripped to the ground.
> He was unable to find anyone who would back him in the venture, yet he refused to give up the idea of producing the play.
> "You will obey it," he wrote, "or you will seek employment elsewhere."

In general, the comma is used if the subjects of the two clauses are different. It is usually needed for clarity.

However, the trend is toward eliminating the comma when the clauses are short, thus:

It is odd but it happens.

You can play it safe by using the comma, leaving it to the editor to omit it if he considers it unnecessary.

The trend toward eliminating the comma before the coordinating conjunction *and* in compound sentences is much stronger than the trend toward eliminating the comma before the conjunction *but*.

When the subject is the same for both clauses and is not repeated in the second clause, a comma must be used if the conjunction is *but*. But if the connective is *and,* and if the two statements are closely related, the comma should be omitted.

The justice of the peace heard the man's arguments, but was still unconvinced.
He has had seven years of experience on papers in Detroit and Louisville and is thoroughly competent.

Be sure to note that *so* is not listed with the coordinating conjunctions. The good journalist will avoid the use of *so* by changing one of the independent clauses to a dependent clause or a phrase.

POOR: The detectives knew that Smith still had a room at the Blotz boarding house, so they waited for him to return there for his clothes.
BETTER: As (or *Because*) the detectives knew that Smith still had a room . . ., they waited . . .
Or: Knowing that Smith still had a room . . ., they waited . . .

2. Commas are used to separate words or figures which might be misunderstood.

What the major problem is, is not clear.

3. Commas are used to indicate the omission of a word common to both parts of the sentence and easily understood.

Talent is often inherited; genius, never.

4. Commas are used to separate words, phrases or clauses used in a series when the coordinating conjunction is omitted from the series.

When the conjunction, usually *and* or *or,* is used before the last word or phrase or clause in the series, no comma need be inserted before the conjunction. This is universal journalistic style.

A frank, blunt statement was made to the press by Mayor Young.
South Dakota State University, Oklahoma Baptist University and the University of New Mexico are members.

He had a pale face, shifty eyes and a battered right ear.

Mantle could cover center field capably, could bat from either side of the plate and could hit game-winning home runs consistently.

He wrapped a scarf around his neck, turned up his overcoat collar and hurried through the door.

In another hour he must decide whether to push on, to pause for a brief rest or to camp for the night.

Bigamy Jones was a first-rate man with a gun, with a horse or with the women.

He demanded to know immediately whether we would make the trip, if he could bring his wife and when we could arrive.

If the conjunction is omitted at the end, the comma must be used.

The injured man painfully made his way over the ridge, down the hill, through the shallow stream.

You note that when adjectives are used in a series, the comma is not placed after the last adjective: a *frank, blunt* statement. Make sure that the parts of the series are coordinate. Can they be joined by *and*'s? If not, the comma is not needed, for one word usually modifies the meaning of the second word, even if they are not joined by a hyphen: *a white brick* house; a *dull green* finish. Use of a comma in these expressions would be an error.

Sometimes the final adjective in a series is so closely associated with the noun that follows that the two appear to be a compound noun: an old *oaken bucket;* a sharp *steel blade;* her new *spring bonnet.* No comma is used in such constructions.

5. Commas are used to set off a nonrestrictive clause. The *nonrestrictive* clause is not needed for one to understand fully and completely the meaning of the sentence in which such a clause occurs.

Ralph Wolfe, who has served two terms as mayor, announced today that he would not seek reelection.

John Thomas, the man who is standing near the dais, is the mayor's cousin.

Note that the identity of the subjects in the sentences above is made perfectly clear by giving their proper names, Ralph Wolfe and John Thomas. The clauses "who has served . . . as mayor" and "the man . . . near the dais" give additional information about the subjects, but are not needed to identify them. Nonrestrictive clauses, then, are enclosed by a pair of commas to show that these clauses are of secondary importance. You will do well to consider the pair of commas that enclose a nonrestrictive element as one punctuation mark: you cannot use one comma without the other. Don't fail to insert the second comma!

In the following examples of nonrestrictive clauses, note the use of only a single comma in the first two sentences, since the nonrestrictive clauses come last.

> The latest entrant in the race for mayor is Margaret West, who has served two terms in office.
>
> Pitching in top form are Knapp and Tanana, who are expected to lead the Angels to a Western division title.
>
> "Angel dust," which is used to cure rubber and to tranquilize large animals such as elephants, has risen above alcohol and heroin as the "major drug of abuse" in the nation's capital.
>
> Bob Dandridge and Elvin Hayes, upon whom Coach Dick Motta relies to win the NBA championship, were in top form in the second game.

If the clause is *restrictive*—if it is necessary to the meaning of the sentence—no commas are used.

In the sentence below, the subject *man* is not clearly identified without the *who* clause. Note how the clause points out a definite person.

> The man who is standing near the dais is the mayor's cousin.

Try reading the sentence without the *who* clause. You will find that you do not know which particular man is being spoken about. The *who* clause restricts or specifies the meaning of the vague subject *man*. Because the clause is essential to the meaning of the sentence, it is *not* enclosed by commas.

And finally, consider a sentence in which the clause introduced by *whom* is necessary to complete the meaning of the sentence: The three men upon whom Coach Motta relies to win the NBA championship are Dandridge, Hayes and Unseld.

6. Commas are used to set off words and phrases that are used as appositives. Appositives, like non-restrictive clauses, are not essential to the meaning of the sentence.

The *appositive* is usually a phrase that means the same thing as or explains the word it follows.

> Sen. Hubert H. Humphrey, the "Happy Warrior" of American politics, died Friday night after a long and gallant struggle against cancer. He was 66.
>
> Herbert Schmertz, vice president of public affairs for Mobil, said that corporations should be entitled to the same First Amendment protections as newspapers and radio and television stations.
>
> The board elected a new man, Frank Williams, to the presidency.
>
> Eastman Kodak, the world's biggest photographic company, set records in both sales and earnings during the July-September quarter.
>
> The sole heir, his son John, will inherit the entire fortune.

China reportedly has bought anti-tank missiles from France, Peking's first order of advanced Western weapons since Mao Tse-tung's death.

Streaking farther and farther from earth Sunday toward man's first rendezvous with the moon was a lonely speck of life, Apollo 8.

When the use of a comma or commas would be confusing to the reader, writers should use a dash or dashes to set off appositives or other parenthetical material.

Because three officers—Brown, Margerum and Dorries—were out of the city, the board meeting was postponed.

It takes guts to make a movie as bleak and uncompromising as this new Dustin Hoffman vehicle—misplaced guts.

It is becoming common practice for journalists to use the dash instead of the comma to give emphasis to an appositive or other parenthetical material at the end of a sentence, as was done in the preceding Dustin Hoffman sentence. A journalist today probably would use a dash instead of the comma before *Apollo 8* in that particular sentence, and possibly would use a dash between *France* and *Peking's* in that sentence. Further examples of the use of the dash for the comma will be found on pages 259–60.

The only exception to the rule of setting off an appositive is the use of a single word as a restrictive appositive in such sentences as these:

Her daughter *Mary* has gone to England.

This occurred in the reign of Alexander *the Great*. (The appositive is part of the name.)

We *boys* will attend to the moving of the furniture.

7. Commas are used to set off parenthetical words and phrases that are not essential to the meaning of the sentence. Such words and phrases are known as sentence modifiers because they modify the whole sentence rather than any part of it. Every writer will use transitional devices, at least occasionally, to guide the reader. And in journalism there is a strong trend toward using transitional words and phrases in both newspapers and magazines.

Although transitional words and phrases can contribute much, remember that they are not essential in the sentence. Therefore, they must be set off by commas—just as *Therefore* is punctuated in this sentence. Note the use and the punctuation of transitional expressions in the sentences that follow.

Meanwhile, two congressional committees began formal study of the $4.8 billion arms package.

The rival forces, *meanwhile*, prepared to meet Wednesday to patch up a peace.

However, the couple found it impossible to care for the "bubble baby" at home.

Or: The couple, however, found it. . . .

His story, *in the first place*, does not sound accurate. *On the other hand*, it does sound plausible.

He says the report points up the need for more in-house auditing. *"Otherwise*, you will have programs running wild."

Increasingly, attention is being focused by opponents on the problem of what to do with the nuclear waste that is piling up.

In sum, the Israeli reaction to the terrorist killings was not eye-for-eye reprisal but. . . .

Incidentally, the pay scale is to be raised Jan. 1. *Or:* The pay scale, *incidentally*, is to. . . .

8. Commas are used to set off nominatives of direct address. Also, the introductory *yes* or *no* is set off by a comma.

She said, "You know, *Joe*, that Ruby will be your tennis partner."

Gentlemen, start your calculators.

It is evident, *Mr. Chairman*, that the club must raise about $3,000 more for the project. *Or: Mr. Chairman*, it is. . . .

Yes, there really is a Lynchburg, Tenn., just like (*as*) it says in the Jack Daniel's whiskey ads, and *yes*, it has a population of just under 400, same as always.

9. Commas are used to set off the year in a date, and also to set off the month and the exact date following the day of the week.

It was Aug. 23, 1968, that the Soviet Union and four of its Warsaw Pact allies invaded Czechoslovakia and seized virtual control of the government.

The ceremony took place Friday, May 16, in Los Angeles.

When a phrase lists only a month and a year, spell out the month and do not set off the year with a comma: January 1978 was Cleveland's coldest month.

10. Commas are used to set off the name of the state or country when it follows the name of a city.

The car thief was arrested and booked in Bloomington, Ill., Tuesday.

Harrison was born in Colorado, but his parents moved to Tucson, Ariz., when he was three.

Mrs. O'Brien came here from Dublin, Ireland, when she was 16.

11. Use a comma for most figures higher than 999: 1,229. (But see 12 for addresses, telephone numbers, etc.)

12. Commas are used to set off explanatory figures, such as the age of a person or his address or telephone number.

The woman injured in the accident is Mrs. R. L. Hillinger, 22, of 1023 Oak Street.

Mrs. R. L. Hillinger, 22, of 1023 Oak Street, was injured in the accident.

Jones gave his telephone number, 741-7741, to the reporter.

13. Commas are used to set off party affiliations, degrees and titles given after a name.

> Sen. Strom Thurmond, R.-S.C., led the filibuster.
> The next head of the university may be Wayne A. Danielson, Ph.D.
> It was signed by J. H. Brokaw, First City Bank president. (Note that a title following a name is not capitalized except for persons of great distinction.)

14. The press associations and most newspapers do *not* set off Jr. and Sr. after a name: Robert Stewart Jr. was elected vice president.

15. Commas are used to separate direct quotations from explanatory matter.

> "It may have served its purpose, but now we can go in a different direction," Mrs. Haskins said.
> "If the traffic needs change to require a rail system," Mayor Folsom responded, "I'm sure the City Council would seriously consider such a proposal."
> "The question is how far we get with an investigation like that," said Ms. Foster, who explained that most of the board's information about programs comes from the administration.

16. Commas are used to set off participial and infinitive phrases or long prepositional phrases which precede the main clause.

Remember that the participial phrase is used as an adjective or an adverb. The introductory infinitive phrase may be used as a noun or as an adverb.

> PARTICIPIAL PHRASES:
> *Having suffered heavy losses,* the troops slowly withdrew. (The participial phrase modifies the noun *troops.*)
> *Slowed by collapse today of a company negotiator,* efforts to reach an agreement in the Lone Star Steel dispute made limited headway. (The participial phrase modifies the noun *efforts.*)

Note that a participial phrase which *follows* the noun it modifies also must be set off: Muhammad Ali, stung by criticism of his overweight display against Jimmy Young, floated onto the scales at a trim 220 pounds Sunday. . . .

You may need to be warned about confusing a gerund—which is always used as a noun—with the present participle. The gerund or gerund phrase is never set off by commas.

> Bargaining to end the nation's 75-day-old coal strike collapsed Saturday night. (*Bargaining* is a gerund here, and the gerund phrase is the subject of *collapsed.*)
> "Swimming and jogging are excellent sports for persons of all ages," he declared. (The compound gerund *Swimming and jogging* is the subject of *are.*)

INFINITIVE PHRASES:

To provide an incentive for raising higher-grade livestock, the Iowa State Fair next fall will offer livestock premiums totaling $60,000. (The infinitive phrase modifies the verb *will offer.*)

To win ball games, a team must have high-grade pitching. (The infinitive phrase modifies the verb *must have.*)

Note that no comma is needed in the following sentence, in which the infinitive phrase is used as a noun, subject of the verb *became.*

To balance agriculture with industry became a chief goal of the South three decades ago.

PREPOSITIONAL PHRASES:

With a pinstriped railroad cap cocked on his blond head, young L. M. Crandall Jr. deftly engineered his way into the finals of the Texas Public Links Golf Association championship Saturday.

The prepositional phrase *With a . . . cap cocked on his blond head* modifies *Crandall.* Although it is used as an adjective, it is so long that it requires a comma.

After days of desperate filibustering, the Senate finally passed the bill late Friday night.

The prepositional phrase *After days of . . . filibustering* modifies *passed.* A comma is needed for clarity.

If the prepositional phrase is short, no comma may be needed. Note these examples:

In the last few minutes he finished the report.

Throughout the night they searched the forest for the lost boy.

Note: Although the length of the introductory prepositional phrase is the chief guide in determining whether or not to use a comma, remember that the main purpose of all punctuation is to make the meaning clear. If a short prepositional phrase needs a comma to make the meaning readily apparent to the reader, use the comma. Note how the comma contributes to clarity in the following constructions.

In Beirut, the Palestinian Liberation Organization said its Saturday attack was a strike . . .

On separate continents, the two men who first conquered Mount Everest celebrated the 25th anniversary of the historic climb.

Every day, Elda Troy used to come home with a headache from her high-pressure job in a busy purchasing department.

In the halls of Harvard, faculty members of America's oldest college are locked in serious debate.

> *In the drowsy early-morning hours,* passers-by and visitors to the Tulsa police
> station often stop and listen to the harmonizing of the department's first quartet
> to be organized in a decade.

Most editors would agree that the comma after *hours* helps to make the
meaning clearer.

17. Commas are used to set off nominative absolutes. The *nominative
absolute* is another independent element of the sentence. It is not grammatically necessary to the sentence; hence it must be set off.

> *The inauguration (being) over,* Washington began to return to normal Tuesday.
> *Her right hand paralyzed from the snake bite,* the child could not lift the box.

18. Commas are used to set off introductory dependent clauses. This is
one of the most important usages of the comma—and one which journalists
too often violate. Unless the introductory clause is very short, the comma
should be used to set it off.

> Because small business cannot afford the cost of complying with nitpicking
> federal paperwork requirements, some premeditated violations do occur. (The
> long introductory cause clause must be set off.)
> While (Although) UMW President Arnold Miller predicted that the contract
> would be ratified overwhelmingly, other coal officials and miners were more
> skeptical. (The long introductory clause of concession must be set off.)
> If there was such a message from Beirut to Washington, it was not getting
> through. (And this introductory clause of condition, although not as long as
> the foregoing clauses, also needs to be followed by a comma.)

If the introductory dependent clause is short, the comma may often be
omitted.

> If he gets in late he will telephone.
> When the actress arrived she greeted her mother first.

However, you will not be in error if you place a comma after these clauses.

If the dependent adverbial clause comes in the middle of the sentence, it
must be set off with commas, like the nonrestrictive clause.

> The president of the Machinists Union said the anti-inflation program, if it is to
> succeed, must stop "unbridled corporate power."

If the dependent clause follows the independent clause, no comma is
needed usually. Be governed by the sense of the sentence.

> The city manager said that the community will suffer an acute water shortage
> unless a new lake is built within six years.
> Lacovara said he quit because Flynt balked at helping him obtain subpoenas and
> information from the Justice Department and the CIA.
> The three tired astronauts were catching as much sleep as they could before their
> spaceship reentered through the earth's atmosphere.

When Not to Use the Comma

1. No comma is used before an *of* phrase indicating place or position.

Sen. James B. Allen of Alabama died yesterday in . . .

2. No comma is used between two nouns that identify the same person.

The general was quite proud of his *son John*.

3. No comma is used in such phrases as: five feet three inches; 2 gallons 1 pint; 10 hours 20 minutes 8 seconds.

The featherweight fighter is only five feet three inches tall.

4. No comma is needed before either a partial quotation or an indirect quote.

He declared that the result would be "utter confusion."
The maxim of "every man for himself" should not apply in this case, he argued.

(The *Associated Press Stylebook* advises avoiding fragmentary quotes. This subject is treated on page 256.) It is obvious, of course, that the indirect quote is not set off by a comma: The governor declared that he would quit politics for good if he is not reelected.

5. No comma is needed to set off restrictive clauses.

The car *that is stalled* is the one the colonel was using.
The man *who set the player's arm* is Dr. Benjamin Carroll.

6. No comma is used to separate the clauses of a complex sentence when the dependent clause follows the independent clause and is closely related to it. This rule applies largely to adverbial clauses that are essential to the meaning of the main clause and to the meaning of the whole sentence. In a sense, such clauses restrict the meaning of the main clause. Therefore these adverbial clauses, like the restrictive clauses discussed on page 250, should not be set off by commas. Note the following examples:

Hart will start at quarterback in the Pro Bowl because Staubach was injured in the Super Bowl game.
Or: Hart will start at quarterback . . . if Staubach can't play.
Mrs. Kleeb says she had the distinction of being the youngest and the shortest girl in the Rockette line when she started.
Women workers won an important legal victory Tuesday as the Supreme Court outlawed all pension plans requiring them to contribute larger portions of their salaries than men.

However, if the dependent clause following the independent clause is not necessary to the meaning of the sentence, it needs to be set off. All such clauses do is to introduce additional information that is really nonrestrictive.

The comma is needed in such a nonrestrictive clause: They found no one in the apartment, although lights were burning and the TV set was on.

7. No comma is used before the coordinating conjunction that connects the last two items in a series.

> The flag is red, white *and* green.
> A tall, dark-haired *and* handsome man was Jackie's companion.
> He wanted to know how he could get there, what he was to bring *and* what he was expected to do on arrival.

8. No comma is needed between adjectives which could not be separated by *and* and make sense. The noun and its preceding adjective may often be considered as a compound noun:

> The *tall eye surgeon* in the *bright red outfit* is Dr. Renee Richards.
> The knife had a *sharp cutting edge*.
> That's a *beautiful race horse*.

9. The comma no longer is used after the coordinating conjunctions *and* and *but* when used to begin a sentence.

> *And* in Southgate, Ky., townspeople gathered for a service at the town's war memorial, a short distance from the site of the Beverly Hills Supper Club fire that killed 165 people in May 1977.
> *But* before Eric Sevareid signs off Wednesday, there will be one last gulp, one last slow turn of that magnificent face, and just before that little light goes off, one last word. . ."Walter". . . .

10. Do not use the comma before the abbreviations *Jr.* and *Sr.*: Joseph P. Kennedy Jr.

SEMICOLONS

The journalist should use the semicolon sparingly. In general, use the semicolon to indicate a greater separation of thought and information than a comma can convey but less than the separation that a period implies. Its chief use is in compound sentences, and the reporter will avoid using sentences in which the conjunction is omitted between two independent clauses.

1. Use a semicolon to separate independent clauses that are not connected by a coordinating conjunction such as *and* or *but* or *for*. Note the following examples in which these conjunctions were omitted and the semicolon had to be used:

> "Holovita means whole life; my ministry means whole life," Mrs. Stapleton said Sunday.
> The women are ready to march; the men are not (ready to march).
> The Creighton center cannot get up; he is hurt.
> "A few years from now, Concorde flights will probably be rarities; possibly they may not exist," he predicted.

In the first two foregoing examples, some editors would accept the comma as correct punctuation. As Copperud pointed out recently, the comma now may be sufficient punctuation if the clauses are brief, closely connected and parallel in form. These are called "contact clauses." Copperud advises journalism students to learn the rule for avoiding the comma splice but also to learn to recognize the exception of contact clauses that are acceptable. These two might be accepted: "Holovita means whole life, my ministry means whole life,". . . . The women are ready to march, the men are not. . . . (Of course a writer may always play it safe by using the semicolon.)

2. Use a semicolon between clauses of a compound sentence that are joined by conjunctive adverbs like *however, therefore, otherwise, consequently,* etc.

> The disease will occur in the best regulated kennels; however, dogs which have been inoculated are less likely to contract the disease.
> Neither side will yield an inch; therefore the conference apparently will end in failure.
> The secretary of state must recover from his illness rapidly; *otherwise* he cannot represent the United States at the conference.
> More than $90 million is flowing into the Saudi treasury every day; consequently, the Saudis have more money than they can spend, waste or give away.

3. A semicolon is used to separate coordinate phrases and clauses which are punctuated internally with a comma or commas.

> The new officers are: James Johnston, president; Raymond Nix, vice president; Mrs. Melba Myrick, secretary; and Miss Jane Brown, treasurer.
> A. M. Myrick, president of the company, is expected to arrive at noon; and Sam Katz, vice-president, should arrive this afternoon.

4. A semicolon is used to separate independent clauses that are joined by a coordinate conjunction if the clauses are long or have internal punctuation.

> The youngster, who was a raw but willing recruit, found that brawn still helps; but he learned quickly that today's rookie cop must have a nimble mind, an even temper and mature personality—qualities which get the young applicant past the first hurdles of intelligence tests.

5. A semicolon is used to separate phrases which contain commas, particularly when the meaning otherwise would not be clear.

> In the group were J. K. Thomas, the president of Wisconsin Service Company; Mrs. Jane Brown, his secretary; T. K. Thomas, his brother; Mrs. R. B. Thomas; two accountants; and a statistician.

COLONS

1. The colon is used before a long, formal quotation, such as statements and excerpts from speeches or writings.

If the quotation is longer than one sentence, it should start a new paragraph.

> Asked if he felt Fakuda made a firm committment to reduce the trade balance which heavily favors Japan now, Vance replied:
> "I do. I think there is a strong committment on that issue.
> "I think we are working together on this. I am confident we are going to make further progress."

2. The colon is used after a statement that is followed by an amplifying clause or expression.

> We are here for just one purpose: We are going to drill, drill, drill.
> He has only two ambitions: to marry rich and to "make the jet set."

Note in the first example that *We* is capitalized. The rule is to capitalize the first word following the colon only if it is a proper noun or the start of a complete sentence.

3. The colon is used after a clause that introduces a list.

> Try this menu: armadillo chili, fried beans, green onions and tortillas.
> The following officers were elected: A. P. Smith, Tallahassee; G. A. Morgan, Tucson; and Walter Cross, San Antonio.

If the words *the following* or *as follows* are not used, the colon need not be used, but it is correct to include it.

> Among the delegates are Smith, Morgan and Cross.
> The cities and their new populations are: Canterville, 50,500; Poplarside, 48,200; Sunnyvale, 43,500.

4. The colon often can be effective in giving emphasis to a word or a phrase.

> He had only one hobby: sleeping.
> Don't forget the biggest flop of the year: the two-dollar bill.
> We have set ourselves an ambitious goal in America: a high standard of health care for everyone, at manageable cost.

5. A colon is used between the numbers giving the chapter and verse of a Scripture passage.

> You will find it in Genesis 1:1–5.

6. A colon is used in writing figures that show time and timed events in sports.

> McHam is expected at 4:30 p.m. Thursday.
> They won in 1:02:45.8 (one hour, two minutes and 45.8 seconds).

Reporters will find two other uses for the colon. It is used for dialogue, especially in covering a trial, and it is used for question-and-answer interviews:

> Wade: When did you discover the body?
> Jones: I would say about a quarter to ten.

> Q: Is there a way to discourage a burglar from stealing things if you're not around to hear him?
> A: Probably the best deterrent is a dog in the house—preferably a nervous little dog that barks a lot.

APOSTROPHES

The use of the apostrophe in possessives has been treated in detail in Chapter 7. Review that chapter if you need to.

Here are the chief uses of the apostrophe:

1. An apostrophe is used to form possessives.

Mr. Dale's house	the Dales' automobile	Dickens' novels
the baby's rattle	the children's toys	the church's needs

2. An apostrophe is used to form the plurals of singular letters: Use two m's. He made two A's and three B's this term. The A's may win another pennant.

But add only an *s* to multiple letters: She learned her ABCs early. The same rule may be applied to figures, according to the press associations: It was the 1930s . . . Temperatures will soar to the high 90s.

Note, however, that some dictionaries call for use of *'s* here.

3. An apostrophe is used to indicate omission of a letter or letters or of a figure.

wasn't	they'd	o'clock	I've	aren't	class of '64
don't	hasn't	I'll	it's	can't	Spirit of '76

QUOTATION MARKS

1. Double quotation marks are used to enclose direct quotations—the exact words of a speaker or writer when reported in a story or article. Study the examples that follow.

> "I'm happy to be here," said the reticent 18-year-old riding wonder who will be aboard co-favored Affirmed in Saturday's 104th Kentucky Derby.
> "Everybody in Walton knows Steve (Cauthen)!" replied Doug. "When he comes home he is like everybody else."
> After stepping onto the moon, Armstrong said, "That's one small step for a man, one giant leap for mankind."

You might note variation in placement of the source of the quote in each of the examples. It is placed last in the first sentence, in the middle in the second example and first in the third sentence.

And here's a good example of use of the partial quote:

> Sen. Birch Bayh, D-Ind., chairman of the Senate Intelligence Committee, which produced the bill as its first piece of legislation, said the act "will bring to an end the practice of electronic surveillance by the executive branch without a court order."

You will note in the preceding example that partial quotations are enclosed just as are complete quotes. The first word of the partial quotation is not capitalized.

Journalists should guard against overusing fragmentary quotations. The *Associated Press Stylebook* advises: "If a speaker's words are clear and concise, favor the full quote. And if cumbersome language can be paraphrased fairly, use an indirect construction, reserving quotation marks for sensitive or controversial passages that must be identified specifically as coming from the speaker."

Observe the careful use of partial quotes in the sentences that follow.

> The Kremlin spokesman claimed that the Canadian spy charges were a "groundless" move in an officially inspired campaign "with obviously provocative aims" to smear Soviet-Canadian relations.
>
> John H. Perkins, president-elect of the American Bankers Association, noted that Miller (G. William Miller) has a reputation as "a strong leader" in the business fraternity and predicted "he's going to try to do a good job."
>
> The tobacco industry is hardly overjoyed at the promise of HEW Secretary Joseph Califano to launch "the most vigorous and hard-hitting program against smoking that this country has ever had."

There are four rules to be remembered in connection with the use of direct quotations: (1) Set off explanatory expressions with commas; (2) Capitalize the first word of the quotation if it is a complete sentence; (3) Place a period or a comma within the quotation marks; (4) Place a question mark inside the quotation marks if the quotation is a question; otherwise, put the question mark outside the quotation marks. Note these examples of the four important rules:

> "If we can have the support of every citizen," the governor declared, "we can solve this problem."
>
> *Or:* "If we have the support of every citizen, we can solve this problem," said the governor.
>
> "Shortage of water is not our only problem," the governor reiterated. "Soil conservation is also important."
>
> *But:* The governor said that "we can solve this water-shortage problem." (Partial quotation not capitalized.)

Reread the preceding examples and note that the commas and periods are always placed inside the quotation marks regardless of the meaning.

Note placement of the question mark in the following sentences:

> "When will they be ready?" he asked.
> But would you accept his statement of being "always conscious of the importance of the position"?

When a quotation runs to two or more paragraphs in length, the quotation marks are placed at the beginning of each paragraph and at the end of the last paragraph of the quotation.

> "Change the rules in the middle of the game?" asked Miss Jordan, rhetorically.
> "It's no game, Mr. Chairman. We're talking about the rules of living, breathing, viable, working human beings, individuals.
> "We're talking about the Constitution of the United States and something that needs to be done to make it still more perfect. It's no game."

2. Single quotation marks are used to designate quoted matter that is given within a direct quotation.

> "The people who work with Wallenda in the act ran around in a panic, screaming 'Oh my God, oh my God,'" Gary Williams, a local newspaper photographer, said . . .
> The man testified, "I asked her, 'Did you find this copy of the book lying beside the body?' but she did not answer my question."

3. Newspaper usage calls for double quotation marks with titles of books, movies, plays, operas, songs, poems, television program titles and the titles of lectures, speeches and works of art. Use quotation marks around the names of all such works except the Bible and books that contain primarily reference material, such as dictionaries, encyclopedias, handbooks, etc.

Examples: "The Rise and Fall of the Third Reich," "God Bless America," the NBC "Today" program, the "CBS Evening News," Leonardo da Vinci's "Mona Lisa," "The Gin Game," "Gone With the Wind," Webster's New Collegiate Dictionary, Encyclopedia Britannica, Copperud's A Dictionary of Usage and Style.

Of course journalists should know that quotation marks are *not* used with newspaper and magazine titles: The New York Times, The Atlantic Monthly. In printing, such names are often italicized or printed in caps and small caps, in the text only.

In all titles, capitalize the principal words, including prepositions and conjunctions of four or more letters. Capitalize an article—*the, a, an*—or a word of fewer than four letters if it is the first or last word in a title.

4. Double quotation marks are used to set off slang expressions or words that are used ironically.

258 / Punctuation and Spelling

The blonde is the burglar's "gun moll," police believe.

She used a new version of the "pigeon drop" scheme.

The miser's "generosity" consisted of leaving two thousand dollars to his dog and cutting out the servants from his will.

5. Quotation marks are now used with nicknames when the nickname is inserted into the identification of the individual: Daniel "Chappie" James Jr., who risked court-martial to fight segregation and eventually became the first black four-star general, died Saturday at 58.

However, in sports reporting, nicknames may be substituted for a first name without using quotation marks: Bear Bryant. But if the full name is used, it is Paul "Bear" Bryant.

Also, no quotation marks are needed with a nickname used in place of a person's given name in news stories: Jimmy Carter. Be sure, however, that is the way the person wishes to be known.

6. Finally, there are three more points to keep in mind in using quotations.

In quoting two or more persons in the same story, put quotations of the separate individuals into separate paragraphs.

Most editors will insist that you do not mix one or more complete sentences of direct quotation with one or more complete sentences of non-quoted material within the same paragraph.

A common error of journalism students is the failure to close the quotation—to insert the second pair of quotation marks. Be alert to avoid this error.

PARENTHESES

Journalists are warned by newspaper editors and the press associations to avoid the use of parentheses, which are jarring to the reader. If you are tempted to use parentheses, try to write the sentence some other way. But if a sentence must contain incidental material, use commas or two dashes as alternatives. Such punctuation usually is much more effective. However, when writers think parentheses are necessary, they should follow certain guidelines.

1. Parentheses are used to set off loosely connected parenthetical material that is incidental to the meaning of the sentence. The material is inserted by the writer to explain or to amplify the thought being expressed.

The kidnappers wrote that they were "executing the (death) sentence on Aldo Moro."

"We are pinning all our hopes and our attention on the use of the gerund executing," a Christian Democratic statement said. "They (the kidnappers) could have used the past tense and we all know the Red Brigades choose their words carefully."

Use synonyms for such common words as *walk* (*strode, limped, hurried,* etc.) and *said* (*declared, asserted, shouted,* etc.)

2. If a parenthesis ends a sentence, the final mark of punctuation for the sentence is placed outside the parenthesis unless the statement in the parenthesis is a complete sentence in itself. Note the placement of the period in the examples in the preceding section. And here are some other examples:

> We believe there will be other occasions for the use of this device (and many more, at that).
> The speaker used two quotations from the Bible (one from Genesis and one from Luke).
> The speaker used the same quotation twice in is speech. (The quotation was from the first chapter of Genesis.)

3. Parentheses are sometimes used to insert the name of the state after the name of a city in the title of a newspaper or an organization.

> The Stillwater (Okla.) News-Press was founded by his grandfather.

BRACKETS

The journalist will have practically no use for brackets. Since brackets cannot be transferred over news wires, the press services advise staff members to use parentheses instead or to rewrite the material.

Brackets are used largely by editors to enclose interpolated matter in a passage being quoted: ''At that time [1820] Mexico was ruled by the aristocracy,'' the historian stated.

DASHES

Too many writers overwork the dash. Many editors will point out to you that a period, a semicolon or a colon may be used to better advantage. Learn to use the dash sparingly but effectively. In typing, be sure to strike the hyphen bar twice to make a dash, and do not leave space on either side of the dash.

1. A dash is used to indicate a sudden break in the thought or the speech.

> She stammered, ''But—but—I did not—''
> He is tall, dark—and ugly.
> The slaying of Floyd's son was mysterious—the most mysterious murder in the history of Texas, in fact.
> Trigger man in the slaying—the other side does not deny it—is Juan Julio Perkins.
> If the Terrorists win the election—God forbid!—right-thinking men and women will be driven from the country.

2. A dash is sometimes used before a repetition, for effect.

> Men grow weary of life—weary of constant struggle for existence.
> There is but one love common to all—the love of life.

3. A dash is sometimes used to set off a statement or a summary of particulars.

> Wine, women, money—all make men falter.
> She has left it all—love, money, fame—for a life devoted to the poor. (Note that the use of commas instead of dashes would have been confusing here.)

4. The dash is often used to indicate questions and answers in a verbatim report of testimony.

> Q.—Did you see the man in the tavern?
> A.—No, I did not.

5. Dashes, rather than commas or parentheses, may be used most effectively to emphasize material that is parenthetical but which contributes importantly to the meaning of the sentence. In fact, there is a strong trend toward using dashes in this way, both in newspapers and magazines. Note in the examples that follow how writers made parenthetical material emphatic by using dashes. You will observe that the parenthetical material is used appositively. Ordinarily, appositives are set off by commas, but certainly the use of dashes can make such material more emphatic.

> Scientists believe there are vast reservoirs of undiscovered energy—hot water— beneath the surface of the Atlantic coastal plain from southern New Jersey to northern Florida.
> A devastating anticancer drug—capable of killing all cancer in mice with a single dose—has been produced by scientists in California.
> The expert pointed out that Hughes had a unique way of crossing his t's and dotting his i's—a trait that appears in the disputed will.
> For Saudi Arabia has the United States, and the rest of the industrial world, over a barrel—of oil.

HYPHENS

The journalist's use of the hyphen is largely in compounds. The most difficult problem with English compounds is whether to write them as (1) separate words or (2) hyphenated words or (3) solid words.

Use of the hyphen in compound words is so varied that writers need to consult the dictionary or the stylebook when in doubt. But at this point, the following guidelines on uses of the hyphen should be helpful.

1. The hyphen is used to form compound adjectives that precede the noun they modify.

Failure to follow this rule is one of the most common faults of journalism students and of practicing journalists, and they are urged to accept this pertinent advice offered in the AP Stylebook: Use hyphens to avoid ambiguity or to form a single idea from two or more words. Use a hyphen whenever ambiguity would result if it were omitted: The president will speak to *small-business* men (not to small business men). Also: After he *recovered* his health he decided to *re-cover* the roof himself.

When a compound modifier—two or more words that express a single concept—*precedes* a noun, use hyphens to link all the words in the compound except the adverb *very* and all adverbs that end in *ly*: a first-quarter touchdown, a bluish-green dress, a part-time job, a well-known actor, a better-qualified woman, a know-it-all attitude, a very good time, the newly completed bridge.

Note the use of hyphens in compound modifiers in sentences taken from four metropolitan newspapers and from *Editor & Publisher*:

> Tracy Austin, the fragile-looking 15-year-old girl from Rolling Hills, Calif., took her biggest step to reaching tennis stardom by ending the 37-match victory streak of Dallas' Martina Navratilova. . . .
>
> Calvin Coolidge is not the most quoted of our former presidents, but it's just possible he was one of the first tell-it-like-it-is public figures. He once opened his mouth and out came, "Business will be better or worse."
>
> Sen. Dick Clark, D.-Iowa, also introduced another farther-reaching, second-round bill that would raise price-support targets for wheat, corn. . . .
>
> A three-woman, three-man probate court jury ruled Wednesday that the late billionaire Howard Hughes was a legal resident of Texas and that the so-called "Mormon will" was a forgery.
>
> Two men convicted of first-degree murder in the 1976 car-bomb slaying of newspaper reporter Don Bolles were sentenced to die in the gas chamber.

Here's a list of commonly used (note that *commonly used* is not hyphenated) compound adjectives that precede the noun:

good-looking woman	happy-go-lucky way	ready-to-wear clothes
200-meter run	Houston-Maryland game	first-class mail
terror-stricken face	mob-connected figure	hit-or-miss manner
left-handed pitcher	old-fashioned dress	a 40-inch cut
a full-time job	a well-educated person	snow-covered mountain

You are reminded that the hyphen is not used between an adverb ending in *ly* and a participle (adjective) that precede a noun: the *brightly lighted* room; a *widely advertised* product.

There is no universal rule to follow in hyphenating or not hyphenating the compound adjective when it *follows* the noun. The reason for this is that usage is constantly changing in the spelling of compound words. Compound words usually go through three stages in spelling. Usually they are first written as two words, then hyphenated and finally written as one word.

For the spelling of a compound, then, you need to consult a current dictionary or a stylebook. The dictionary will show what are true compounds—words that must be hyphenated, such as *self-employed, self-conscious, gold-filled, good-natured, time-consuming* and so forth.

Dictionaries, however, differ on use of the hyphen in compounds. For example, the word *week end* or *week-end* or *weekend* was a two-word compound to begin with. Currently it is listed in *Webster's New Collegiate Dictionary*, surprisingly enough, as *week end* as a noun, *week-end* as an intransitive verb, and with no solid spelling (*weekend*). On the other hand, *Webster's New Twentieth Century Dictionary* prefers the solid form, *weekend*, with *week-end* as second choice.

You may, then, turn to the stylebook as your best guide. Say you need to check on whether or not to hyphenate a compound modifier that *follows* the noun. If you turn to the *Associated Press Stylebook*, you will find this answer: Many combinations that are hyphenated before a noun are not hyphenated when they occur after the noun: The team scored in the first quarter. The dress, a bluish green, was very attractive on her. She works full time. His attitude suggested that he knew it all.

But when a modifier that would be hyphenated before a noun occurs instead after a form of the verb *to be*, the hyphen usually must be retained to avoid confusion: The man is well-known. The woman is quick-witted. The children are soft-spoken. The play is second-rate.

(Editors of the AP and UPI 1977 stylebooks chose as their main reference *Webster's New World Dictionary of the American Language*.)

Writers who do not have ready access to the stylebook of a newspaper, magazine or press association may wish to use *A Manual of Style*, University of Chicago Press, or *The Style Manual* of the Government Printing Office.

2. The hyphen is used in suspended compounds: a 12- or 16-page booklet; low- and middle-income workers.

3. The hyphen is used in prepositional phrase combinations.

attorney-at-law	out-of-doors	stick-in-the-mud
mother-in-law	door-to-door (poll)	matter-of-fact

4. A hyphen is used in compound numerals from twenty-one to ninety-nine, and also in fractions: sixty-five years, a two-thirds share.

5. The hyphen is used to distinguish different meanings in words of like spelling.

The shoplifter eventually reformed.
The line was re-formed at the end of the field.
Without proper recreation, the youths are likely to become delinquents.
They decided on the re-creation of certain rules they had abolished.
He recovered in time to re-cover his roof.

6. A hyphen is used between some prefixes and nouns or adjectives, and always between the prefix and a proper noun or proper adjective.

Prefixes that take a hyphen include *ex, un, all, pro, anti* and *pan.* The suffix *elect* also requires the hyphen:

ex-governor Briscoe   pro-life   un-American   governor-elect Hill
pro-British   All-American or all-American   Pan-American countries
anti-communist

7. The hyphen is used to take the place of the preposition *to* in figures indicating an extension.

The treasurer is preparing the April-July report of income.
Refer to pages 130-158 for a table on income.
The reception for the Hopes will last from 2-4 p.m.

8. A hyphen is used to divide a word at the end of a line of type or of writing.

Words are divided only between syllables. Most printers do not advocate dividing words of two syllables, and of course words of one syllable may not be divided. Most newspaper editors advise reporters to avoid all hyphenation of this kind, ignoring an uneven right margin. If you do divide a word at the end of the line, be sure to place the hyphen at the end of that line. Also, make sure that you follow the division of the word that is given in the dictionary. This does not always follow the division of the word as spoken. Notice these examples:

rec-om-men-da-tion	pref-er-ence	sup-po-si-tion
pri-vate	im-ag-ery	bar-bi-tu-rate or bar-bit-u-rate
skill-ful-ness	pre-ferred	su-preme-ly
non-ad-dic-ting	ped-a-go-gy	proc-la-ma-tion
pro-cess-or	jour-nal-ism	re-vi-sion

18

Correct Spelling is a "Must" for the Journalist

Originality in style of writing has been stressed. One place, however, where the journalist must not display originality is in his spelling.

If you need special encouragement to improve your spelling, recall the findings of a survey in which almost two-thirds of 100 American newspaper editors rated deficiency in spelling as the second greatest fault of journalism graduates whom they have employed. Only deficiency in grammar was called a greater fault. This should convince you that correct spelling and good grammar are important assets for success in the field of journalism.

Knowledge of a few basic rules of spelling and the habit of using the dictionary when in doubt will see you through. You want to succeed at your first job, and you want to rise in the journalism ranks with maximum speed. Learn to spell correctly, then, and to use good reference books when you need to.

BASIC RULES OF SPELLING

There are five basic rules of spelling you need to know. You will use these largely in spelling verbs. However, note that the rules apply also to nouns, adjectives and adverbs.

Rule 1. Words of one syllable that end in a single consonant preceded by a single vowel double the consonant before adding a suffix that begins with a vowel.

The vowels are *a, e, i, o* and *u*; sometimes *y* is regarded as a vowel. All the other letters are consonants.

Take the verb *trap* and test it with the rule above. Is it a one-syllable verb? Yes. It ends in a single consonant, *p*. The consonant is preceded by a single vowel, *a*. The suffixes *ed* and *ing* begin with a vowel. Hence when one of these suffixes is added to *trap*, the *p* must be doubled: *trapped, trapping*. This is a foolproof rule you may follow for *all* one-syllable verbs.

Some of the suffixes to which this rule applies are: *-able, -ably, -age, -al, -ed, -ent, -est, -ing, -ish*. Try out the rule on the following words, thus: bag, bagged, bagging, baggage; beg, begged, begging, beggar; man, manned, manning, mannish; etc.

bag	dot	flip	jam	plot	slam
bar	drag	get	lag	putt (in golf)	stop
beg	drop	grab	man	run	trip
brag	fan	hop	pin	ship	wet
dab	flit	knit	plan	sit	wrap

There are some exceptions to this rule, but you should have no trouble with these. Words that end in the consonants *k, v, w, x* and *y* do not double the consonant before a suffix with a vowel. Examples are:

box, boxing, boxed   row, rowing, rowed   play, playing, played

Another exception is the verb *bus* (*bused* or *bussed, busing* or *bussing*).

Rule 2. Words of more than one syllable that end in a consonant preceded by a single vowel double the final consonant before adding a suffix beginning with a vowel—*if* the word is accented on the last syllable.

Take the word *commit*. It ends in the consonant *t*. The final consonant is preceded by the single vowel *i*. The word is accented on the second syllable: com-mit′. The consonant *t* is doubled before adding a suffix like *-ed* or *-ing*: *committed, committing*.

Other words that follow this rule are:

admit	confer	excel	omit	regret
allot	control	impel	propel	repel
begin	defer	incur	rebel	submit
compel	deter	infer	recur	transfer
concur	dispel	occur	refer	

The verb *equip* is considered as belonging under this rule because the *u* has the sound of the consonant *w: equip, equipping, equipped*.

You might note that many of the verbs listed above may add suffixes like *-able, -ably, -al, -ent, -er*, etc., to form nouns, adjectives and adverbs. Note that the consonant is doubled, according to the rule, in these words: controller, controllable, regrettable, regrettably, concurrent, deterrent, referral, repellent. However, if the word you form must have the accent on the first syllable, don't double the consonant, as in the adjective pref´erable.

If the words are accented on any syllable other than the last, the consonant is not doubled before adding a suffix beginning with a vowel.

hap´pen, happening	ben´e-fit, benefiting
o´pen, opened, opening	de-vel´op, developer
ex-hib´it, exhibitor	dif fer, different
can´cel, canceled	pro-hib´it, prohibited
mod´el, modeling	sum´mon, summoning

There are a few words that may double the final consonant or not double it, either form being considered correct. The dictionary shows both forms, with the preferred form given first, thus: *tra ´vel, -eled* or *-elled, -eling* or *-elling*. Other examples are *counsel* and *kidnap*. Use the preferred form in your writing.

Rule 3. Words that end in silent *e* drop the *e* before adding a suffix beginning with a vowel (*-ing, -able, -ance, -ibly, -ous, -ish,* etc.)

advise, advising, advisable	guide, guidance	use, usable
change, changing	notice, noticing	dine, dining
come, coming	desire, desirable	desire, desirous
argue, arguing, arguable	force, forcibly	blue, bluish
interfere, interfering	sale, salable	resemble, resemblance
judge, judging, judgment	believe, believable	love, lovable[1]

The exceptions to this rule include words in which the dropping of the *e* would confuse the meaning, and words ending in *ce* or *ge* in which the *c* or the *g* has a soft sound, like *s* or *j*.

eye, eyeing	canoe, canoeing	change, changeable
dye, dyeing	peace, peaceable	courage, courageous
hoe, hoeing	notice, noticeable	manage, manageable

Note the difference between *die, dying,* and *dye, dyeing*.

Words that end in silent *e* retain the *e* before adding a suffix beginning with a consonant: arrange, arrangement; stale, staleness; hope, hopeful; sincere, sincerely; nine, nineteen, etc.

Rule 4. (a) Verbs ending in *y* preceded by a consonant change the *y* to *i* before adding *-es* to form the third-person singular, present tense, or before adding *-ed* to form the past tense.

---

[1] Webster's now lists *judgement, saleable* and *loveable* as secondary variants. The stylebooks say, "Don't use."

try, tries, tried	study, studies, studied
cry, cries, cried	reply, replies, replied
deny, denies, denied	carry, carries, carried
hurry, hurries, hurried	worry, worries, worried

The exception is for the ending *-ing*: try, trying, etc.

(b) Nouns and adjectives ending in *y* preceded by a consonant change the *y* to *i* before adding *-es, -est* and other suffixes that do *not* begin with an *i*.

lady, ladies	dry, drier, driest	busy, busily
city, cities	mercy, merciful	noisy, noisily
sky, skies	happy, happiness	theory, theories

But: gray*er*, gray*est*, etc.

Rule 5. When *i* and *e* occur together in a word, the *i* usually precedes the *e* except after the consonant *c*.

The journalist will do well to remember the old jingle:

Use *i* before *e*
Except after *c*
Or when sounded like *a*
As in *neighbor* and *weigh*.

True, there are more exceptions to this rule than to the others, but the rule is often helpful. The more important exceptions should be learned, and the dictionary should be consulted when there is any doubt.

Words that follow the rule are:

achieve	conceit	friend	piece	relief
alien	conceive	frontier	pierce	siege
believe	deceive	grief	receipt	thief
chief	fierce	grieve	receive	yield

The most common exceptions to the rule are: counterfeit, either, financier, foreign, heifer, height, inveigle, leisure, science, their, weird.

You will see that there are several exceptions to Rule 5, but remember that the first four rules may be followed with few exceptions. You will save yourself many trips to the dictionary by using all five rules. But when there is no safe rule to use or whenever you have any doubt about the spelling of a word, the safest rule to follow is to look it up in the dictionary!

FORMING PLURALS AND POSSESSIVES

Journalism students have been found to be particularly weak in the correct use of the possessive case. A review of Chapter 7 will refresh your memory on many points.

Forming Plurals

Nine essential things to remember are discussed here.

1. Most nouns, particularly those ending in a consonant, form their plurals by adding *s* or *es*.

 lens, lenses   point, points   gas, gases

2. Nouns ending in *o* preceded by a vowel add *s* to form the plural.

 cameo, cameos   hoe, hoes   radio, radios

3. Nouns ending in *o* preceded by a consonant usually add *s* to form the plural, but sometimes add *es*.

 halo, halos   buffalo, buffaloes
 Eskimo, Eskimos   potato, potatoes

4. Nouns ending in *y* preceded by a vowel form the plural by adding *s*.

 guy, guys   key, keys   alloy, alloys

5. Nouns ending in *y* preceded by a consonant form the plural by changing *y* to *i* and adding *es*.

 baby, babies   army, armies   soliloquy, soliloquies

In *soliloquy* the *u* is pronounced like *w*, so the word follows this rule.

6. Some nouns form their plurals irregularly.

 man, men   woman, women   child, children   foot, feet

7. The plurals of letters, figures, signs, abbreviations and words named as words are formed usually by adding an apostrophe and *s* (*'s*).

 three r's   five B-29's   too many *and's*

8. Nouns ending in *f*, *fe* or *ff* *usually* form the plural by adding *s*.

 proof, proofs   cuff, cuffs   handkerchief, handkerchiefs

A few of these nouns change the *f* to *v* and add *es* to form the plural.

 loaf, loaves   half, halves   thief, thieves   wife, wives

9. Foreign words sometimes retain their foreign plurals.

 datum, data   crisis, crises   addendum, addenda   alumnus, alumni

Forming Possessives

You will do well to turn back to pages 94–96, 100–01 to review the detailed discussion of forming possessives of nouns. You will find below only a brief summary of the rules for forming possessives.

1. The possessive of singular nouns, with a few exceptions, is formed by adding *'s*.

child's toy   baby's crib   Charles's book (or Charles' book)

Remember, if a noun ends in *s*, and *'s* makes the word disagreeable to the ear or difficult to say, the apostrophe alone may be used. In fact, newspaper and wire service stylebooks now advise adding only the apostrophe in such cases: Charles' boat; Moses' tablet.

2. The possessive of plural nouns ending in *s* is formed by adding the apostrophe only.

the Blakes' car   my two sisters' home

3. The possessive of plural nouns not ending in *s* is formed by adding *'s*.

two men's reports   several children's parents

4. The possessive pronouns do not have an apostrophe.

mine   hers   his   its   yours   ours   theirs

SPELLING HINTS FOR THE JOURNALIST

The pages that follow have a list of the words most commonly misspelled by journalists. You should make it a "must" to learn to spell these words correctly. Concentrate on the words that give you trouble. The so-called "spelling demons" are designated by asterisks(*).

You are urged to follow these nine steps with any words you misspell regularly:

1. Look up the word in the dictionary.
2. Study the spelling of the word and its meaning.
3. Fix in your mind the exact appearance of the word, paying particular attention to the sequence of letters and to the division of the word into syllables. (Many words are misspelled because the writer has failed to divide them into their correct syllables. Example: *in/ci/dent/ly* for *in/ci/den/tal/ly*.)

You may find that you have been misspelling a word because you mispronounced it. You may have been inserting an unnecessary consonant in a word, as in saying "drownded" for *drowned*. On the other hand, you may have been adding an unnecessary vowel to the word in writing it, as in writing "athelete" for *athlete*. Do you make the mistake of using an unnecessary *i* in writing *similar*? (The misspelling of "similar" as "similiar" is common because of confusion with "familiar," which does have an additional *i*.) You may be omitting a necessary vowel in some words. The word *sophomore* is often misspelled "sophmore." Or you may be omitting a consonant, as in gover(n)ment.

Another fact you may have failed to learn is that many English words contain silent letters. You must learn to spell these words correctly. Note the following words. The letters in parentheses are not sounded, but they must be included when you write the words:

(p)neumonia kil(n) (w)rapped tho(ugh) thoro(ugh)

4. Pronounce the word aloud several times, syllable by syllable.

5. Type or write the word ten times to fix it in your mind.

6. Now study the word again. Take a pencil and write the word divided into syllables with a slant line between each two syllables, like this: in/ci/den/tal/ly.

7. Underline the parts of the word that give you trouble, thus:

embarrass   fiery   separate   familiar   picnicking   disappoint
weird   believable   similar   questionnaire   judgment²
arctic   recommend   marshal   cemetery

8. Devote as much time as you feel is necessary to reviewing the words that give you trouble.

9. Make sure that you can now spell the word correctly without using the dictionary.

However, whenever you are in doubt about the spelling or the syllabication of a word, *look it up in the dictionary.*

WORDS COMMONLY MISSPELLED

Asterisks (*) indicate "spelling demons"

abandon	abscess	academy
abbreviate	abscond	accede
abdomen	absence	accelerator
abduct	absorb	acceptable
aberration	absorption	accessibility
abet	absurd	accessory (ies)
abeyance	abundance	*accidentally
abhorrence	abysmal	*accommodate
abreast	abyss	accompanist
abridgment³	academic	accompanying

---

²Webster's considers *judgement* a secondary variant, but stylebooks do not accept it.
³Webster's gives *abridgement* as a secondary variant.

accomplish
accumulate
accurate
accustomed
acetylene
ache
achievement
acknowledge
acknowledgment
acoustics
acquaintance
acquiesce
acquire
acquitted
acrid
*across
acumen
adaptability
additionally
addressed
adjacent
adjoining
adjutant
ad-lib
administrator
admirable
admissible
admittance
admitted
adolescent
advantageous
advertise (ment)
advice (*noun*)
advisable
advise (*verb*)
adviser
advisory
aeronautics
aesthetic
affidavit
affiliate
agenda
aggravate
aggregate
aggressive

aggressor
agreeing
alias
alienate
align
allege
allegiance
alleys
allied
allies
allocate
allotment
allotted
*all right
almanac
almost
already
although
altogether
aluminum
always
amateur
ambidextrous
ambiguous
ammonia
amnesia
amok or amuck
among
analogous
analysis
analyze
anemia
anemic
animosity
ankle
annihilated
annual
anoint
anonymous
answer
antarctic
antecedent
anticipate
anticlimax
antidote

antiseptic
antitoxin
anxiety
anxious
apartment
aperture
*apologize
apology
appalling
apparatus
apparel
apparent
apparition
appealed
appearance
appellate
appetite
appraise
appreciate
approaching
appropriate
apropos
aquarium
architect
arctic
arguing
argument
arising
arithmetic (al)
armament
arouse
arousing
arrangement
arranging
arrival
arthritis
article
artificial
artillery
ascend
ascent
ascertain
asinine
asked
aspirin

*assassin
assassinate
assault
assessment
assistance
association
astronaut
*athlete
*athletic(s)
atmosphere
attacked
attendance
attitude
attorney
auctioneer
audible
audience
authentic
author
authoritative
authorities
authorize
autumn
auxiliary
awkward

baccalaureate
bachelor
bacteriology
bailiff
balance
ballad
ballet
ballistic(s)
balloon
ballot
bananas
bankruptcy
Baptist
*baptize
barbarous
bargain
barrel(ed)
baring
barricade

barring
basically
*battalion
bearing
becoming
beggar
begging
beginning
behavior
beige
believable
*believe
believing
belligerent
beneficial
*benefit(ed)
benign
beverage
bicycle
biennial
bigoted
binoculars
biscuit
boisterous
bona fide
bookkeeper
boulevard
boundary (ies)
bouquet
breath (*noun*)
breathe (*verb*)
brethren
brief
brilliant
bristle
Britain
Briton
broccoli
brochure
brogue
bronchitis
built
bulletin
buoyant
bureau

burglar
buries
bury
bus
bus(s)es
business
bustle

cache
cadaver
caesarean (section)
caffeine
*calendar
caliber
calm
calumny
camouflage
campaign
cancel
cancellation
cancel(l)ed
*candidate
*can't (cannot)
cantaloupe
*captain
carburetor
career
careful
Caribbean
carriage
carrying
cartridge
cashier
catalog (ue)
catastrophe
catechism
categorically
category
caucus
cauliflower
cavalry
ceiling
Celsius
*cemetery
census

centigrade
*certain
champagne
*changeable
changing
chaperon(e)
characteristic
characterize
chargeable
charismatic
chassis
chatter
chauffeur
chauvinist
chief
chiffonier
chili *or* chilli, chile
chimney
chocolate
choir
choose
choosing
chord (in music)
chose
chosen
chronology
circuit
circular
circumstantial
cite
cities
civilize
clientele
climactic (ally)
climatic
clique
cloth (*noun*)
clothe (*verb*)
clothes (*plural*)
coconut
coincide
coincidence
coliseum

collar
collateral
collegiate
collide
collision
colloquial
cologne
colonel
*color
colossal
column
combatant
combat(t)ing
coming
commemorate
commentator
commercial
commission
commissioner
commitment
committed
*committee
communication
community
comparable
comparatively
compatible
compel
compelled
competent
competition
competitive
complexioned[4]
complimentary
comprise
compulsory
comrade
comradeship
concede
conceit
conceive
conceivable
concentration

concerned
concession
conciliation
concise
condemn
confectionery
confer
conferred
confident (*adj.*)
confidentially
connoisseur
conqueror
conscience (*noun*)
conscientious (*adj.*)
consciousness (*noun*)
*consensus
consider
consistency
consonant
conspicuous
consul
consumer
contagious
contemporary
contemptible
contemptuous
contentious
continually
continuously
contradictory
control
controlled
*controversy
convalescent
convene
convenience
convenient
conveyed
coolly (*adv.*)
cooperate
copies
copyright
*corner
corps

[4] Webster's now accepts *complected.*

corpus delicti
corral (led)
correlate
correspondence
correspondent
corroborate
corsage
cosmic
cosmonaut
costume
cough
countenance
counterfeit
countries
coup
courageous
courteous
courtesies
courtesy
credibility
*cried
cries
criticism
*criticize
crochet
cruelty
curiosity
curriculum
customary
cylinder
czar

data (*plural*)
datum (*sing.*)
dealt (*past of* deal)
debatable
debater
debris
debtor
deceased
deceitful
deceive
decide
*decided
decision

defendant
defense *or* defence
defer
deferred
defiance
deficiency
deficit
*definite
demagogue
denied
deny
denying
dependent
depositary (*person*)
depository (*place*)
deprivation
depth
derived
descend
descendant
descent
*describe
description
desiccate
*desirable
desirous
despair
desperate
desperation
despicable
destroy
deteriorate
detriment
devastating
*develop
developed
development
dexterous (pref.)
diagnose
diagonally
dialog (ue)
diarrhea
dictatorial
dictionary
*dietitian

difference
diffidence
digestible
dilapidated
dilemma
diligent
diminish
*dining
dining-room (*adj.*)
diocese
diphtheria
dirigible
disability
*disappear
*disappoint(ed)
disastrous
disavowal
disavowed
discernible
disciple
discipline
discuss (ed)
discussion
disease
disinfectant
dissatisfied
dissect
dissension
dissipate
dissipation
distinction
distinguish
distribute
distributor
*divide
*divine
division
doctor
doesn't
dominant
don't
dormitories
dormitory
drastically
drought

drowned
drudgery
drunkenness
duffel
dullness
dumbbell
dumbfounded
durable
*dyeing
dying (expiring)

easily
eccentric
economically
economize
ecstasy
Ecuador
eerie
effect
effective
efficiency
*eighth
eligible
eliminate
eloquence
emanate
*embarrass
embed (ded)
emergencies
emergency
emotionally
emphasis (*noun*)
*emphasize (*verb*)
emphatic
emphysema
employe (e)
encourage
encouragement
encouraging
encyclical
endeavor
endurance
enemies
enemy
enough

enthusiastic
entirely
entrance
enunciate
envelop (*verb*)
envelope (*noun*)
envelopment
environment
epidemic
epidemiology
epoch
equable
equilibrium
equip
equipment
equipped
*equivalent
erroneous
escape
especially
espionage
essence
essential
etc.
ever
every
everybody
evidently
exaggerate
examine
examination
exceed
excel
excelled
excellent
except
exceptional
exceptionally
excess
excessive
excitable
excitement
exercise
exhaust (ed)
exhibit

exhibition
exhilarate
*existence
exorbitant
exorcist
expense
experience
experiment
explanation
explicit
extension
extraordinary
extravagance
extremely
eyeing

facilitate
facilities
Fahrenheit
fallacies
fallout (*noun*)
*familiar
familiarity
famous
fascinate
fascinating
feasible
featherbedding
*February
fictitious
field
fierce
*fiery
fifth
filibuster
finally
financial
financially
financier
flier *or* flyer
fluoridation
focal
forehead
*foreign
foremost

foresee
foreword
forfeit
fortieth
*forty
forty-four
forward (not forwards)
fourth
fragrant
frantically
fraternity
fraudulent
freight
frequency
*freshman (*adj.*)
friend
friendliness
frivolous
frontier
fulfil (l)
fulfilled
ful(l)ness
fundamental
furniture
further
fusillade

gagging
gaiety *or* gayety
gallant
gamble
gambling
gases
gauge
gelatin
generally
generous
genius
genuine
ghost
gizmo
glamour *or* glamor
glamorous *or* glamourous
glycerin
gnawing

gobbledygook
goddess
goodby (e)
*government
governor
*grammar
grammatical
grandeur
grandiose
grateful
grief
grievous
gruesome
guarantee
guard
guardian
gubernatorial
guess
guidance
guillotine
guru
gypsy *or* gipsy

halcyon
Halloween
handful
handkerchief
handle
handling
handsome
haphazard
harass
hardening
harebrained
hastily
haul (led)
haven't
hazardous
*height
helpfulness
hemorrhage
herald
hereditary
heresy
heroes
heroine

hesitancy
hesitantly
hindrance
hearse
heliport
hodgepodge
hooky
hope
hopeless
hoping
hopping (leaping)
hospitable
huge
humidity
humorous
hundred
hundredths
hurried
hurriedly
hurrying
hygiene
hygienic
hymn
hymnal
hypnosis
hypnotize
*hypocrisy
hysterical

icicle
identity
ideologies
idiocy
idiomatic
idiosyncrasies
illicit
illiterate
illogical
illustrate
imaginary
imagination
imagining
imitation
immaculate
*immediately
immensely

immigrate
immigration
immovable
impetuous
impostor (pref.)
imprisonment
impromptu
impugn
inaccessible
inaccuracy
inadequate
inadmissible
inaugurate
incalculable
incentive
incessant
*incidentally
incipient
incomparable
incompetent
incorrigible
incredible
incredibly
incredulous
incur (red)
incurable
indefinitely
independence
*independent
Indian
indict (ment)
indigestible
indiscreet
indispensable
induce
inebriated
inefficiency
inescapable
inevitable
inexhaustible
infectious
inferred
infinite (ly)

inflammable
influence
influential
infuriate
ingredient
inherent
initiation
initiative
innocence
innocuous
innovate
innuendo
*inoculate
inseparable
insignia
insistence
instance
instantaneous
instead
instill *or* instil
insulin
intellectual
intelligence
intelligent
intelligible
intentionally
intercede
intercepted
interested
*interesting
interfere
intermittent
interpret
interpretation
interrupt (ion)
intolerable
intricacies
introduce
invariably
inveigle
iridescent
irrelevant
irreligious

irresistible
irresponsible
island
isthmus
itemize
itinerary
*its (*pron.*)
*it's (it is)
itself

January
jaundice
jealous
jeopardize
jewelry
jodhpurs
*judgment[5]
ju-jitsu
judicial

kaleidoscope
keenness
khaki
kidnap (p) ed
kidnap (p) er
kilometer
kimono
kindergarten
knack
knickknack
knowledge (able)
knuckle

label
*laboratory
ladies
*laid (*past of* lay)
laryngitis
larynx
later
latter
laundered
lavender
*led (*past of* lead)

[5] Webster's accepts *judgement* as a variant, but stylebooks do not accept it.

legerdemain
leggings
legible
legionnaire
legislative
legislator
legitimate
leisure
leisurely
*length
lenses
lethargic
leukemia
liable
*liaison
*libel
library
license
lieutenant
likable
likelihood
likely
lilies
limousine
lingerie
*liquefy
liqueur
liquidate
liquor
listener
literary
literature
livable
livelihood
liveliness
loneliness
loose (to untie)
*lose
*losing
*lovable⁶
loveliness
loyalty
lucid

luminous
luscious
luxurious
*lying

macaroni
machinery
Mafia
magazine
magnificence
mahogany
maintain
maintenance
malaise
malfeasance
manageable
managing
mandatory
maneuver
manual
manufacturer
many
marijuana
marriage
marries
*marshal
Massachusetts
material
mathematics
mattress
maximum
*meanness
*meant
medicine
medieval
mediocre
menswear
menu
mercenary
merciful
messenger
middleman
mileage

militia
millinery
millionaire
mimicking
miniature
minimum
minuscule
minutely
miscegenation
miscellaneous
*mischievous
mislead (*present*)
*misled (*past*)
Mississippi
missile
*misspell (ed)
mobilize
moccasin
model (ed)
modifying
momentous
monopolize
monotonous
monsignor
monstrous
*morale
mortgage
mosquitoes
mountainous
movable
municipal
murmur (ing)
muscle
museum
musical (e)
mustache
myriad
mysterious

naive
*naphtha
natural (ly)
nearby

*Webster's lists *loveable* as a variant.

nebulous
*necessary
necessarily
necessity
necessitate
necessities
neighbor
*neither
neutral
nevertheless
nickel
niece
nineteen
nineteenth
ninety
ninth
nitpicking
nomenclature
nominative
nonagenarian
notable
noticeable
notoriety
nowadays
nowhere (no *s*)
nucleus
nuisance
nullify
nutritionist

obedience
obeisance
obligation
oblige
obliging
obscene
observer
obsolete
obstacle
obstreperous
*occasion
*occasionally
occur

*occurred
occurrence
o'clock
oculist
odor
offense
offered
official
omission
omit
*omitted
oneself
operate
opinion
opponent
*opportunity
oppressive
optimism
optimistic
optimistically
ordinarily
organization
origin
*original (ly)
oscillate
outrageous
overrun

pageant
*paid (*past of* pay)
palliative
pamphlet
pantomime
paraffin
*parallel (ed)
paralysis
paralyzed
paraphernalia
pari-mutuel
parishioner
parley
parliamentary
participle

*particularly
partner
passed (*past of* pass)
past (*adj.*)
passenger
passers-by
pasteurization
pastime
pathos
patronize
pavilion
peaceable
peasant
peculiar (ly)
peculiarity
pell-mell
pendulum
penicillin
perceive
perceptible
perception
percent[7]
peremptory
perform
perhaps
peripatetic
permanent
permissible
perpendicular
per se
perseverance
persistence
persistent
personal (*adj.*)
personally (*adv.*)
personnel (*noun*)
*perspiration
persuade
persuasion
pertain
pertinent
pervade
pessimistic

[7] Stylebooks and dictionaries now require the solid form for *percent.*

phenomenal
Philippines
philosophy
physically
physician
pianist
picnic
*picnicked
*picknicker
pilgrim
pimiento
pitiful
plainness
plaintiff
*planned (*past of* plan)
plaque
platoon
plausible
playwright
pleasant
pleasure
pliers
plurality
pneumonia
poignant
poinsettia
politician
politicking
politics
polluted
portray (ed)
Portuguese
positively
*possess (ion)
possessive
possibility
possible
possibly
potato (es)
practicable
practical (ly)
practice *or* practise
  (*verb*)
practice (*noun*)
practitioner
prairie

*precede
precedence
precedent (s)
preceding
precious
predecessor
predicament
predominant
prefer (red)
preferable
preference
prejudice
preliminary
premonition
preparation
preparatory
prepare
preposterous
pressure
prestigious
pretend
pretense
prevalence
prevalent
preventive
primitive
prisoner
*privilege
probably
*procedure
*proceed
process
prodigy
profess (ed)
profession
*professor
proffered
proficiency
profligate
program
programed
  or programmed
prohibition
promenade
prominence
promissory

promptness
pronunciation
propel (led)
propeller
proportion
prosperous
protrude
prove
proving
prowess
prudence
psalm
pseudonym
psychic
psychology
ptomaine
publicize
puerile
purchase
purchasing
pursue
pursuing
pursuit
putting
*pyorrhea

quandary
quantity
quarantine
quarrel (ed)
quarter
quartet
*questionnaire
*queue
quietly
quiz (zed)
quizzes

raccoon
racial
racketeer
radiator
rapid (ly)
*rarefy
rarity
readiness

ready
realistically
realize
*really
rearrangement
rebellious
recede
receipt
*receive
reciprocate
*recognize
*recommend (ation)
reconcile
reconciliation
reconnaissance
recur (red)
   (*not* reoccurred)
recurrence
reference
referred
regard
region
regrettable
rehearsal
reign
reimburse
reinforced
relapse
relevant
reliable
relief
relieve
religious
remarkable
*remembrance
reminiscences
reminiscent
remittance
remuneration
renaissance
repair (ed)
repellent (or *ant*)
repentance
repetition
repetitious

*replied
replies
representative
reptile
requirement
rescind
resemblance
reservoir
resistance
*respectfully
*respectively
responsible
restaurant
*restaurateur
retaliate
revelation
reverence
rheumatic
rheumatism
rhyme
rhythm
rhythmical
ricochet (ed *or* ted)
ridiculous
riding
rock 'n' roll
running
rural
rutabaga

sacrifice
sacrificing
sacrilegious
safety
*salable
sandwich
sarcastically
satellites
Saturday
sauerkraut
saxophone
scarcely
scarcity
schedule
scheme

science
scion
scissors
scream (ed)
scrupulous
secede
secession
secondary
secretary
*seize (d)
*sensible
*separate
serendipity
*sergeant
serviceable
several
severely
shepherd
*sheriff
shiftless
*shining
shoulder
*shriek
*siege
sieve
signature
significance
significant
silhouette
*similar (ly)
*similarity
simile
simplify
simulate
simultaneous
sincerely
siphon
*sizable
skeleton
skier
skiing
skillful (ly) *or* skilfully
sleight-of-hand
smooth
sobriquet

solemn	suite (of rooms)	*tied
soliloquy (-quies)	*summarize	till
soluble	*superintendent	toe (ing)
somber	*supersede	together
somnambulist	superstitious	tomato (es)
sophisticated	supervision	toward
*sophomore	supervisor	traceable
sororities	supine	tragedy
souvenir	suppress	tranquil(l)ity
sovereign	sure (ly)	transfer (red)
spaghetti	*surprise	transient
sparse	surveillance	transmission
specially	*suspicious	transmitter
specialty	swimming	travel (l) ed
specifically	switch	treacherous
specimen	syllable	treasure
specious	symmetrical	treasurer
specter	symmetry	tries
speech	sympathize	trolley
spoonful (s)	synonymous	trouble
sputnik	syrup or sirup	trousseau
step (ped)		truant
*stop (ped, ping)	tablespoonfuls	*truly
stopper	taciturn	tuberculosis
stories	tactfully	Tuesday
*straight	taking	twelfth
strait jacket	tantamount	tying[8]
strategic	tariff	typical
strategy	temblor	typify
*strength (en)	temperament (al)	typing
strenuous	temperance	typography
*stretch	temperature	tyrannically
strictly	temporarily	tyranny
studious	tenant	
studying	tendency	ukulele
subscription	tentacles	ulterior
substantial	tentative	ultimatum (s)
subtle	*theater	unanimous
succeed	their (*pron.*)	unconscious
success (ful)	there (*adverb*)	uncontrollable
succession	therefore (*conj.*)	under way
suddenness	they're (they are)	undesirable
sufficient	*thorough	undoubtedly
suffrage	thousandth (s)	universally

[8] Webster's has *tieing* as secondary variant, but the stylebooks do not accept it.

*unnecessary
unparalleled
unprecedented
*until
unusual (ly)
up-to-date
usable
usage
useful (ly)
*using
*usual (ly)
utility
utilize
utterance

vacancy
vaccinate
vacuum
valiant
valleys
valuable
valves
varicose
vaudeville
vegetable
vehicle
vender *or* vendor
vengeance
verbatim
verified
vermilion
vertebra
vertebras *or*
    vertebrae (*pl.*)
*veteran
veterinarian

vexatious
vice versa
vicinity
vied, vying
vigilance
vignette
vilify
*village
*villain
*villainy
virile
virtuous
visa
visible
visibly
vitreous (of glass)
volume
voluntary

warrant
wasteful (ly)
weakness (es)
weather (ed)
*Wednesday
weigh (ed)
*weird
weirdo (s)
welcome
welfare
wherever
*whether
whir (red)
whistle
wholly
who's
whose

*wield
*wiener
*wil (l) ful
wintry
wiry
wizard
woeful
woman
women (*pl.*)
won't
wool (l) y
writer
*writing
written
wrought

X-ray (*n., v., adj.*)
xylography
xylophone

yacht
yearlong
yield
yokel
your (*poss.*)
you're (you are)
yourself (yourselves)

zeal
zealot
zealous
zephyr
zinc
zodiac
zoning
zoology

TROUBLESOME HOMONYMS
AND OTHER WORDS EASILY CONFUSED

Homonyms are words that sound alike but which are spelled differently and which have different meanings. There are hundreds of such words in the English language, but the ones that will give you the most trouble are listed below.

Possibly of even more importance than the list of homonyms is the listing of other words and phrases that are easily confused. The list has been greatly expanded in this edition of *Grammar for Journalists,* with the purpose of making it a helpful supplement to the new Glossary of Usage.

Study the list carefully. Concentrate on the words with which you have difficulty. Your objective in using this list is to ground yourself thoroughly in the correct spelling, the exact meaning(s) of the word and how it may be used correctly and effectively in a sentence.

To determine the meaning and the correct use of a term, such as *refute* for example, first see if it is listed in the Glossary of Usage. We have included in the glossary only those words which we think present the greatest usage problems for journalists, and you will find there a *refute, rebut, dispute* entry that shows *refute* often is misused for *rebut, dispute* or *deny.* A sample sentence shows that *disputed* should have been used instead of *refuted.*

If you don't find in the glossary the term you wish to check, look it up in a good dictionary to determine its exact, correct usage. You also may find many of the easily confused words listed in *The Associated Press Stylebook and Libel Manual* and in *The United Press International Stylebook.* Because word usage changes constantly, be sure to use a current edition of a dictionary or a stylebook.

You likely will find you can spend many profitable hours studying homonyms and other words that are easily confused.

A LIST OF HOMONYMS AND OTHER WORDS EASILY CONFUSED

accept	allude	area	baring
except	elude	aria	barring
access	allusion	artful	bearing
excess	illusion	artistic	bath
adverse	altar	ascent	bathe
averse	alter	assent	berth
affect	alumna	auger	birth
effect	alumnae	augur	beside
aid	alumnus	average	besides
aide	alumni	median	better
aisle	anecdote	mean	bettor
isle	antidote		bloc
alleys	angel	awhile	block
allies	angle	a while	blond
all ready	appraise	bail	blonde[8]
already	apprise	bale	

[8]*Blonde* is being replaced by blond but is still preferred as the feminine noun form.

bolder
boulder

border
boarder

born
borne

brake
break

breach
breech

breath
breathe

brunet
brunette[9]

bullet

cartridge
shell

cannon
canon
canyon (cañon)

canvas
canvass

capital
capitol

carat
caret
karat

career
careen

carton
cartoon

cast
caste

caster
castor

cavalry
Calvary

censer
censor

censure

ceremonial
ceremonious

chafe
chaff

childish
childlike

choose
chose

chord
cord

cite
site
sight

clamber
clamor

clench
clinch

climactic
climatic

cloth
clothe

coarse
course

common sense (noun)
commonsense (adj.)

compare to, with
contrast

complacent
complaisant

complement
compliment

comptroller
controller

connote
denote

conscience
conscious

consul
council
councilor
counsel
counselor

contemptible
contemptuous

continual
continuous

corespondent
correspondent

credulous
credible
creditable

decent
descent
dissent

dependant (noun)
dependent (adj.)

deprecate
depreciate

desert
dessert

device
devise

disapprove
disprove

discreet
discrete

disinterested
uninterested

draft
draught

drought
drouth (preferred)

dual
duel

dyeing
dying

efficacy
efficiency

egoist
egotist

emigrate
immigrate
emigrant
immigrant

eminent
imminent

ensure
insure

envelop
envelope

ever
every

faint
feint

farther
further

faze
phase

fiance
finacee

flack
flak

flair
flare

flaunt
flout

[9]Either *brunet* or *brunette* may be used as noun or adjective.

flier
flyer
flounder
founder
forbear
forebear
forego
forgo
foreword
forward
formally
formerly
forth
fourth
fortuitous
fortunate
foul
fowl
freezing
subfreezing
friendlily
friendly
gourmand
gourmet
grill
grille
guarantee
guaranty
hair
hare
heir
hangar
hanger
healthful
healthy
hoard
horde
hoping
hopping
human
humane

idle
idol
idyl
imaginary
imaginative
impassable
impassible
imply
infer
inflammable
inflammatory
ingenious
ingenuous
instant
instance
interment
internment
its
it's
later
latter
laudable
laudatory
lead
led
lend
loan
lessen
lesson
liable
libel
loose
lose
luxuriant
luxurious
magnate
magnet
mantel
mantle
manual
manuel

marital
martial
masterful
masterly
material
materiel
memento
momento
militate
mitigate
miner
minor
modern
modernistic
monster
monstrous
moral
morale
naked
nude
nauseated
nauseous
naval
navel
noisome
noisy
notorious
famous
observance
observation
oneself
one's self
ordinance
ordnance
orient
orientate
pander
panderer
passed
past
peace
piece

peak
peek
pique
peal
peel
pedal
peddle
peer
pier
perpetuate
perpetrate
perquisite
prerequisite
persecute
prosecute
personal
personnel
perspicacious
perspicuous
persuade
convince
pistol
revolver
plain
plane
planed
planned
pole
poll
pom-pom
pompon
pore
pour
practicable
practical
pray
prey
precede
proceed
procedure
premier
premiere
premise

premises

prescribe

proscribe

principal

principle

prophecy

prophesy

quiet

quite

racket

racquet

rain

reign

rein

raise

raze

rapped

wrapped

ravage

ravish

refute

rebut

relation

relative

repertoire

repertory

resin

rosin

respectfully

respectively

reverse

converse

opposite

vice versa

rhyme

rime

right

rite

write

rout

route

sanitarium

sanitorium

scene

seen

scrip

script

seasonable

seasonal

secular

sectarian

sense

since

sensual

sensuous

sententious

sentient

serge

surge

sew

so

sow

sewage

sewerage

shear

sheer

shone

shown

soar

sore

sole

soul

some time

sometime

sometimes

stair

stare

stanch

staunch

stationary

stationery

statue

stature

statute

steal

steel

straight

strait

strategy

tactics

surely

surly

tenants

tenets

than

then

their

there

they're

therefor

therefore

thrash

thresh

threw

through

throne

thrown

to

too

two

tortuous

torturous

toward

towards

track

tract

triumphal

triumphant

troop

troupe

trooper

trouper

turban

turbine

under way (adv.)

underway (adj.)

unexceptionable

unexceptional

uninterested

disinterested

usage

use

vain

vane

vein

vale

veil

vice

vise

viscous

viscus

waive

wave

waiver

waver

wander

wonder

weather

whether

weighed

weighted

whole

hole

wholly

holey

holy

whose

who's

woman

women

lady

your

you're

Glossary of Usage

This glossary of usage—a new section in *Grammar for Journalists*—has been prepared primarily for journalism students and practicing journalists. It consists largely of terms—words and expressions—that are often confused and misused. The list is far from complete, but it does contain most of the words and phrases that are misused frequently. Journalists and other writers should not be guilty of such misuse.

(As a supplement to the glossary, a greatly expanded list of Troublesome Homonyms and Other Words Easily Confused is available in Chapter 18, as well as a list of Words Commonly Misspelled. Be sure to make full use of these lists as well as the Glossary.)

In Chapter 16 we discussed (1) words and expressions that should be avoided altogether; (2) words and phrases that generally should be avoided; and (3) words and phrases that may be used by the journalist whenever appropriate. Although we have not keyed the commonly misused terms to the three usage groups, we do refer in many of the glossary entries to such faults as *wordiness, vulgarisms, stereotypes, slang, jargon* and *gobbledygook*, and to some acceptable forms such as *idioms* and *colloquialisms*.

Remember that colloquialisms particularly may be used correctly by journalists, especially by those in television and radio and those in advertising. And newspapers and magazines find many colloquial words and phrases to be acceptable in some contexts, especially in quotations.

When in doubt about the use of a word or a phrase that is not covered here or elsewhere in *Grammar for Journalists*, refer to a good dictionary to determine the term's exact, correct usage. You also may find many troublesome words and phrases listed in *The Associated Press Stylebook and Libel Manual* and in *The United Press International Stylebook*. Be sure to use a *current* edition of a dictionary or a stylebook, since word usage changes constantly, and what was regarded as incorrect yesterday may be found correct today—or by tomorrow.

ACCIDENTLY. A vulgarism. Add *ly* to *accidental*.

AD. The shortened form of *advertisement* should be used only colloquially by journalists. Other such forms are *auto, phone, math, photo*.

AFTERWARD, AFTERWARDS. *Afterward* is the preferred spelling.

AIN'T. A substandard contraction. Use only in quoted matter or special contexts.

AIR. *Air* for *broadcast* is highly approved, and it fits well into headlines. But copyeditors are warned not to use *air* in headlines when *discuss, expose* or *explore* would be more specific.

ALLEGE(D). Journalists must avoid the common error of using *allege(d)* redundantly: He was *indicted* for *alleged* burglary. He was *charged* with alleged burglary. Used in connection with the verbs *indicted* and *charged*, *alleged* is unnecessary in both sentences.

ALRIGHT, ALL RIGHT. Webster's lists *alright* as standard usage, but the stylebooks say, "Never use *alright*."

ANTICIPATE, EXPECT. *Expect* may be used correctly for *anticipate* almost always: We *expected* (not *anticipated*) rain. But, We ordered 300 extra chairs in *anticipation* (not in *expectation*) of drawing a larger crowd.

ANY MORE. *Any more* is correct in a negative statement in which a contrast in times is implied: We can hardly expect him to work for us any more. Or, It's hard for us to get together any more. But don't use *any more* in a positive statement: He intends to work only four days a week any more.

ANYONE OR ANY ONE; EVERYONE OR EVERYONE; SOMEONE OR SOME ONE. Be careful to distinguish the difference between *anyone* and *any one*, etc. See page 115.

ANYWHERE(S), BACKWARD(S), SOMEWHERE(S). The adverb *anywhere* never adds an *s*. *Backward* and *somewhere* are preferred spellings. See page 140.

APT, LIABLE, LIKELY. Avoid using *apt* and *liable* for *likely*: He's *likely* (not *apt*) to be late. He's *likely* (not *liable*) to be late. Use liable in the sense of an undesirable action: You are *liable* to fall. You are *liable* to be sued.

AS. . .AS, SO. . .AS. It has been argued that in negative comparisons, formal English prefers *so. . . as*. However, Copperud says this form is not required and that *as. . . as* is now preferred usage: He means to run the union *as* (not *so*) long *as* he can.

AS FAR AS. Journalists should avoid the common error of failing to use *is* (or *are*) concerned following *as far as*. *As far as* charisma (*is concerned*), you get an Ali once in a lifetime. Septien has no limit *as far as* field goals *are* concerned (correct).

AS, THAN. Don't confuse *as* and *than* in making comparisons. See page 135.

AT THAT (THIS) POINT IN TIME. Today's most common, inane circumlocution. See page 228.

AVOID. Don't use *avoid* for *prevent*. To *avoid* is to keep away from, to sidestep; to *prevent* is to keep from happening or existing: He turned quickly to *avoid* the stone wall. Volunteers quickly began to throw up sandbags to *prevent* (not *avoid*) the dam from breaking.

AWAIT (OR AWAITING) FOR. The *for* is not necessary. Don't imitate this top sportscaster reporting a championship fight: "We are *awaiting for* the decision."

AWFUL, AWFULLY. *Awful* as an adverb meaning *very* or *extremely* and *awfully*, with essentially the same meaning, are now accepted by Webster's, but journalists will do well to use such terms as *awfully tired* only colloquially. Referring to such terms as "atomic flyswatters," Bernstein says, "When such powerful words as *awful, dreadful, fearful* or *horrible* are used as mere commonplace expressions of disapproval, the primary meanings of the words are displaced and depreciated. At the same time the new meanings remain debased, so that there is a gross loss all around."

BAD, BADLY. Don't use *bad* as an adverb. Use it as a predicate adjective instead of *badly*: Looking up from his hospital bed, he said he felt *bad*. Use *badly* as an adverb only: The team slumped *badly* in midseason. See pages 49–50, 135.

BESIDE, BESIDES. Do not confuse these. See page 148.

BETWEEN, AMONG. Use of *between* or *among* is a bit tricky. See page 148.

BID. Don't use *bid* in the sense of *try* or *attempt*. Its use in a headline may be excused since *bids* is shorter than *attempts*: NASA Bids to Save Skylab. However, there is no excuse for the journalist to use *bid* for *try* or *attempt* in the text.

BOTH. Avoid using *both* unnecessarily. It is often used redundantly with such words as *equal, alike, agree, together*. *Both* indicates duality, or twoness, which is established by such words as those cited, Copperud observes. Therefore "Both are equally liberal" should read, "They are equally liberal." And "Both appeared together in a new show" should be "They appeared together." "Both agreed" should be "They agreed," and "Both looked alike" should be "They looked alike." Too, don't use *both* with *as well as*: *Both* students *as well as* teachers protested the ruling. Make it either "Students as well as teachers. . ." or "Both students and teachers. . . ."

BREAK OR BROKE (her leg). See *Sustain*.

BURGLARY, ROBBERY, THEFT, HOLDUP AND LARCENY. These have different meanings. Check the dictionary or the stylebook.

CAN, MAY. Although *can* and *may* are now interchangeable in informal English, journalists should follow the old guidelines, using *can* to express ability, power and so on, and using *may* to express permission or possibility. *Can* for *may* should be used only colloquially by writers.

CANNOT HELP BUT. Don't use this double negative. Instead of *cannot help but feel* (*believe, think,* etc.), write it: *cannot help feeling* (*believing, thinking,* etc.) Example: I cannot help feeling he will win.

CAN'T HARDLY. Another double negative. See *Hardly*.

CHAIR. Used as a verb with the meaning *serve as chairman of*, *chair* is the best example of the modern practice of making verbs out of nouns. *Chair* used as a verb has been accepted by Webster's, of course, and it is widely used now in newspapers, magazines and on the air. The trend toward making verbs out of nouns (*chaired* the meeting, *authored* a best-selling novel, etc.) has been resisted by language authorities, but it appears that *chaired*, at least, has won acceptability. But is it all right to say that Miss Eleanor Norton, head of the Equal Employment Opportunity Commission, is a *chair*? She is not chairman of the EEOC, she would have you know; neither is she chairwoman, nor even chairperson. Miss Norton is a *chair*. If that is not ridiculous enough, consider another example from a leading journal for journalists. Heaven forbid that many editors will permit staff members to go as far as this usage: ''The second panel was *membered* by Howard R. Fibich, news editor, *Milwaukee* (Wis.) *Journal*; Richard D. Blum, vice president, *Dallas News*;. . . .

CITE. *Cite* is not synonymous with *charge* or *accuse*. You can *cite* only something that exists—a fact. Incorrect: He *cited* the suspect's record of arson. This says that such a record exists. It is only possible to say that the suspect was *accused* of having a record as an arsonist.

COLLIDE, COLLISION. Two objects must be in motion before they can *collide*, the stylebooks point out. A car cannot collide with a tree, for example.

COMMENTATE. Now accepted usage.

COMPILE. Don't use for *write* or *compose*. *To compile* is to collect into a volume. The author does not *compile* a book; he *writes* it.

COMPRISE, COMPOSE. *Comprise* means to *include* or to *embrace*: The German empire *comprised* a number of separate states. Do not use it in the passive sense ''to be comprised of.'' Instead, use ''to be *composed* of,'' as in: The committee is *composed* of five representatives.

CONNOTE, DENOTE. *Connote* simply *implies* something; *denote means* something. As Webster's points out, the terms are complementary rather than strictly synonymous and cannot be interchanged without significant loss of precision. The word *home*, for example, *denotes* the place where one lives, but to one person it may *connote* comfort, intimacy and affection and to another misery, estrangement and abuse.

CONSIDER. *Consider* should not be used when *believe* or *suppose* will do: The manager *believed* the complaint to be unjustified, but he wanted more time to *consider* it. (*Consider* involves thinking it over.)

CONVINCE, PERSUADE. Don't use *convince* when you mean *persuade*. One is *convinced of a fact* or *that something is so*, whereas *persuade* means *talk into* or *induce*. As Copperud observes, incorrect usage results from having an infinitive object follow convince: They hope the governor can be *convinced* to call a special session of the legislature. The correct word is *persuaded*, with the meaning of *talk into*:. . . can be *persuaded* to call. The infinitive *to call* is the object of *persuade*. The infinitive could not be the object of *convince* because *convince* cannot idiomatically be followed by *to*. It must be followed by *of* or by a relative clause beginning with *that*:. . . can be *convinced* that he should call. . . .

COUPLE (OF). *Couple* must be accompanied by *of*. Think how "a couple apples" would look in print.

CRITERIA, CRITERIONS. *Criteria* has kept integrity as the *plural* of *criterion*, but *criterions* also is correct. See pages 86–87 for a list of foreign words, particularly Latin-root words, that are now used correctly in either the foreign plural or the English plural. Only a few Latin-root words retain the foreign plural only. They include: alumnus, alumni; crisis, crises; datum, data; and thesis, theses. Press association stylebooks add to this list *addenda, curricula, criteria* and *media* (when referring to newspapers and magazines).

DEMOLISH, DESTROY. The stylebooks say the meaning here is *to do away with completely*. They say that something cannot be *partly demolished* or *destroyed* and that there is no need to say *totally* destroyed. Copperud disagrees. He argues that *partly destroyed* is not a contradiction in terms and that it sometimes gives a clearer picture of the extent of the damage: the part of it so described with the word *demolished* or *destroyed* is completely gone—but some of the whole remains. Better check with the editor on this.

DIE OF, DIE FROM. Die *of* is still preferred usage. Die *from* would be preferred in such a construction as *die from fatigue*.

DIFFERENT FROM, DIFFERENT THAN. Use *from*, not *than*, in most instances. However, *than* is correct when it introduces a condensed clause: "It has possessed me in a different way *than* (it) ever (did) before," Cardinal Newman declared. The use of *than* is becoming more common. See page 150.

DIFFER FROM, DIFFER WITH. Use *differ from* to indicate dissimilarity and *differ with* to indicate disagreement. See page 150.

DISCLOSE, REVEAL. Don't use these for routine news that you need only *report* or *announce*. *Disclose* and *reveal* should be used only for that which has been concealed.

DROWN(ED). Don't use *drown* in the passive voice. A person drowns; he or she is not drowned. And you certainly know not to spell it *drownded*.

DUE TO, BECAUSE OF. See page 139.

EACH, EITHER. *Either* means one or the other, not both. *Each* side and *either* side are considered correct now, but *each side* sounds more natural and is preferred: There was shrubbery on *each side* of the door.

EACH OTHER, ONE ANOTHER. See page 115.

ECOLOGY, ENVIRONMENT. They are not synonymous. *Ecology* is a science concerned with the interrelationships of organisms and their *environments*.

ENTHUSE. Although Webster's and other dictionaries now accept *enthuse* as a verb, with the meaning of *to make enthusiastic* or *to show enthusiasm*, most editors advise that it be used only colloquially: "We were really enthused to come from behind and win," the coach chortled.

FAD WORDS. This is Bernstein's term for such objectionable usage as: *phase out* for *reduce*; *stepped up* for *increased* or *accelerated; task force* for *committee, panel* or *investigative body; know-how* for *skill*; etc. Bernstein also lists and discusses *crash program, balding, breakthrough, chain reaction, kudos, marginal, spell out, target* and *trigger*. Others that could be added are *shape up, size up, trade-off, go public* and *bottom line*.

FARTHER, FURTHER. See pages 133–34.

FEWER, LESS. In general, use *fewer* to refer to *number*—for individual items—and *less* for *quantity, amount* and *bulk*. Use *fewer* employees, not *less* employees; *less* (an amount) than $40, but *fewer* than four $5-bills.

FINALIZE. Don't use *finalize* when *complete, finish* or *end* will do. See pages 233–34 for jargon and gobbledygook, such as *politicize, accessorize, prioritize, minimize, maximize, decriminalize, sensitize, illegalize,* etc.

FRESHMAN OR FRESHMEN. Never use the plural *freshmen* as an adjective. *The singular freshman* is the adjective form: Jones was elected *freshman* president. See page 142.

FULSOME. It does not mean *full, copious* or *bounteous*, Bernstein points out. It means *overfull* and *offensive, repulsive, odious*. Beware especially of the phrase "fulsome praise."

GOOD, WELL. Using *good* for *well* (He's hitting *good*) is now accepted by Webster's, and Flesch says it is now standard usage. But most editors won't accept such usage, even in sports writing and sportscasting. Certainly it should be used only colloquially.

GRADUATE, WAS GRADUATED. The active voice is now preferred: Cheryl Tiegs *has graduated* (from modeling), not *has been graduated*; Christopher Dealey *graduated* (not *was graduated*) Friday.

HANGED, HUNG. See page 64.

HARDLY, SCARCELY, BARELY. Not to be used with a negative: The snow was so heavy that I *could hardly* (not *couldn't hardly*) see the road.

HEAD UP. An excellent example of two faults: converting a noun (*head*) into a verb, which in turn results in a redundant expression. If *head* is accepted as a verb in "He will *head* the committee," it does not require the preposition *up*. He simply will *head* the committee. (For a list of wordy expressions, see pages 228–29.

HEALTHFUL, HEALTHY. *Healthful*, meaning conducive to health, is rapidly being replaced by *healthy*: The New Mexico climate is *healthy*. Some editors will still insist it should be *healthful*.

HEART ATTACK, CORONARY, CARDIAC. *Heart attack* is preferred as a noun to *coronary* and *cardiac*, which are properly adjectives: He had a *heart attack* (not a *coronary*).

HOPEFULLY. *Hopefully* is misused far too often. It should be used only to describe how a subject *feels*: Hopefully, I *will* (or *shall*) present my plan for approval. (He is *hopeful* it will be approved.) But you can't attribute hope to a nonperson. Incorrect: Hopefully, price increases will begin leveling off in the fourth quarter. Although *hopefully*, with the meaning of *it is hoped*, has been accepted in the dictionaries, the stylebooks disallow its use.

HYPHENATION. Failure to hyphenate compound adjectives preceding a noun is one of the most common errors found in the printed media. Note the hyphenation of compound adjectives in this sentence: Tracy Austin, the *fragile-looking 15-year-old* girl from. . . took her biggest step. . . by ending the *37-match victory* streak of Martina Navratilova. Do not hyphenate a compound with an adverb ending in *ly*: *recently completed* bridge, *stylishly dressed* woman. Use of the hyphen in such constructions is another common error found in the media.

IMPACT. *Impact* is overused. It is too strong a word to be used for *effect or influence*. Also, it has become gobbledygook, as in *federally impacted areas*. Avoid using *impact* as a verb.

IMPLY, INFER. To *imply* is *to hint at* or *suggest*; to *infer* is *to draw a conclusion*, as Copperud points out. Don't use *infer* for *imply*: They *implied* (not *inferred*) that we were accepting rake-offs.

IN BACK OF, IN BEHIND. These are wordy expressions for *back of* and *behind*. Correct: His car was *behind* (or *back of*) mine.

INCLUDE. Don't use *include* to mean *are*. Don't write that schools in the conference *include* when you list the names of all schools in the conference. *Include* is used when you mention only some of the units. If all schools are named, it should be: Schools in the conference *are*. . . .

INSIST AND CONTEND. Don't use *insist* or *contend* when a simple *says* or *points out* or *asserts* is all that's called for in a statement with which no disagreement is indicated and in which emphasis is not needed. Incorrect: Parents can help children learn to read in home study, using a simple phonics system, the principal *insists* (or *contends*).

INTERPRETATIVE, INTERPRETIVE. *Interpretive* is gaining favor, but most editors insist on using *interpretative*, certainly in such a construction as *interpretative reporting*.

IRREGARDLESS. A double negative listed as nonstandard in all dictionaries. Use *regardless*.

ITS, IT'S. See page 101.

KIND OF, SORT OF. See page 109.

LADY, WOMAN. *Woman* has replaced *lady* except in titles, names of societies and in the salutation "Ladies and gentlemen."

LAST, LATEST. These are now listed in dictionaries as interchangeable, but stylebooks still insist on avoiding the use of *last* as a synonym for *latest* if it might imply finality. See page 134.

LAY, LIE. See page 63.

LEAVE ALONE, LET ALONE. *Leave alone* for *let alone*, in the sense of "Don't bother her," is now standard. AP approves *letting* her alone but advises the use of *leave alone* in a construction like this: When I entered the room I saw the two were sleeping; so I decided to *leave them alone*.

LIKE, AS, AS IF. Avoid using *like* as a conjunction: It looks *like* (*as if*) it will rain. *Like* is used largely as a preposition: It looks *like* rain. But it may be used as a conjunction in some instances. See pages 146–47.

LEND, LOAN. The use of the verb *loan* for *lend* is standard usage, but *lend* has much more versatility.

LOCATE, SETTLE, SITUATE. Until recently it was incorrect to say that a person *located* (for *settled*) in a certain community. Now *locate* is accepted as synonymous with *situated* and also with *settled* or *living*: He has located in La Crosse; his home is located at 3501 Madison.

MAD. *Mad* is now accepted to mean *angry*. It still is used for *insane*, but largely in literature.

MAJORITY, MOST OF. Majority means *more than half*. Don't use a *majority of* for *most of*, a stronger expression: *Most of* (not *a majority of*) the tenants protested the raise in rent.

MARSHAL, MARSHALL. *Marshal* is the spelling for both the noun and the verb: The field *marshal* will *marshal* his forces. *Marshall* is a proper noun.

MATERIALIZE. Don't use for *develop*, *appear* or *arrive*, as in: Snow failed to *materialize*.

MEAN, AVERAGE, MEDIUM. *Mean* and *average* are synonymous. Each word refers to the sum of all components divided by the number of components. *Median* is the number that has as many components above it as below it.

MEDIA, MEDIUM, MEDIUMS. *Media* and *mediums* are plural and require the plural verb. Never say the mass media *was* used. . . . *Mediums* is the English plural of *medium*, one of many Latin-root words—like *appendix* and *memorandum*—the plural of which may be formed by adding an *s* or *es*. But of course it must be mass media (not mass mediums) when referring to publications and broadcasts. (See pages 86–87.)

MORE THAN, OVER. *Webster's* now accepts *over* as interchangeable with *more than*, but the stylebooks do not agree. AP says *over* refers to spatial relationships: The plane flew over the fairgrounds. *More than* is used with figures: More than 600 homeowners overflowed the council room.

MYSELF. Don't use a reflexive pronoun like *myself* instead of the nominative form as part of a compound subject. And don't use a reflexive pronoun instead of a pronoun in the objective case as part of a compound object of a verb or a preposition. This is one of the most common errors made on television and radio today. It also appears in the print media, where it should be used only in quotations. Incorrect: The committee chairman and *myself* (*I*) will confer today on the proposed bill. The speaker praised the chairman and *myself* (*me*) for our work on the bill.

NOTORIOUS, FAMOUS. Don't use *notorious* for *noted* or *famous*, or *notoriety* for *notable*. Notorious means widely and *unfavorably* known. Consider this headline in a metropolitan paper: Arlington Girl Vaults to *Notoriety*. The story was about a teenage (or teenaged) gymnast.

NOT TOO, NOT VERY. Don't use *not too* for *not very*. He's *not very* (not *not too*) experienced. (Editors condemn the use of *very* and would advise writing it: He doesn't have much experience.)

NOUNS USED AS VERBS. See *Chair*.

OBLIVIOUS. Don't use this high-sounding word for more specific words like unaware (of) and unmindful (of): She was *unaware of* (not *oblivious of*) the possible consequences.

OCCUR, TAKE PLACE. Use *occur* in the sense of *to happen*, such as an accident. Use *take place* for anything that is planned or prearranged.

OF, HAVE. Don't write *of* when you mean *have*. He should *have* (not *of*) known.

O.K. Use only colloquially for *correct* or *all right*.

OPTIMISTIC. Don't misuse for *hopeful, favorable*, etc. He is *hopeful* (not *optimistic*) the Yankees will repeat. There are several *favorable* (or *encouraging*) (not *optimistic*) indications that. . . .

ORAL, VERBAL. Use *oral* to refer to spoken words; use *written* to refer to words committed to paper. *Verbal* may apply to *spoken* or *written* words. It simply means "in the form of words," as compared with other forms of communication such as gestures. Copperud advises writers to choose between *oral* and *written* and not to take a chance by using *verbal*.

OVER, MORE THAN. See *More than, over*.

PARALLELISM. Ideas or thoughts in a series in the same sentence require *parallel construction*. For extensive treatment of parallellism, see pages 190–92.

PARTIALLY, PARTLY. Use *partly*, not *partially*, to mean *in part*. *Partially* can imply showing favoritism. Example: The debate was *partly* (not *partially*) recorded.

PEOPLE, PERSONS. In general, use *people* when speaking of a large or uncounted number of individuals: Thousands of *people* were evacuated from their homes. The *people* are speaking up on taxes. *Persons* usually is used when speaking of a relatively small or exact number, but *people* also may be used, according to press association stylebooks. In fact, Copperud says that *people* is now preferred to *persons* in speaking of a small or exact number: Three *people* attended. Some editors, however, still follow the traditional distinction between *people* and *persons*.

PERCENT, PER CENT. *Percent*—one word with no period—has replaced *per cent*.

PERSONAL, PERSONALLY. Don't use these words unnecessarily: He is a *personal* friend of mine. He could not attend *personally*.

PLUS. Avoid using *plus* in place of the conjunction *and*. Incorrect: The assistant principal *plus* (*and*) two teachers are being considered for the position. Use *plus* only colloquially as meaning *and more*: Phyllis George has *personality plus*.

POLITICS. Politics, plural in form, is singular when referring to politics as a science or study: Do you think American *politics is* (not *are*) honest? AP says politics may take a plural verb in such a construction as this: My *politics are* my own business. (The speaker does not refer to politics as a study or science, but to the way he casts his secret ballot.)

PRACTICALLY, ALMOST. Don't use *practically* for *almost*: His fortune is *almost* (not *practically*) gone.

PRESENTLY, AT PRESENT. These should not be used unnecessarily: He is *presently* chairman. He lives in Queens *at present*. Delete *presently* and *at present*. Journalists should never use *presently* to mean *currently*; they are not truly synonymous.

PRIOR TO, BEFORE. Use *before*: The manager called a ten-minute meeting *before* (not *prior to*) the game. Also, don't use *prior* as an adjective for *previous* or *earlier*: He served *an earlier* (or a *previous*) term (not *prior* term) for theft.

PRINCIPAL, PRINCIPLE. *Principal* is used primarily as an adjective with the meaning of *chief* or *main*: the *principal* parts of verbs; the *principal* bank officer. But it also is used as a noun: She is *principal* of the school. She receives 6½ percent interest on the *principal*. The noun *principle* means a fundamental law, doctrine or truth or a guiding rule or a code of conduct: the *principle* of racial equality; the *principles* and practice of English grammar.

PROVEN, PROVED. Use *proven* largely as an adjective: a *proven* remedy; a *proven* oil field. *Proved* is preferred as the past participle in a verb phrase: He has *proved* (not *proven*) his ability to manage the business.

RAISE, REAR. Both are now used in the sense of *bringing up* (a child). *Rear* is more formal. Flesch advises: Don't use *rear* when *raise* will do.

REAL, SURE. Webster's now accepts *real* and *sure* as adverbs for *really* and *surely*, but journalists are advised to use them only colloquially.

REDUNDANCIES. For a list of *redundant* expressions, see pages 228–29.

REFUTE, REBUT. *Refute* is not synonymous with *rebut*. It means "proved wrong by argument or evidence." Usually the right word is *rebut* or *deny* or *dispute*: He *disputed* (not *refuted*) his opponent's arguments.

RELUCTANT, RETICENT. A person is *reluctant* if he doesn't wish to act: He is *reluctant* to make the race. He is *reticent* if he doesn't want to speak: On that subject, he is *reticent*.

REOCCUR, REOCCURRENCE. Nothing *reoccurs*, it simply *recurs*. And this is a *recurrence*, not a *reoccurrence*.

RESPECTIVE, RESPECTIVELY. These words—meaning *separate, separately* or *in the order given*—are usually unnecessary, as in this sentence: Lee Evans, Tommie Smith and Jean Roberts finished first, second and third, *respectively*, in the 400-meter finals. However, *respectively* is needed here: The charges could bring sentences of between five and 99 years and two and 20 years, *respectively*.

SAY, SAID. *Said* is the most serviceable word in the journalist's language, but synonyms should be used when appropriate. Just don't strain for synonyms for *said*. See page 225.

SECURE, OBTAIN, GET. Don't use *secure* for *obtain* or *get*. Use *secure* only with the meaning of getting possession or control of. Certainly you would not say, "Police *secured* the information they wanted," when all you need to say is that they *obtained* or *got* the information. But, He *secured* the deed to the property.

SET, SIT. See pages 63–64.

SHALL, WILL. *Will* is displacing *shall* in first-person constructions, and it is used, of course, in the second and third persons unless determination is expressed. *Shall*, not *will*, is now used to express determination. See pages 79–80.

SIMPLISTIC, SIMPLE. Don't use the fashionable word *simplistic* when *simple* is the correct usage. Simplistic means *oversimplified*. Correct: She offered a *simple* (not *simplistic*) solution to the problem.

SLANG. In general, journalists will avoid using slang, except perhaps colloquially. Some slang survives to become useful in written and oral English, but most slang—such as *blow my mind, A-OK, Swell!* and *Neat!, Do you dig me?* and *tell it like it is*—don't last. See pages 232–33.

SO. Avoid the use of *so* to connect clauses: Jones sprained his ankle, so we had to leave him behind. If you do insist on using *so* in such a weak construction, at least learn to use a semicolon before *so*. However, editors urge that a *so* type of sentence be reconstructed: After Jones sprained his ankle, we had to leave him behind. See pages 154–55.

SURE, REAL. See Real, sure.

SUSTAIN. Avoid using *sustain* as a synonym for *receive* or *suffer* or *incur* (an injury). And if it was a leg that was broken, why not say so: The chauffeur's leg *was broken*. You might avoid saying that *he broke* his leg, if you think this may imply he did it purposely, but Copperud calls this good idiomatic usage.

TEMPERATURES. Temperatures can't get cooler or warmer; They get higher or lower. Make it: Temperatures *will rise* (not *warm up*) tomorrow.

THAT, WHICH. *That* introduces restrictive dependent clauses; *which* introduces non-restrictive clauses. See pages 116–17.

TOO, VERY. *Too* should not be used for *very*: He won't stay *very* (not *too*) long. However, most editors who object to the use of *very* would say to simply write it: He won't stay long.

TOTALLY DEMOLISHED OR DESTROYED. See Demolish, destroy.

TRANSPIRE. Webster's now accepts *transpire* as synonym for *occur, happen, take place, come to pass, leak out*. But it is only a fancy word that is misused as a verb with the meaning of *becoming known* or *coming to pass*. Many grammarians see it as loose usage. Examples: What *happened, took place* or *occurred* (not *transpired*) at the meeting was withheld from the press. Despite attempts to conceal its strategy, the group's secret *leaked out* (not *transpired*).

TRY AND, TRY TO. *Try and* should be used only colloquially for *try to*. See pages 147–48.

UNDER WAY, UNDERWAY. *Under way* (two words) is correct whether it concerns a ship, a sprinter or a presidential campaign, according to Bernstein. The stylebooks agree. Use *underway* as an adjective: They resorted to *underway* refueling.

UNIQUE. Because *unique* is regarded as *the only one of its kind*—unequalled—you are advised not to write *more* or *most* or *somewhat* unique. Copperud argues, however, that such usage as *more unique, most unique* and *quite unique* is acceptable.

UP, UPPED. Webster's now accepts *up* as a verb, with the meaning of *to raise*, as in: *upped* the prices. However, most editors advise that it be used only colloquially.

UPCOMING. It's called journalese. It should be avoided when *coming* alone will do. Or you may use *forthcoming* or *approaching*. Example: The *coming* (not *upcoming*) election should be a close one.

USING NOUNS AS VERBS. See Nouns as verbs.

VERY. Newspaper editors frown on the use of *very*. See page 136.

WHO, WHOM. For correct use of *who* and *whom*, see pages 96–97, 116–19, and 122–23.

Bibliography

Works of reference most often consulted and cited by the author in this Third Edition of *Grammar for Journalists* were mentioned in Chapter 1. They are:

The American Heritage Dictionary of the English Language. William Morris, ed. New York and Boston: American Heritage Publishing and Houghton Mifflin Co.

Angione, Howard. *The Associated Press Stylebook and Libel Manual*, 1977. The Associated Press, 50 Rockefeller Plaza, New York, N.Y. 10020.

Bernstein, Theodore M. *The Careful Writer: A Modern Guide to English Usage*. New York: Atheneum, 1965, 1973.

Copperud, Roy H. *A Dictionary of Usage and Style*. New York and London: Hawthorne Books, 1964.

Flesch, Rudolf. *Look It Up: A Deskbook of American Spelling and Style*. New York: Harper & Row, 1977.

Webster's New Collegiate Dictionary. Springfield, Mass.: G. & C. Merriam, 1977.

Webster's New Twentieth Century Dictionary of the English Language. 2nd ed. Cleveland and New York: The World Publishing Company.

Although the following books were not used as primary references in the process of revising this text, the author can recommend them as helpful books of reference for the journalism student and the practicing journalist:

Baskette, Floyd K., and Sissors, Jack Z. *The Art of Editing*. 2nd ed. New York: Macmillan, 1977.

Bernstein, Theodore M. *Dos, Don'ts & Maybes of English Usage*. New York: Times Books, 1977.

———. *Reverse Dictionary*. New York: Quadrangle Books, 1975.

Bremner, John B. *Words, Words, Words: A Dictionary for Writers and Others Who Care About Words.* New York: Columbia Univ. Press, 1980.

Copperud, Roy H. *American Usage and Style: The Consensus.* New York: Van Nostrand Reinhold, 1980.

Crowell, Alfred A. *Creative News Editing.* 2nd ed. Dubuque: William C. Brown, 1975.

Curme, George O. *Principles and Practice of English Grammar.* New York: Barnes & Noble, 1947.

Davis, Esther, and Devol, Kenneth. *Writing Style for Journalists.* Los Angeles: A Best Publication (A Brewster Educational Series Text Publication), 1962.

Dunbar, Howard H.; Marcett, Mildred E.; and McCloskey, Frank H. *Writing Good English.* Boston: D. C. Heath, 1951.

Flesch, Rudolf. *The Art of Readable Writing.* New York: Harper & Brothers, 1949.

———. *The ABC of Style: A Guide to Plain English.* New York: Harper & Row, 1964.

Fowler, H. W. (See Listing for Nicholson, Margaret.)

Funk & Wagnalls Editorial Staff. *Standard Handbook of Prepositions, Conjunctions, Relative Pronouns and Adverbs.* New York: Funk & Wagnalls, 1953.

Garst, Robert E., and Bernstein, Theodore M. *Headlines and Deadlines: A Manual for Copy Editors.* 3rd ed. New York: Columbia Univ. Press, 1980.

Gibson, Martin L. *Editing in the Electronic Era.* Ames: Iowa State Univ. Press, 1979.

Gunning, Robert. *The Technique of Clear Writing.* New York: McGraw-Hill, 1952.

Hopper, Vincent F., and Gale, Cedric. *Essentials of Effective Writing: A Practical Grammar and Handbook of Basic Writing Techniques.* Great Neck, N.Y.: Barron's Educational Series, 1961.

Kent, Ruth. *The Language of Journalism: A Glossary of Print-Communications Terms.* Kent, Ohio: Kent State Univ. Press, 1970.

Leggett, Glen; Mead, C. David; and Charvat, William. *Prentice-Hall Handbook for Writers.* Englewood Ciffs, N.J.: Prentice-Hall, 1970.

McCrimmon, James M. *Writing With a Purpose.* 6th ed. Boston: Houghton Mifflin, 1977.

Miller, Bobby Ray. *The United Press International Stylebook, 1977.* United Press International, 220 E. 42nd St., New York, N.Y. 10017.

Miller, Shirley M., ed. *Webster's New World Word Book: The 33,000 Most Used Words Spelled and Syllabified.* Rev. ed. New York: The World Publishing Company, 1971.

Morris, William, and Morris, May. *Harper Dictionary of Contemporary Usage.* New York: Harper & Row, 1975.

Newman, Edwin. *Strictly Speaking: Will America Be the Death of English?* New York: Bobbs-Merrill, 1974.

The New York Times Manual of Style and Usage. Revised and edited by Lewis Jordan. Chicago: Quadrangle Books, 1976.

Nicholson, Margaret. *American-English Usage Based on Fowler's Modern English Usage.* (Published as a Signet Book by arrangement with Oxford University Press).

———. *A Practical Style Guide for Authors and Editors.* New York, Chicago and San Francisco: Holt, Rinehart and Winston, 1971.

Opdycke, John B. *Get It Right*. New York: Funk & Wagnalls, 1941.

Payne, Lucile Vaughn. *The Lively Art of Writing*. New York: The New American Library, Follett Publishing, 1965.

Prejean, Blanche G., and Danielson, Wayne A. *Programmed News Style*. (Basic Skills in Journalism Series). Englewood Cliffs, N.J.: Prentice-Hall, 1978.

Safire, William. *On Language*. New York: Times Books, 1980.

Shaw, Harry. *Dictionary of Problem Words & Expressions*. New York: McGraw-Hill, 1975.

Shaw, Harry, and Shaffer, Virginia. *McGraw-Hill Handbook of English*. 4th ed. New York, Toronto, London: McGraw-Hill, 1977.

Simon, John. *Paradigms Lost: Reflections on Literacy and Its Decline*. New York: Clarkson N. Potter, 1980.

Strunk, William Jr., and White, E. B. *The Elements of Style*. 3rd ed. New York: Macmillan, 1979.

U.S. Government Printing Office Style Manual. Washington, D.C.: U.S. Government Printing Office, 1973.

Walsh, J. Martyn, and Walsh, Anna Kathleen. *Plain English Handbook: A Complete Guide to Good English*. Cincinnati: McCormick-Mathers Publishing, 1972.

Webster's New World Dictionary of the American Language. Cleveland: William Collins World Publishing Co., 1978.

Westley, Bruce H. *News Editing*. 3rd ed. Boston: Houghton Mifflin, 1980.

Wimer, Arthur, and Brix, Dale. *Workbook for Radio and TV News Editing and Writing*. 5th ed. Dubuque: Wm. C. Brown Company, 1980.

Wooley, Edwin C.; Scott, Franklin W.; and Bracher, Frederick. *College Handbook of Composition*. 5th ed. Boston: D. C. Heath and Company.

Wylie, Bob. *Fuzzified Phrases Fracture Reader Attention*. This very helpful article, adapted from a talk Wylie gave at the annual conference of the National Council of College Publication Advisers in October 1978, was published in *Community College Journalist*/Winter 1978.

Zinsser, William. *On Writing Well*. New York: Harper & Row, 1976.

Index

Spelling, rules for (*cont'd.*)
  doubling final consonant
    before suffix, 264–66
  ei and *ie*, 267
  final -*e*, before suffix, 266
  final -*y*, in forming plural,
    266–67
  similar words with different
    meanings, 283–88
  study of word formations, 269–70
  troublesome homonyms and
    other words easily confused,
    283–88
  use of dictionary for, 269–70
  words commonly misspelled, list
    of, 270–83
Split infinitives, 72–73, 141–142
Split verb phrases, 71–72
Squinting modifiers, 180, 183
Stereotypes, 230–32
Structure of sentence. *See*
  Sentence(s)
Subject of sentence
  agreement with predicate, 11–12,
    67–68, 102–110, 112–26
  case of, 89–90, 96–97
  complete, 11–12
  compound, 16
  defined, 9–12, 54
  gerund as, 54, 69, 189–90, 213
  importance of, 54
  infinitive as, 54, 69, 209–10
  noun, 9–13, 207–08
  noun clause as, 19, 210–11
  phrase as, 68–69, 208–10
  pronoun, 9–13, 214
  shifting of, 193–94
  simple, 9–13, 48, 54
    importance of recognizing,
    9–13, 48, 54
  understood, 22
Subjective case. *See* Nominative
  case
Subjective complement. *See*
  Predicate nouns and
  pronouns
Subjunctive mood, 66–67
Subordination. *See also* Clauses,
  subordinate

Subordination (*cont'd.*)
  for emphasis, 199–200
  misuses of. *See* Unity in
    sentences
  for unity, 172–74
Superlative degree, 132–35
Sure, real, 298
Sustain, 299
Syllabication, 263–70
Syntax (sentence structure), 48–55

Tautology, 228
Temperatures, 299
Tense
  correct use of, 57–58, 73
  defined, 57
  errors in use of, 73–81
  of infinitive, used after verb in
    past or past perfect tense,
    76–77
  kinds of, 57–59
    future, 57, 79–80
    future perfect, 58, 75–77
    past, 57, 73–78
    past perfect, 58, 75–78
    present, 58, 75–78
    present perfect, 58, 75–77
    progressive, 58, 75
  of participle, 77
  principal parts of verbs, 59–63
  shifts in, unnecessary, 74, 78,
    194–95
Than
  after *no sooner*, 155
  for *from*, 138
  for *when*, 140
That
  overuse of, 155
  or *which*, 116–17
The. *See* Articles
There, as expletive, 37, 55, 214–15
*This, that kind of; these, those
  kinds of*, 109
Titles
  of people
    article with *Rev.*, 131
    commas with, 248
    quotation marks with, 257